BILL SEVERN'S BEST MAGIC

Severn, Bill.
Bill Severn's Best magic : 50 top tricks to entertain and amaze your friends on all occasions / Bill Severn ; illustrated by Timothy Wenk. -- 1st ed. -- Harrisburg, Pa. : Stackpole Books, c1990.
viii, 210 p. : ill.

04244117 LC:89011569 ISBN:0811722295 (pbk.)

1. Tricks. 2. Conjuring. I. Wenk, Timothy. II. Title: Best magic. III. Title

805 90DEC10 h8/ 1-00530476

BILL SEVERN'S BEST MAGIC

50 TOP TRICKS TO ENTERTAIN AND AMAZE YOUR FRIENDS ON ALL OCCASIONS

Bill Severn

Illustrated by Timothy Wenk

Stackpole Books

Published by
STACKPOLE BOOKS
Cameron and Kelker Streets
P.O. Box 1831
Harrisburg, PA 17105

Printed in the United States of America

10 9 8 7 6 5 4 3 2

First Edition

Cover design by Tracy Patterson

Library of Congress Cataloging-in-Publication Data

Severn, Bill.
Bill Severn's best magic: 50 top tricks to entertain and amaze your friends on all occasions/Bill Severn; illustrated by Timothy Wenk.—1st ed.
p. cm.
ISBN 0-8117-2229-5
1. Tricks. 2. Magic. I. Wenk, Timothy, ill. II. Title.
GV1548.S364 1990
793.8—dc20 89-11569
CIP
AC

Contents

Introduction

Here are more than fifty tricks and routines, enough to provide you with a dozen magic acts—close-up tricks to entertain just a few friends, and others for a larger audience. They are the tricks I consider the best, the most entertaining, of all that I have published during the fifty-some years I have been writing about magic.

Collected for the first time in one volume, they include some material from books now out of print and no longer available. Everything has been revised and updated, sometimes extensively, with the hindsight of practical knowledge that I've gained from frequently performing these tricks over the years.

They are all based on the use of simple props, easily put together at home, and they require no special equipment, unusual skills, or prior knowledge of magic. But they will require of you some rehearsal and some creative acting to make the most of them. Magic *is* theater, and its charm is in creating the basic theatrical illusion of make-believe.

The secret of a trick, as far as the magician is concerned, should be the least important thing about it. He will want to keep the secret, by performing well enough to conceal it, but far more important is *entertaining* the audience. What makes magic entertaining is not tricks in themselves, no matter how clever the method nor how expertly they are done, but the presentation that surrounds them—the plot, the patter, the planned buildup to an unexpected magical surprise. Every trick should be *acted out*, not just shown.

For each trick in this book, the presentation is given first, so that as you learn the trick you can always keep in mind how it should look to those who see it. Next comes a list of props you will need, then a bare-bones explanation of the secret, with careful directions for putting the props together and setting them up so the trick is ready to show. Finally you will learn *what you do* from step-by-step instructions for performing the trick.

The basic methods of magic are a common heritage of all magicians. Although some methods have been put to new uses here, they generally are those that have become accepted as standard and practical. Credit for them belongs to a long line of magicians who, through trial and error, have worked them out over the years.

New tricks are endless because each basic principle can be dressed up in presentations that are limited only by the magician's own imagination and creative talent. I hope this book will help to inspire you to make up your own magic, and that you will find ideas here that will add to your pleasure of inviting audiences to pretend with you in the theater's oldest game of make-believe.

ONE

Magic Wherever You Are

These are tricks to show at home, outdoors, at the office, or wherever you happen to be with a few friends.

Each trick is planned as a "happening" rather than as part of a set-up magic show. It is a magical surprise in which something suddenly seems to happen that those watching know can't really happen at all.

The more surprising you can make it, the more magical it will seem, and the more fun to watch. With this sort of magic, that fun of the unexpected is far more important than whether or not you fool anybody. But if you do these tricks well, they should leave your friends puzzled as well as entertained and amazed.

The Bewildering Bandage

How it looks

There is a bandage around the tip of your right first finger and when you are asked what happened, you explain that you cut yourself practicing magic.

"I had a trick I wanted to show you," you say, "but it's pretty hard to do with my finger bandaged. At least, it doesn't hurt much. I can hardly remember which finger I cut."

As you speak, you wave your hand and the bandage seems to vanish from your first finger. Suddenly it reappears on your second finger. It vanishes again and then jumps back into view on your first finger. Once more it disappears. This time you reach in under your jacket and bring out your finger with the bandage again on the tip.

"I'm glad I didn't cut the rest of my fingers," you say, "or I couldn't do this trick at all." You hold up your hand and bandages pop into view at the tips of all four fingers!

What you need

A roll of 1" bandage
A roll of 1/2" adhesive tape

Three bobby pins and two small safety pins
Thin cardboard and a pair of scissors
Sports jacket

The secret

The first bandage is made as a thimble-like device that slips on and off your finger when it is manipulated. The other bandages are in a holder beneath your jacket, where you secretly slip them into place on your fingers when you reach inside your jacket to reproduce the first bandage. (The method is the standard one magicians use for the manipulation and production of thimbles at the fingertips, but in this version fake bandages are used instead.)

How you fix it

Cut four strips of cardboard, each about 1-1/2" wide and 3" long. Take one strip and make a small tube of it by bending it around the tip of your first finger. Fasten it together with a piece of adhesive tape. It should fit snugly but allow you to slip your finger in and out of it easily.

Cut an 18" length from the roll of bandage. Wind the bandage around the sides and over the top of the tube to cover the cardboard completely except for the finger hole at the bottom. Fasten this bandage with a circling strip of adhesive tape.

The result should be a fake bandage you can fit over the tip of your finger as you would a thimble. With the remaining strips of cardboard, make fake bandages the same way for your three other right-hand fingers.

You will need to construct a simple holder to hide three of the bandages under the front of your jacket so you can secretly slip your fingers into them. To make this, cut a piece of cardboard 2" wide and 4" long. Slide the three bobby pins down over the top edge of it as if they were paper clips. Fasten a safety pin at each side edge of the cardboard, which should be strengthened at the edges with strips of tape so the pins won't tear through.

Clip three fake bandages, mouths upward, to the bobby pins. The pins should be spaced so you can put second, third, and little fingers into the bandages easily and quickly. By pushing straight down until your fingers come clear of the card, you can lift the bandages away on the tips of your fingers.

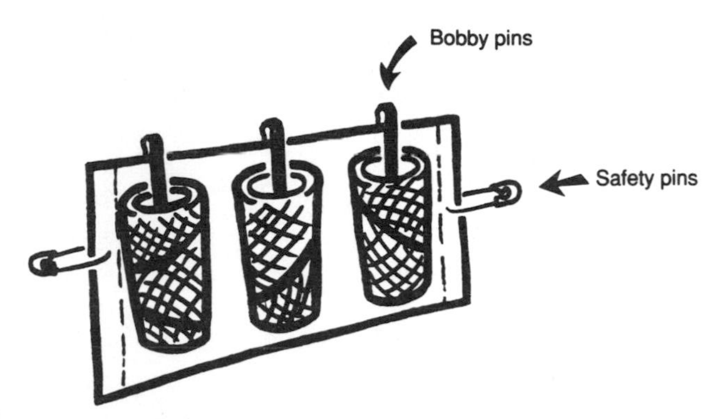

This device will hold the bandages under the jacket.

With the bandages in proper position on the holder, pin it to the left side of your shirt at a slant, so your fingers can slide into the bandages easily when you reach your hand inside your jacket. Put your jacket on to cover the holder. Have the original fake bandage on the tip of your right first finger.

What you do

The first part of the trick, in which the bandage seems to vanish and hop from finger to finger, depends on what magicians call a *thumb palm*. To use it with this bandage, bend your finger in until the tip of the bandage is at the crotch of the thumb. Squeeze your thumb to grip and hold the bandage, pull your finger out of it, and straighten your fingers.

If you do this rapidly, with the back of your hand toward those watching, and move your hand up and down a little at the same time, the bandage will seem to disappear. Practice it in front of a mirror until you can do it smoothly.

When you do this trick, stand with your right side to those watching. Hold up your right hand so its back is toward your viewers and your bandaged right first finger points to the left. Wave your hand, secretly bend in your finger, leave the bandage nipped in the crotch of your thumb, and straighten out your finger again.

Give viewers time to realize that the bandage has vanished. Wave your hand again, bend in your *second* finger, slip it into the bandage, and straighten out your finger. The bandage seems to have

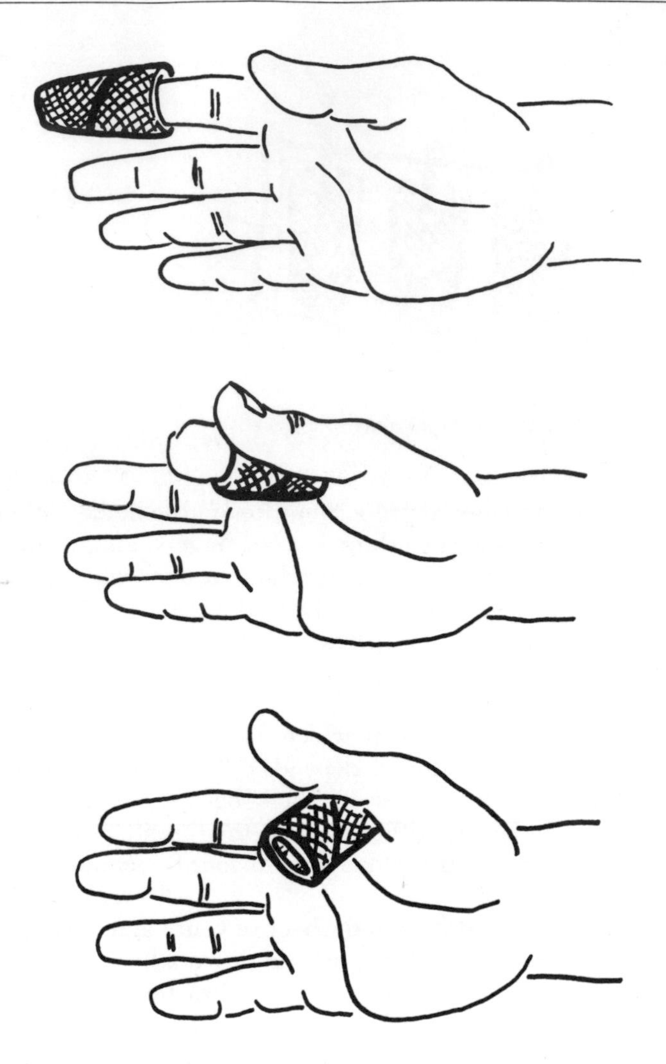

Here's the way you thumb palm a thimble-like bandage.

jumped to that fingertip. Use the same move to make it appear on the first finger once more. Then vanish it again.

Now close the rest of your fingers into a fist and point toward your jacket with your empty first finger. Slip your hand in under your jacket and open your fingers. Bend in your first finger to get the bandage on it from the crotch of your thumb. Slide your other fingers into the bandages in the holder. Move your hand straight down so the bandages slip free of the holder and come away on the tips of your fingers. All this takes only a moment to do.

With your hand still beneath your jacket, point your first finger out with the bandage on it. Close your three other fingers into a fist so the bandages on them will be hidden against the palm of your hand. Withdraw your hand from your jacket and show the bandage on your first finger. It looks as if you merely reached in under your jacket and recovered the bandage that had vanished from your finger an instant before.

Turn your hand so your first finger points toward the ceiling, with the back of the hand still toward those watching. Say, "I'm glad I didn't cut the rest of my fingers or I couldn't do this trick at all." Suddenly open your fingers wide so all the bandages pop into view on all four fingertips.

Whistle-up Chewing Gum

How it looks

"Would you like some chewing gum?" you ask a friend, as you show a pack of gum and hold it up in your hand. "It's magic gum. All I have to do is whistle—and the magic happens."

You whistle loudly and a stick of gum slowly rises up from the pack. As you hand the stick to your friend and put the rest of the pack away, you say, "Just don't try to whistle while you chew it. You might take off and fly to the moon."

What you need

A pack of chewing gum
A one-foot length of strong thread (color doesn't matter because it won't be seen)
A pair of sharp-pointed scissors
Slacks with pockets, sports jacket

The secret

The pack of gum is threaded inside, and the thread runs out through a hole in the back where it is secretly worked by your thumb.

The props are self-contained so you can carry the gum around in your pocket to show the trick whenever you please.

How you fix it

Peel open the flaps at the top of the pack and cut them off even with the top edge. Wind a strip of transparent tape horizontally around the pack just beneath the top edge, to strengthen it so the thread won't tear through.

Remove all the sticks of gum. Turn the empty wrapper to what will be the back when you hold the pack upright. About one-quarter of an inch down from the top, centered at the back, make a small hole through the tape and wrapper with the point of the scissors.

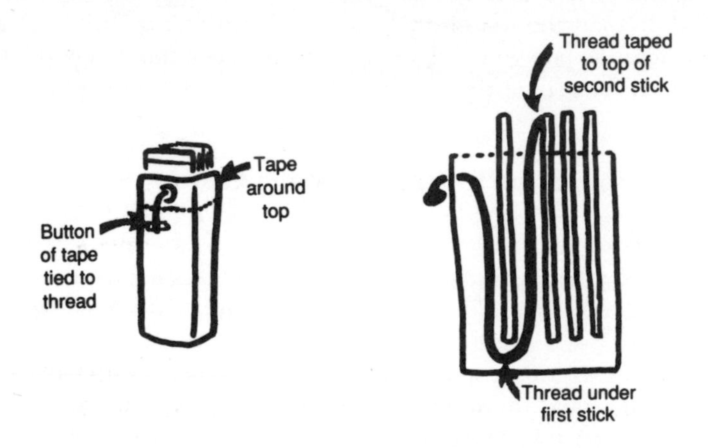

Side view inside the pack of gum.

Put one end of the thread in through that hole and bring it out the top of the wrapper. Fasten that end of the thread to the top of one of the sticks of gum with a strip of tape, first winding the thread several times around the tape so it will hold securely. Put that stick, top end up, back into the wrapper, and draw the thread out through the hole until you have taken up the slack.

Take a second stick of gum and push it down between the first one and the back of the wrapper, so it pushes the thread down under it. Put two more sticks of gum into the wrapper *in front* of the two threaded ones. Take the free end of the thread and gently pull it taut.

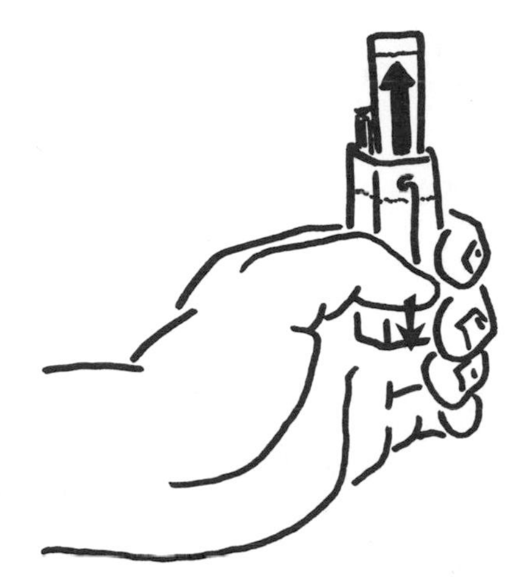

Thumb slides the button down and the gum rises.

Tie that end to a short strip of tape and wind the tape upward around the thread until it is right against the hole at the back of the pack. Wad the tape together so it is like a little button at the end of the thread. Put the pack of gum into an otherwise empty left-hand pocket of your slacks or jacket.

What you do

Reach into your pocket with your left hand. Cover the tape button with your thumb and bring out the pack. Casually show both sides of it as you ask your friend if he would like some gum. With your thumb at the back still covering the button, hold the pack upright and bring your little finger under it, so the bottom of the pack rests on that finger.

"This is magic gum," you say. "All you have to do is whistle—and the magic happens." Keep the pack as it is, and as you whistle, slowly slide your hidden thumb down the back of it, sliding the tape button toward the bottom. That pulls the thread which runs under the stick of gum inside the rear of the pack, and the stick slowly rises.

When it has risen about halfway out of the pack, take the stick with your right hand and give it to your friend. Drop the pack into your pocket, and say, "Just don't try to whistle while you chew it. You might take off and fly to the moon."

Fish Story

How it looks

"I saw an old Western film on television the other night," you say. "It was really wild. There were a couple of guys down by this river—fishing. But they weren't catching a thing. Then an old cowhand rode up and took his rope and started spinning it out over the water."

You show a length of string and snap the end of it out from your hand several times. Suddenly a plastic fish appears dangling from the end of the string as if caught from the air! "I know you won't believe it," you say, "but he *roped* himself a fish—cowboy style."

What you need

A four-foot length of string

A plastic fish, like those used by children as toys, small enough to be concealed in the palm of your hand (These usually are available at variety store toy counters. If you can't find one the right size, make an imitation fish of heavy cardboard, cut to shape and with painted features.)

A sports jacket

The secret

The fish, fastened near one end of the string, is hidden in your hand. In snapping out the string, you secretly switch one end for the other.

How you fix it

Tie the fish tightly to the string, about two inches from one end, by knotting the string around the tail. Loosely gather up the long end of the string and put that at the rear of the right pocket of your jacket, with the part of the string to which the fish is tied toward the front of the pocket.

What you do

Reach into your pocket for the string with your right hand and get the tail end of the fish under the crotch of your thumb. Bring your hand out with its back toward those watching, the fish concealed in the palm.

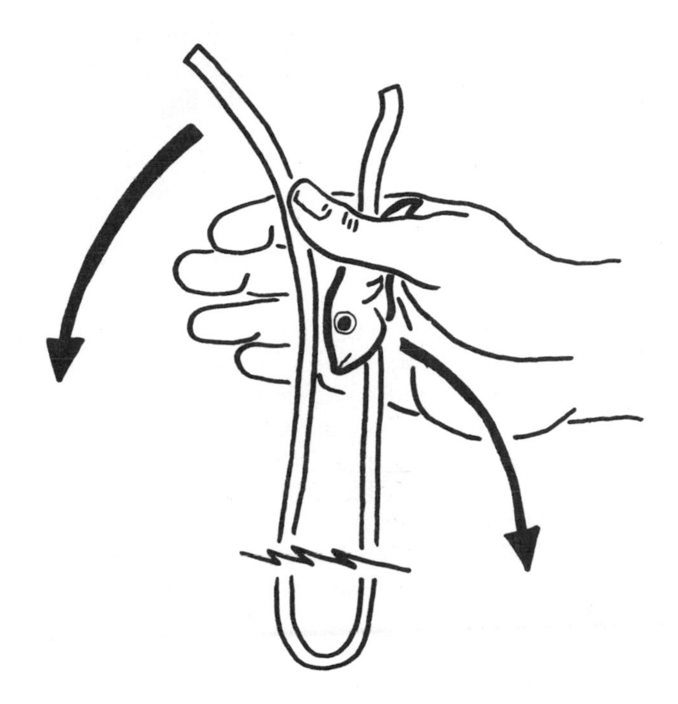

You switch the ends of the string as you snap it out of your hand.

Adjust the string with your left hand by pulling the short end up out of the top of your right hand. Keep that end with your right hand and take the long end with your left hand. Show the string loosely stretched from hand to hand in front of you.

Bring the left end to your right hand. Grip that end between the tip of your right first finger and thumb. Drop your left hand to your side and turn your body slightly to the left. Give your right hand an outward and downward flick and release the end of the string which does *not* have the fish tied to it. Do that as if just giving the string a little snap in the air.

Bring the hanging end back up to the right hand with the left and repeat the same move of snapping it out. Do it several times as you tell the story.

The last time, instead of releasing the free end of the string, keep that gripped with your right first finger and thumb, and open your hand to release the end to which the fish is tied, by snapping that end out into the air. Do it without hesitation, so there seems to be no difference in what you do. To those watching, it should seem as if the fish suddenly were caught from the air at the end of the string.

Fold-up

How it looks

"I've found an easy way to measure things if you don't happen to have a ruler," you say, as you take a paper bag from your pocket. The bag is folded small and flat so everybody can see there could be nothing big inside it. You unfold it, shake it open, and hold it on your hand. "All you have to do is make believe you *have* a ruler—and then use a little magic to make it real."

Reaching down inside the bag with your other hand, you pull out a foot-long ruler, which you show and then drop to the floor so it lands with a solid sound. You fold up the bag again and put it away in your pocket, leaving those who are watching puzzled over how a big solid ruler could have been inside the small folded-up bag.

What you need

A brown paper lunch bag, the flat-bottomed kind, about ten inches high and half that wide
A solid wood or metal ruler
A pair of scissors
A pair of slacks with pockets

The secret

The ruler is hidden down inside the front of your shirt. There is a hole cut in the back of the paper bag. When you reach inside the bag, your hand secretly goes right on out through the hole. You pull the hidden ruler from your shirt, up through the bag, and out the top.

How you fix it

Open out the bag and stand it on its flat bottom. Bags are made with a little half-circle cut from one of the top edges. Turn the opened bag so the side with the half-circle at the top is toward you. Starting about an inch up from the bottom and the same distance

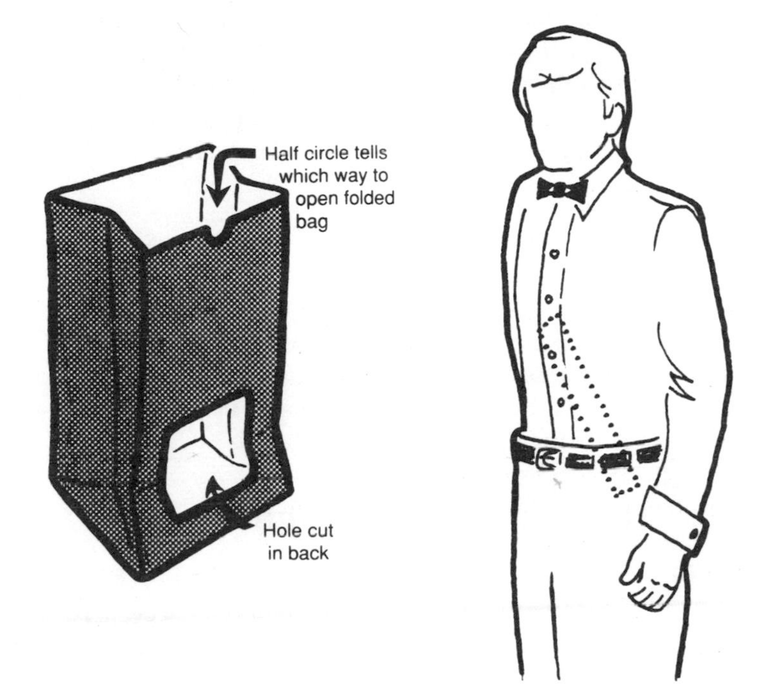

Ruler is hidden under the shirt. The bottom end is held under the belt.

in from each side, cut a hole about three inches square from that face of the bag.

Close the bag and fold the bottom flat against it. Then fold it in half upward and fold it once more. Have it folded that way in one of your pockets.

Slide the ruler inside your shirt near the second button up from your belt and slant it to the left. Push it down until the bottom end goes under the top edge of your slacks and is held beneath your belt. The top end of the ruler should be hidden just inside the front opening of your shirt.

What you do

Take out the folded bag and hold it in front of you so the side with the half-circle at the top edge is toward you. When you unfold the bag, that will be the side with the hole in it. Always keep the other face of the bag toward those who are watching.

Unfold the bag downward and reach inside to open it out so the bottom is flat. With your left hand, take the open bag at the bottom and hold it upright and close to you. Tilt the top a little to the right.

Show your right hand empty and reach down inside the bag and right on out through the hole in the back. Grasp the top end of the ruler and pull it straight out from your shirt, up through the bag, and out the top of the bag to show it.

Hold the "magic ruler" in view for a moment. Then drop it to the floor or on a table so it lands with a thud. Slowly fold up the bag again as it was at the start and put it away in your pocket.

The Auto-Magic Toothbrush

How it looks

"I'd like to show you a new invention," you say, as you take a toothbrush from your pocket. "It's an auto-magic toothbrush that works by magic instead of batteries."

You push it down into your fist and the brush magically rises up through your fingers. It does that several times, as you explain, "It has an up and down brushing motion." You turn your fist sideways, and the brush moves itself out to the side. "And it also brushes across."

You take it in one hand and hold the other hand above it. "The only trouble is that you can't always control the power." Suddenly the toothbrush flies up through the air from one hand to the other. "I'm working on that," you say, as you put it back into your pocket. "But meanwhile I guess I'll have to go on brushing my teeth the old-fashioned way instead of by magic."

What you need

A toothbrush
Fine black thread or monofilament
You should wear a jacket and slacks with pockets when you do the trick

The secret

This is not a close-up trick, but one to do when you are standing a short distance away from those who are watching, because the toothbrush is worked by a thread which might be seen if your viewers are too close.

How you fix it

Use a piece of thread or monofilament about sixteen inches long. Tie one end through the hole at the bottom of the toothbrush handle and the other end to the belt loop of your slacks at your left side. Make sure the knots are securely tied.

Put the toothbrush, handle end down, into your shirt pocket, and then put on your jacket so the thread is covered by it. Leave your jacket unbuttoned.

What you do

Take the toothbrush from your shirt pocket with your right hand and hold it down in front of you at *waist level*, with the thread

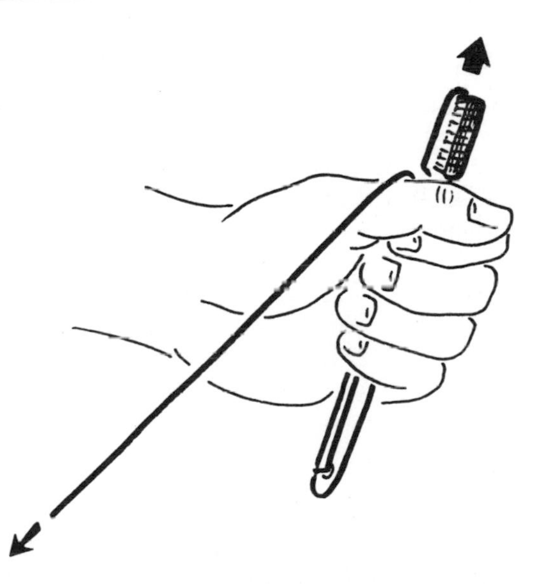

The toothbrush is pushed into your left hand.

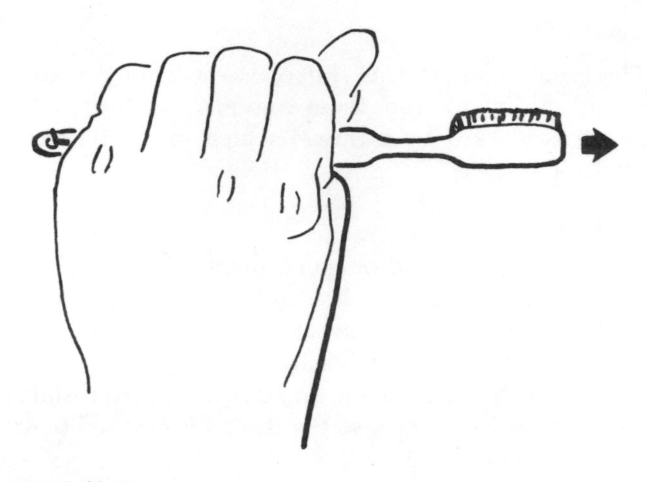

Turn your hand sideways.

running forward from your belt. Close your left hand into a very loose fist, thumb at the top, and push the handle down through that hand until the brush part touches the top edge of your fingers.

Now if you move your left hand *forward* a little, the toothbrush will rise up through your fingers, pulled by the taut thread. Don't lift your hand high; keep it directly in front of your waist.

When the toothbrush has risen a few inches through your left hand, tap it back down with your right hand, and make it rise again. Do that several times, as you explain, "It has an up and down brushing motion."

Turn your left hand sideways, knuckles toward the ceiling, and move your hand forward so the brush pushes itself out to the right. Repeat that, and say, "And it also brushes across."

Take the toothbrush by the *brush* end between your right thumb and first two fingers. Hold it in front of you at waist level with the handle pointing straight up, and let your left hand drop to your side for a moment. Say, "The only trouble is that you can't always control the power."

Bring your left hand up from your side, thumb and fingers spread open wide so that the crotch of your thumb comes under the thread, and without pausing continue to raise your left hand until it is a few inches above the toothbrush. Move your left hand forward

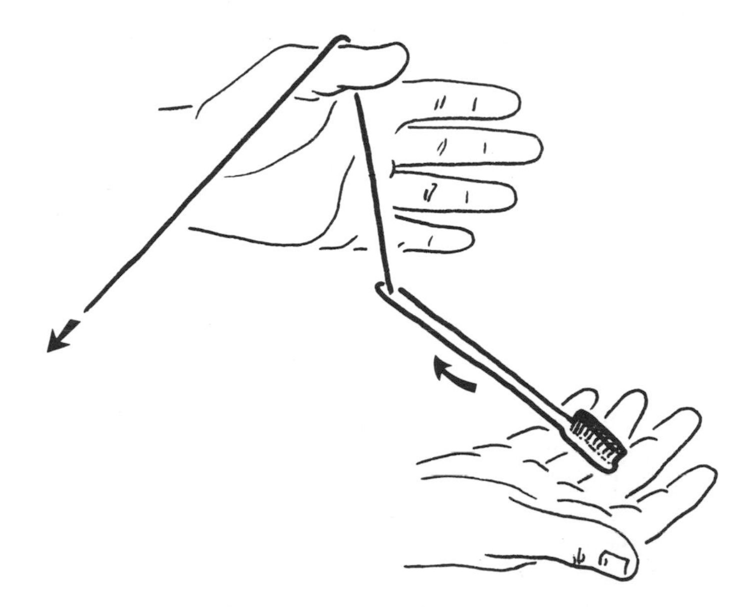

The toothbrush floats through the air from hand to hand.

as you release the brush from your right hand and the brush will seem to float up through the air from hand to hand.

"I'm working on that," you say, as you immediately take it again with your right hand and put it away in your shirt pocket. "But meanwhile I guess I'll have to go on brushing my teeth the old-fashioned way instead of by magic."

The Floating Pencil

How it looks

"I'm going to show you a trick you all can do," you announce. "I'll show you exactly how it's done." You take a pencil from your pocket and make it seem to cling to the tips of your fingers as if held there by magic. Then you pretend to explain the secret.

But those watching soon become more puzzled than ever when you appear to use "real magic" to make the pencil float first at the fingertips of one hand and then the other. It clings to your hand even when a handkerchief is draped between the pencil and your fingers.

What you need

A full-length black wooden pencil
A black tack (This should be slightly longer than the depth of your middle finger. A 1/2" gimp tack (No. 6) is a good one to use.)
A pocket handkerchief
Sports jacket (or shirt) with breast pocket

The secret

The pencil has a small tack extending from one side that you secretly grip between your fingers and that you later remove when wiping the pencil with the handkerchief.

How you fix it

Press the tack into one side of the pencil at its center so that it stands straight out at a right angle to the pencil. You may want to tap it lightly once or twice with a hammer to make sure it will stay in place. Carry the pencil in your shirt pocket or the upper left pocket of your jacket, and have the handkerchief handy.

What you do

Take the pencil from your pocket with your right hand. Hold it so it rests lengthwise across your fingertips with the head of the tack toward you. Your thumb should cover the tack, which lies hidden beneath it. Now if you roll the pencil backwards slightly with your thumb, the head of the tack will revolve so it goes down between your middle fingers.

Grip the tack lightly between your middle fingers and display the pencil as if it were merely resting across your fingertips. Explain

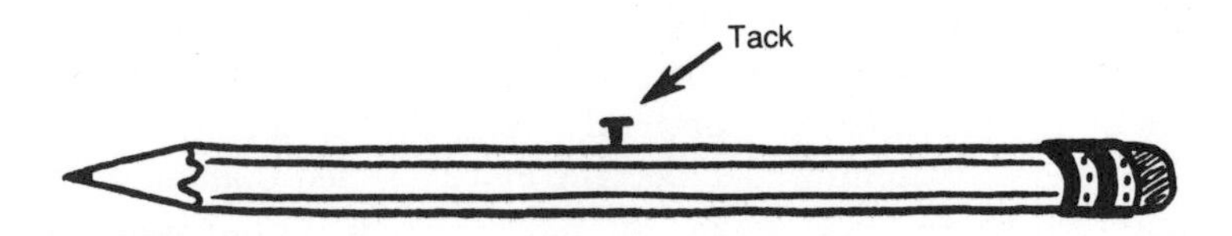

Press the tack into the center of a pencil.

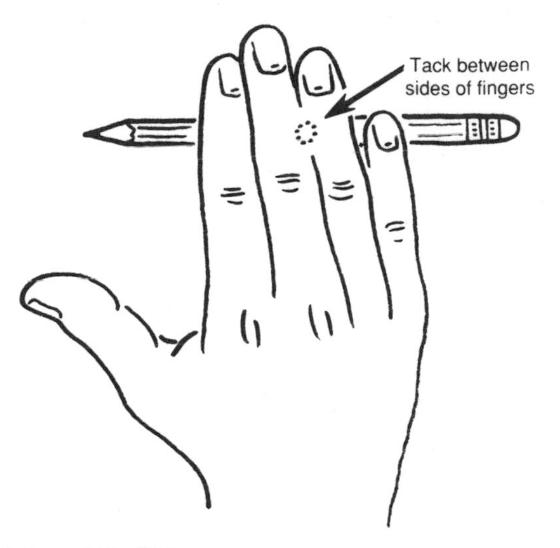

Your palm is toward the floor.

that you are going to show how to do a trick. Say, "But first, we need to create a little static electricity." Take out the handkerchief with your left hand and rub it briskly a few times over the pencil. Tuck the handkerchief back into your breast pocket or drop it on the table where you can reach it.

Keep the palm of your right hand upward with the pencil across the fingertips. Grasp your right wrist with your left fingers underneath the wrist and close them around it. Turn your right palm downward, and as you do, open out your left first finger and put it on the pencil.

Really the pencil clings to your fingers because you are secretly holding the tack between them. But you are going to pretend it is your left first finger that holds the pencil there.

"The pencil seems to cling to the tips of my fingers as if by magic," you say. Hold your hand that way for a moment. "I told you I'd show you how to do it and I will." Lift your hands high and reveal the way your left finger seems to be holding the pencil. "Simple, isn't it?" Lower your hands again so your right palm is toward the floor.

"But there is one thing you have to be very careful about," you say. "You have to be sure to keep your hands down low so nobody

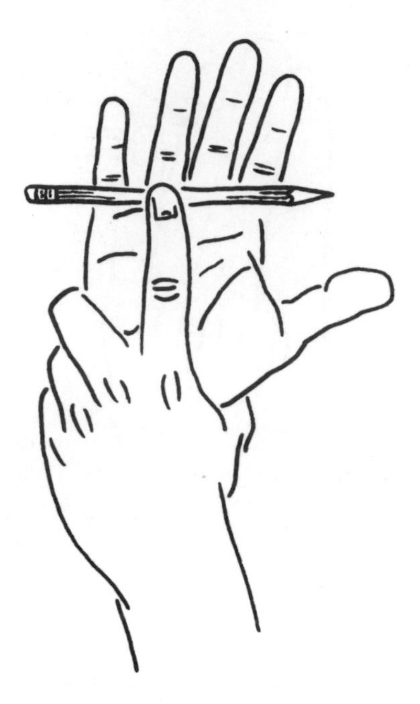

Front view during your fake explanation.

can look up underneath and see that your finger is holding the pencil. Because if they do catch on, then you have to do the trick the hard way—by magic."

As you say the last words, suddenly remove your left hand from your right wrist. Hold your left hand high and snap your fingers. The pencil remains clinging to your right fingers because you secretly hold the tack nipped between them. Gently wave your right hand up and down. The clinging pencil seems to defy gravity.

Hold out your left palm upward and bring your right palm down upon it. Secretly roll the pencil forward slightly with your right fingers. The tack will revolve so its head goes down between the middle fingers of your left hand. Grip the tack between those fingers.

Now take away your right hand and turn your left palm downwards. The pencil will seem to cling to your left fingertips. You can hold your hands, palms together, straight out to one side or the other and transfer the clinging pencil from one to the other. Simply revolve it slightly as your hands touch together and the tack will turn so you can secretly nip it between the fingers of either hand.

Finally hold the pencil by one end with your left fingers, turning it so the head of the tack is toward you and can't be seen by those watching. Say, "Some people think I have some kind of sticky stuff on my fingers, so I'll put the handkerchief between them and the pencil." Take out the handkerchief and drape it across the pencil.

Bring your right hand down to the pencil and secretly grip the head of the tack between your fingers as you did before. You can still hold the tack between your fingers through the single thickness of the handkerchief and work the trick the same way.

Finish it by secretly pressing your thumb hard against the head of the tack, and rubbing the pencil with the handkerchief once more as though you were polishing the pencil. The tack will come away in the handkerchief, which you tuck into your pocket. You can then show all sides of the pencil before dropping it back into your pocket.

Clickety Clips

How it looks

"Have you ever heard magic happen?" you ask. "It usually happens so fast that you can't hear a thing. But once in a while, if you listen real hard, you can hear it."

You take some paper clips from your pocket and have someone count out six of them. Then you give him a rubber band to wrap around them. You cover your hand with a handkerchief and put the paper clips into your hand under the handkerchief.

"Now listen," you say, as you hold the covered hand close to his ear. "Do you hear anything?" He will admit he hears a tiny clicking sound. You say, "That's the sound of the paper clips clicking themselves into one long chain."

You instruct him to remove the handkerchief from your hand, pick up the clips, and take off the rubber band wrapped around them. He discovers that the separate clips are linked together. You say, "Now you can tell people that you once heard magic happen. If they don't believe you—tell them to ask me."

What you need

Slacks with pockets
Fifteen paper clips
A handkerchief
A bundle of about fifty rubber bands (They often are sold in small bundles, but if the ones you buy come in a box you can easily make a bundle of them. Simply hold them together lengthwise and fasten one band around the middle of the bunch.)

The secret

There are two sets of paper clips, one linked and the other unlinked, which you switch under cover of the handkerchief. The handkerchief also covers the secret dropping of the unlinked set, banded together, down your sleeve.

How you fix it

Show the handkerchief and drop it to the table. Talk about hearing magic happen and put your right hand into your pocket. Scoop up the loose paper clips and drop those on the table. Have someone count out six of them.

The reason for starting with more than six is so that your observer will have to count them one at a time. This proves to him that they are all separate without your saying so. If you mentioned "separate paper clips," he might guess you meant to link them together. That would spoil the surprise and make the trick harder to do.

While he is busy counting the clips, reach with your left hand into your left pocket. Scoop the duplicate set of linked and banded clips into your fingers along with the bundle of rubber bands, so that the bundle rests on top of them. Bring your hand out as though it held only the rubber bands, which hide the clips that rest against your fingers.

Pull one of the rubber bands from the bundle with your right hand. Drop the band on the table and tell him to fasten it tightly around the paper clips he has counted. While he is doing that, pick up the handkerchief with your right hand, shake it out, and drape it over your left hand. Reach under it, remove the bundle of rubber bands from your left hand, and put them aside on the table.

That leaves the duplicate banded and linked set of clips lying on the palm of your left hand, hidden under the handkerchief. Hold your covered left hand high and adjust the handkerchief a little to make sure it covers the edge of your sleeve. Ask your friend to drop his banded clips into your right hand. Say, "I'll put them in my other hand under the handkerchief."

But what you really do is reach under the handkerchief and just drop the rubber-banded clips he has given you down into your left sleeve. Take your right hand away. Keep your left hand up and bring it over close to his ear.

Under the handkerchief put your left thumb and second fingertip together so the nails touch. You will find that by making a

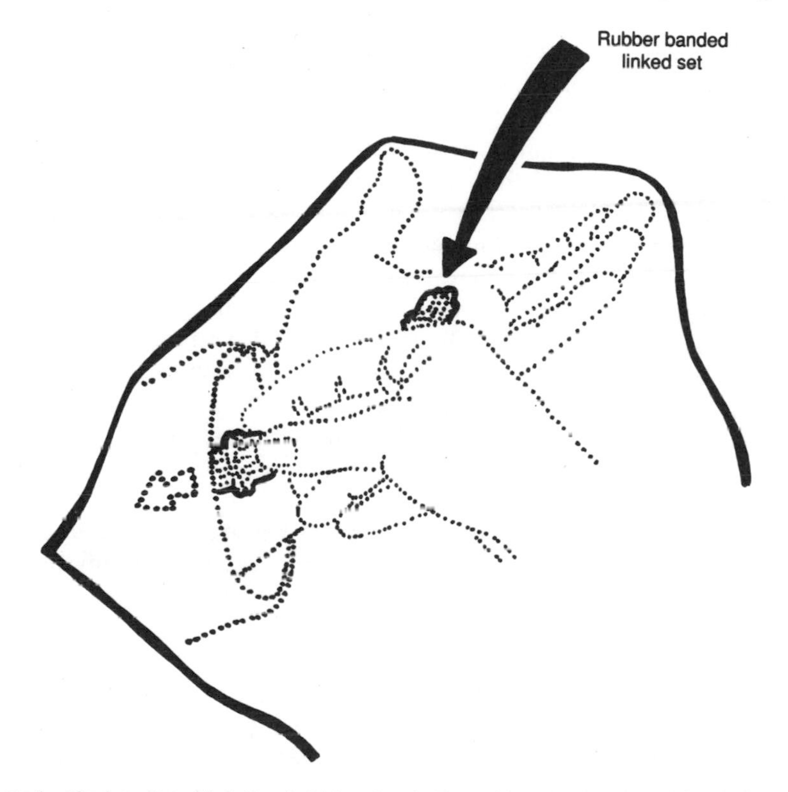

Under the handkerchief, the right hand puts the rubber-banded unlinked clips down the left sleeve.

tiny movement, you can click your thumbnail against your fingernail. The sound will be quite clear.

Ask him if he heard it. Click your nails a few times more while he listens. Have him remove the handkerchief from your hand. Tell him to take the paper clips and unfasten the rubber band. Ask him to hold up the chain for everyone to see.

When those watching have had a moment to realize what has happened, take back the chain of clips. Put them in your left hand. Lower your left hand to your side. The other set of banded clips will fall into your fingers from your sleeve to join those already in your hand. Drop them all together into your left pocket and you will be free to go on with another trick.

The Invisible Magazine Rack

How it looks

"I've found a magic way to store all my old magazines," you say. "I keep them stacked in an invisible magazine rack. That way they don't take up any room."

You show a copy of a magazine, holding it up so everyone can see the front cover. "Whenever I'm finished reading through one issue, I just say a few magic words to myself. Right away the magazine changes from the one I have to the one I want to read."

As you speak, you turn the magazine to show the front of it again. Magically it has changed to a different one, with a cover having a different color and a different picture on it.

"It's a handy thing to take along on a trip, or when you visit the dentist's office or the barber shop." You turn the magazine to show the front cover once more, and it has magically changed again—to a third magazine. "Wherever you go, with an invisible magazine rack, you always have whatever you want to read."

What you need

Three old magazines, such as weekly news magazines, of exactly the same size but with different covers (They can be three different issues of the same magazine or three different magazines that match in size.)
Scissors and rubber cement
Sports jacket

The secret

The front cover is made into a three-way flap that is secretly turned so a different cover shows each time you turn the magazine around.

Fold the first cover in half, right to left, and coat the back with rubber cement. Fasten the back of the left half of the second cover on top of the first cover. Then fold the second one in half. Fasten the third cover in the same way on top of the second.

How you fix it

Start by carefully removing the front covers from two of the magazines. Cut them off right along the spine where the magazine is stapled.

Take the third magazine, with its cover still attached, and fold that cover exactly in half from right to left. With rubber cement, evenly coat the back of the folded part now facing you. Lay one of the extra covers on top of it so their left edges exactly meet, and press it down to stick them together.

Let it dry and then fold that extra cover exactly in half from right to left. Coat the back of the folded part with cement and lay

Back view: As you secretly turn the flap, you hold the magazine upside down.

the left half of the other extra cover on top of it to stick them together. Fold that one in half right to left and open it out again.

You can carry it in one of your jacket pockets by folding it loosely with covers to the inside. But just before performing the trick, place the magazine on a table with the cover side down and with the stapled spine toward the right.

What you do

Pick up the magazine with your right hand, fingers underneath the center of the right edge and thumb at the back. Hold it up to show everyone the cover. You can show both the front and back of the magazine and handle it quite freely. Riffle the pages if you wish, as you talk about your "invisible magazine rack."

Bring your left hand to the left edge so as to hold the magazine upright between both hands, fingers to the front and thumbs at the back. Tilt the magazine over forward until it is upside down, still held upright between your hands at the sides, but with the back of it now toward those watching. The upside-down cover now faces you.

With your right thumb, secretly turn the flap from right to left. Hold the flap under your left thumb, and with the magazine still between both hands, tilt it forward to bring the cover right side up again, facing the audience. Show that the cover has changed.

Repeat the moves to turn (secretly) the second flap and then show that the cover has changed again. Close the magazine, with the covers to the inside, and put it away in your jacket pocket. By magic, you seem to have shown three different magazines!

TWO

Magic with Coins and Bills

Here you will find do-anywhere coin tricks planned for the close-up entertainment of a few friends, new presentations of several classic money mysteries, and novel tricks with dollar bills.

Coin magic, whether close-up or for a larger group, has always had a special appeal, partly because everybody is interested in money and would like to reach out and catch it at the fingertips, or otherwise make it obey each human will and whim. Coins, like cards, are familiar objects, and magic with familiar things always seems more magical.

The basic plots of most coin tricks haven't changed much since early magicians first started showing them to ancient Greeks, probably not long after coins were first minted around 600 B.C. The plots were standard for centuries before Reginald Scot first recorded them in English in *The Discoverie of Witchcraft* in 1584. According to Scot, 16th Century magicians were doing many of the coin tricks magicians still do.

Tricks with paper money are not nearly as old as those with coins, but they were first performed as soon as paper money came into public use. They have much the same appeal. In addition, paper money is more visible and more easily destructible than metal money, and each bill can be identified by its individual serial number.

As with all forms of magic, the variations of basic plots are almost limitless, as are the methods of accomplishing them. However old the plots, fresh presentations make the enjoyment always new.

Cash Offer

How it looks

You take a facial tissue from your pocket, shake it open to show clearly there is nothing in it, and roll it into a small ball in your hands. Holding it up, you ask, "If I offered to sell you this for a dime, would you buy it?"

Without waiting for an answer, you snap your fingers over the ball of tissue, tear it open, and remove a shining half-dollar from inside it. As you show the half-dollar, you say, "For a dime, you should have bought it."

What you need

A facial tissue
A shiny new half-dollar
Sports jacket

The secret

The half-dollar is hidden in your fingers, concealed by the way you show and crumple the tissue.

How you fix it

Open the facial tissue, stuff it loosely into the otherwise empty right-hand pocket of your jacket, and put the half-dollar into the pocket with it.

What you do

Reach into your pocket and get the half-dollar in your hand by closing the three lower fingers loosely around it. Grip the tissue between your thumb and first finger, and take it from your pocket with your other fingers curled inward to hide the coin.

Bring both hands in front of you, their backs toward those watching, and open out the tissue so as to hold it up by one top corner between your right thumb and first finger and the opposite top corner between your left thumb and first finger.

Shake it out to show it is empty, move your left hand forward and all the way over to the right to show the other side of the tissue, and bring both hands back as they were with the tissue stretched between them.

Drop the left corner from your left hand so the tissue hangs down from your right hand. Shake it again with your right hand and show your left hand empty. Cup your left hand in front of you, fingers toward the front, and bring your right hand above it so the bottom corner of the tissue touches the left palm.

Slowly lower your right hand so the tissue loosely folds itself down into your cupped left hand. As your hands touch together,

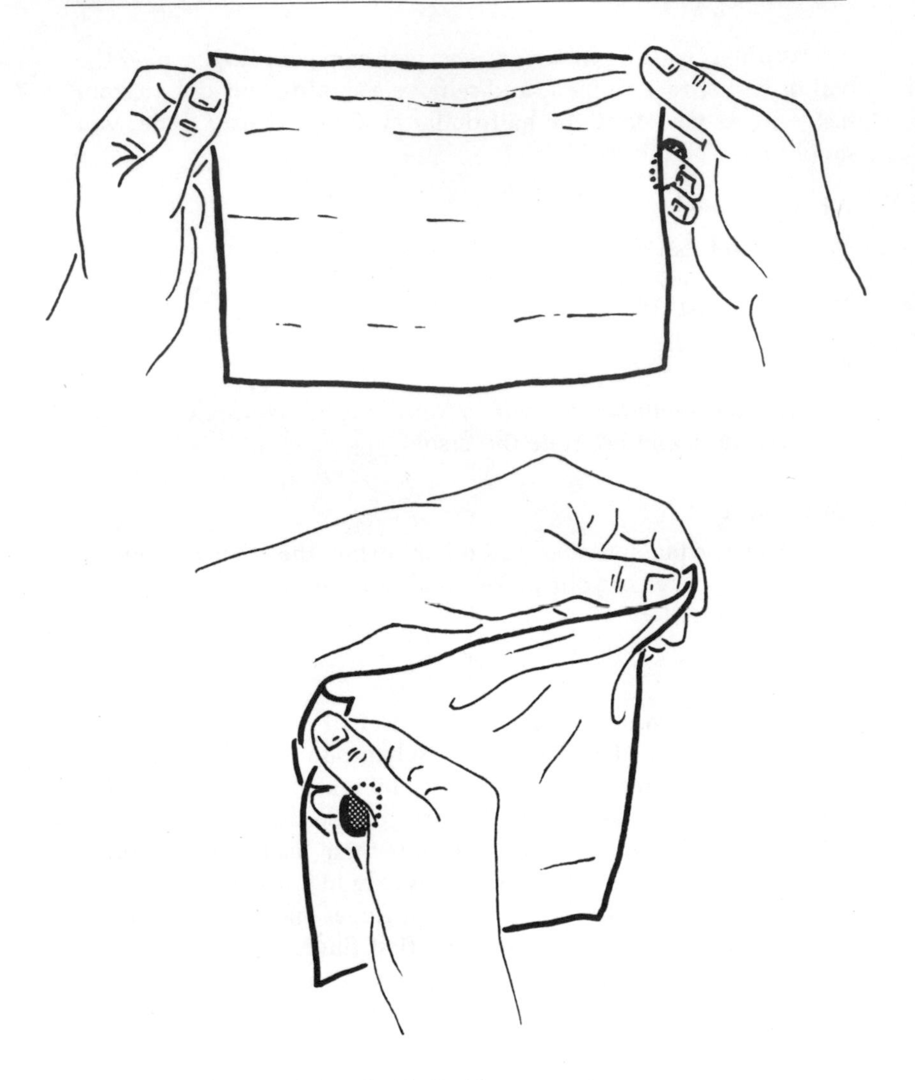

Open out the tissue and show that both sides are empty.

with your right hand inside the folds of the partly crumpled tissue, let the finger-palmed coin slide into it. Keeping your hands together, fold the tissue up around the coin and quickly roll it into a ball.

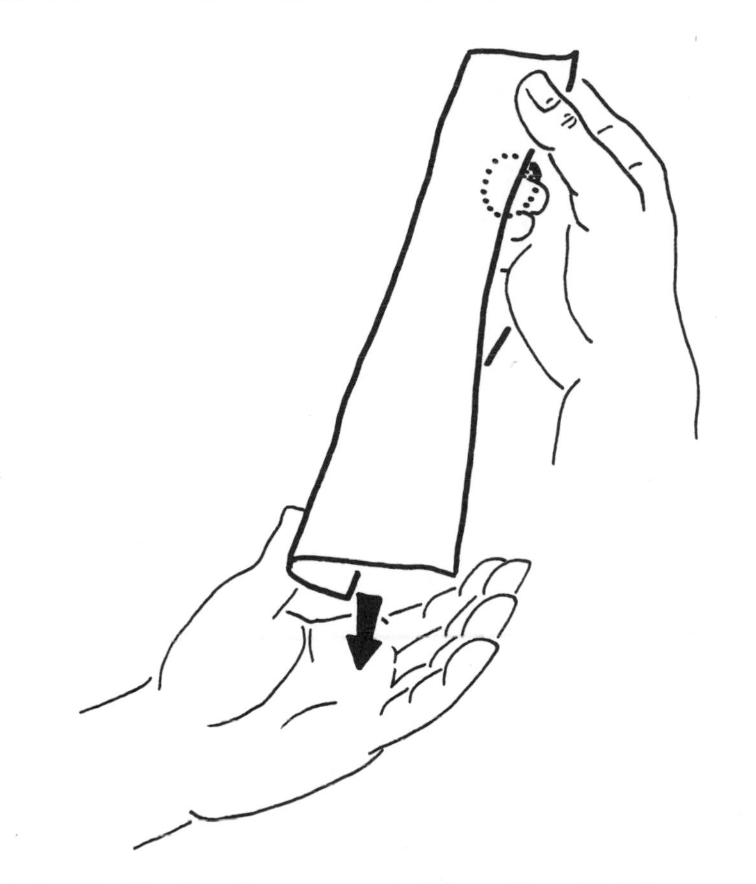

Right hand, holding tissue by one corner, slowly lowers tissue into left.

Hold it on your left palm, with that thumb resting lightly on top of it to keep it from unrolling, and take your right hand away.

Display the ball of tissue on your outstretched left palm, and ask, "If I offered to sell you this for a dime, would you buy it?" Without waiting for an answer, show your right hand empty and snap your fingers over the tissue. Take it with both hands, slowly tear it open, and bring the half-dollar into view. Throw the tissue aside, hold up the half-dollar, and say, "For a dime, you should have bought it!"

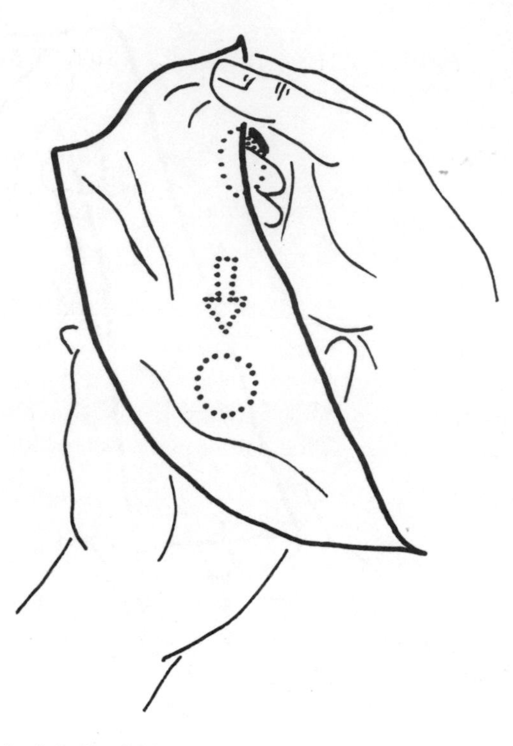

The hidden coin slides into the folds.

Tissue rolled into a ball.

Eyes in the Back of Your Head

How it looks

"Some people are so good at noticing things that we say they have eyes in the back of the head," you say. "You might not believe this, but I've got eyes in the back of my head, too. Magic eyes. Right about here." You point to the base of your skull. "When the light in the room is just right, I've found I can see with the back of my head."

You offer to demonstrate if someone will lend you a quarter. Taking it, you hold the coin against the base of your skull, turning your back so everyone can see it there. With the "eyes in the back of your head," you read the date on the coin, calling it out loud, and then hand it back so the lender can confirm that you did "see" the date correctly.

"With eyes in the back of my head," you say, "I don't always know where I'm going, but I do know where I've been."

What you need

A quarter

The secret

The borrowed coin is switched secretly for one with a date you have memorized ahead of time.

How you fix it

Memorize the date and have the coin in a left pocket that is otherwise empty.

What you do

A short time before you are ready to show the trick, secretly get the coin into your left hand, so it rests against the palm of that hand with the bottom three fingers loosely closed around it.

Ask to borrow the quarter and hold out your right hand for it, so it can be placed on the empty palm of that hand. With your left hand, reach over and pick it up between your first finger and thumb. Hold it up and show it.

Bring your left hand to the back of your neck at the base of your skull and push the borrowed quarter down into your collar, where

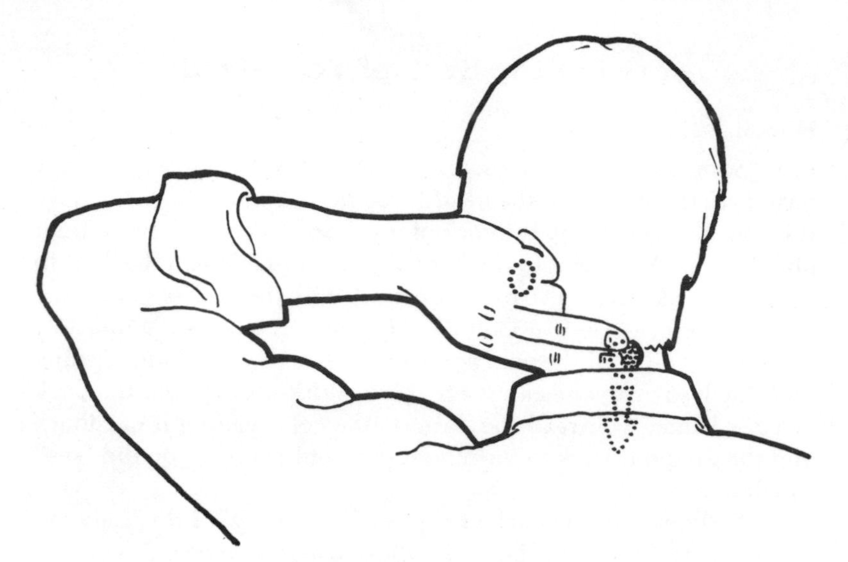

Drop the borrowed coin into your collar.

it will be hidden against your neck. Move your own quarter out to your fingertips and raise your hand a little higher at the back of your head.

Hold it there and immediately turn around so everyone can see it. Slowly call out one number at a time; then repeat the entire date. Lift the coin away from your head, hold it high in the air, turn around, and hand it back to the lender. Ask him or her to read the date aloud to confirm that you saw it correctly with the "eyes in the back of your head."

A Penny for Your Thoughts

How it looks

"I've written you a note, but I don't want you to read it for a minute because it's about something that hasn't happened yet," you tell a friend, as you put a slip of folded paper on the table. You take some coins from your pocket and spread those out across the table. "Three nickels, three dimes, and one penny."

You explain that you are going to take turns eliminating the coins, one at a time, until only one coin is left. "We'll do it this way," you say, "so neither of us can guess which will be the last coin."

You put your two hands down over two coins, ask your friend to touch either one of your hands, and you push that coin aside. Then you invite him to put his two hands over any two coins, and you touch one of his hands and eliminate that coin. You cover two more and he touches one of your hands, and so on, until all the coins have been removed but one.

"You've had half a dozen choices," you say. "But by pure chance, the only one left is a penny." You give him the folded note that has been on the table from the start. He opens it and reads aloud what you have written: "Somehow I knew you would choose to leave the penny."

What you need

Three nickels, three dimes, and one penny
Trousers with pockets
A small slip of paper
A pen or pencil

The secret

It looks like a fair choice each time, but your friend never gets a chance to eliminate the penny. That is always the last coin left, because *you start first* in covering the coins and *you never put either of your own hands over the penny*.

What you do

Explain about the folded note and put it on the table. Show the coins and spread them out a few inches apart from each other. Tell your friend you are going to take turns eliminating the coins, one by one, until only one is left.

Put your two hands over any two coins *except the penny*. Have him touch either of your hands and then you push that coin aside. Then ask him to put his two hands over any two coins. If neither of the coins he covers is the penny, you can touch either of his hands and remove that coin. But if he puts one hand over the penny, you just touch his other hand and remove the coin under it.

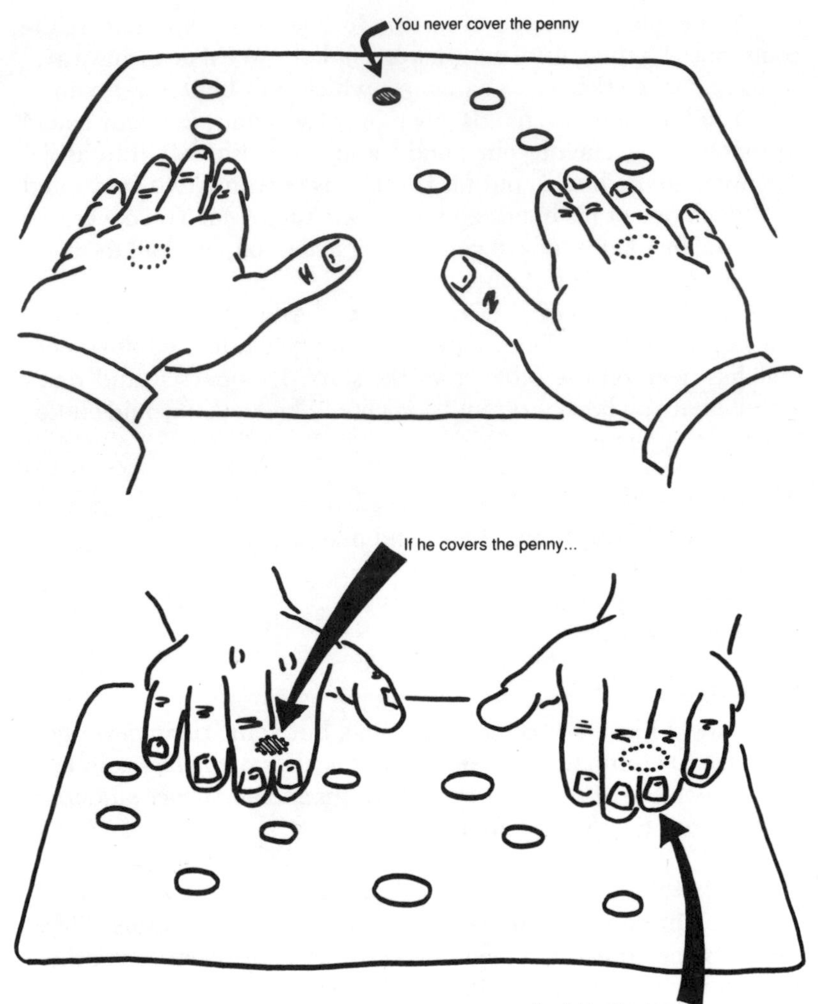

Turn by turn, you continue the same thing. When it's your turn, you never cover the penny; when it's his turn, you always touch one of his hands that is not over the penny. At the end, the penny has to be the only coin left.

"You have had half a dozen choices," you say. "But by pure chance, the only one left is the penny." Then you hand him the folded note and have him read aloud your prediction.

Coins and Kids

How it looks

This is a counting trick for performing before groups of small children. You invite two of them to help you and give each a little clasp purse. Each child is asked to count the coins he finds in his purse. In turn, they count them aloud, dropping them one at a time into an empty paper cup you hold, so everyone can see and hear the counting. After each is finished, you pour the coins back into the child's purse. Each child finds he has exactly five coins.

You pretend to extract one coin and then another from one of the purses and pass the two "invisible coins" into the second purse. When the children count them again, one has three coins in his purse and the other has seven. But to even things up, you reverse the magic, and when the counting is done once more, each has five coins in his purse, as at the beginning.

What you need

Ten quarters or half-dollars
Two small clasp-type pocket purses
A paper drinking cup
A craft knife or sharp-pointed scissors

The secret

The paper cup has a slot in one side near the bottom, so that you can secretly hold back or add coins as they are counted into it.

How you fix it

Cut a lengthwise slot in the paper cup at one side just above the bottom. It should be slightly wider than the coins and a little higher than two coins stacked together. The slot is to allow coins dropped to the bottom of the cup to slide partly out into your fingers held at the side.

Put five coins in each purse and have them on your table along with the cup, turned so its slot is at the rear.

What you do

Invite the two children up, have one stand at each side, and give each of them one of the purses. Pick up the cup with your left hand so your fingers are at the rear, covering the slot, the opening of which should come opposite the space between the middle fingers.

Go to the child at your left and ask him to open his purse. Turn the cup upside down and snap it with your thumb and finger to call attention to the fact that it is empty. Ask the child to take the coins one at a time from his purse and count them aloud as he drops them into the cup you hold. Count aloud with him.

Keep two coins secretly nipped between your fingers.

But as he drops in the first coin, tilt the cup backwards slightly so the coin slides across the bottom of the slot, where you can nip the edge of it between your fingers to hold it. Do the same with the second coin he drops. Tilt the cup forward a little to receive each of the three remaining coins as it is dropped.

Ask again how many coins he has. Have him open his purse wide and turn it upside down to make sure there are no other coins in it. Then have him hold it high, above his eye level, while you pour the coins from the cup back into it. Keep the two coins secretly nipped between your fingers at the rear edge of the slot to hold them back. Only three coins pour from the cup into his purse. Snap the purse shut for him and ask him to keep it between his two hands.

With the two coins nipped between your fingers at the edge of the slot, shake the cup upside down to indicate that it is empty. Let your hand, with the cup, fall to your side.

Now go to the second child and repeat the same counting of coins into the cup. When you finally pour them back into his purse, release the two extra coins so they go in with his five. Snap his purse shut and then rest the cup, slot to the rear, on the table.

Play up the business of making the coins pass across from purse to purse, one at a time, by having the audience shout "Go!" Add to the fun by pretending one of the "invisible coins" fell to the floor and that you can't find it for a moment because it's invisible.

Then have the child with the seven coins count his into the cup. Nip the first two with your fingers, by tilting the cup back to slide them partly through the slot, as he begins to count. Hold those two back when you finally pour the coins into his purse again. The audience thinks he has seven, but he really gets back only five.

Go to the child whose purse has three coins and have him count those into the cup. When you finally pour the coins into his purse again, let the two you have been holding back pour in with them. The audience thinks he has only three, but he really gets back five.

Each child now has a purse containing five coins, but you don't reveal that yet. Put the cup back on the table. Explain to the audience that you must work the magic in reverse. "When I count to three, I want you all to shout the magic word just as loudly as you can," you say. "Everybody shout 'og'—that's 'go' backwards." The audience shouts and you wave your hand backwards and pretend to pass the first "invisible coin." Say, "I'm not sure that was loud enough—let's try again."

Finally, have the coins counted, first from one purse and then the other, each child counting his set out into the cup, to show that each has five coins as at the start.

Comedy Cut Bill

How it looks

You cut a dollar bill in half, hold up the two pieces separately, then put them together and trim off the cut ends. "Will you just snap your fingers?" you ask someone in the audience. When he does, you shake the bill open to show it is whole once more. "There it is. Just as good as new. Well, almost."

Something has gone wrong! The bill is together in one piece, but the two halves are reversed. Half of the back of the bill is joined to half of the face, so the two parts are in opposite directions.

"Which hand did you use when you snapped your fingers?" you ask the spectator. When he answers, you say, "No wonder. That was the wrong hand."

You cut the bill apart again, show the two halves, and trim off the cut ends. "Now snap your fingers," you say. "With the *other* hand." He does and you shake the bill open to show it properly whole again. But it is much smaller than it was at the start because so much has been cut away. "We seem to have lost about forty cents' worth," you say. "But that's how any dollar looks—after taxes."

What you need

Sports jacket
A dozen play money dollar bills
Rubber cement
Talcum powder
An old newspaper
A sharp pair of scissors that will fit into your breast pocket

The secret

This is based on an old trick of repeatedly cutting and restoring a strip of paper that has been treated with rubber cement. The pressure of the scissors as they cut through it automatically sticks the cut edges together so it appears whole again.

How you fix it

Since you will cut up one of the bills each time you practice or show the trick, it is easiest to prepare a batch all at once. Lay all the bills separately in faceup rows on the opened-out newspaper. Thickly coat the entire vertical center of each bill with rubber cement, right down from top to bottom, brushing it out to the edges and covering an area about three inches wide.

When it is dry, apply a good second coat. Allow the bills to dry again and then spread talcum powder liberally over the coated sections, smoothing it with the tip of your finger. Shake off the excess powder, turn all the bills back up, and repeat the same process, so

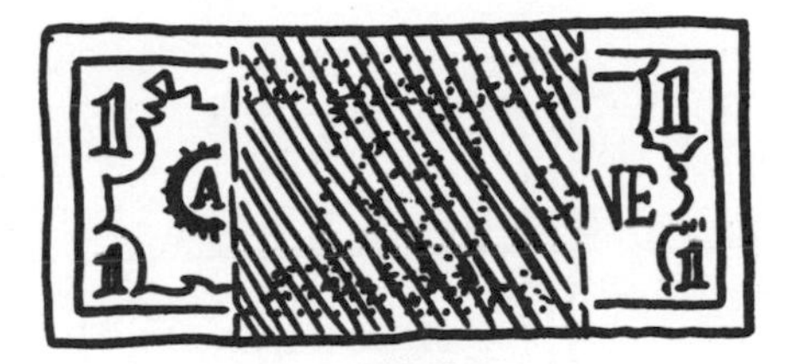

Center of both sides is coated with rubber cement and dusted with talcum.

Cut the bill in half across the center.

Trim off the cut ends by cutting through both together.

The bill is put back together, but the two halves are reversed.

After some more cutting and trimming, the halves match but the bill is much shorter.

the centers of both the fronts and backs are double-coated and powdered. The supply of bills can be stored in an envelope. Because of the powder, they won't stick together.

Turn one of them with its narrow edges top and bottom, and fold it exactly in half, top to bottom. Have it that way in your breast pocket with the scissors.

What you do

Take out the bill and scissors. Unfold the bill, show it, and hold it with your left hand. With the scissors in your right hand, cut across the center crease to cut the bill in two. Hold one half in each hand, show them, and bring the halves together in your left hand so the *back* of one half lies squarely against the *face* of the other half, with both cut edges at the top.

Trim off the two cut edges together, cutting evenly right across through both to trim off about one-quarter of an inch. Let the scraps fall and put the scissors in your breast pocket. Bring your right hand to the bottom edges of the bill and take the outer edge between your right thumb and fingers, still holding the bill with your left hand.

Ask a spectator to snap his fingers. When he does, lift up your right hand so the bill unfolds and hangs open from that hand. Because the rubber cement holds the cut edges, the bill appears to be restored in one piece, but with the two halves reversed, so that half the face is joined to half the back.

"It's together again, but the pieces have hitched themselves up backwards—front to back and back to front." Stare at the strange-looking bill. Then look at the spectator, and ask, "Which hand did you use when you snapped your fingers?" Whatever he answers, say, "No wonder. That was the wrong hand."

Bring the palm of your left hand against the bottom part of the bill that is hanging from your right hand and fold the bill shut. Take the scissors from your pocket. Cut right across through both edges together, again trimming off about one quarter of an inch. Separate the two pieces and show one in each hand.

Now bring them together into your left hand again, one atop the other, but this time so the two pieces are *face to face* or *back to back*. You can easily arrange that as you show the two pieces separately and turn them over.

Hold the two together and trim about half an inch off the already cut edges, cutting evenly through both at once. Put the scissors in your pocket. Hold the bill in your left hand and take the outer bottom edge between your right thumb and fingers.

"Now snap your fingers," you tell the spectator. "With the *other* hand." When he does, hold up the bill with your right hand so it unfolds and hangs open, properly restored but now so much shorter it looks like a midget-sized bill.

"We seem to have lost about forty cents' worth," you say. "But that's how any dollar looks—after taxes." Fold the small bill and put it away in your pocket.

Cup and Bill

How it looks

You borrow a dollar bill, crumple it into a small ball, and drop it into a paper cup. Then you pour the bill from the cup into your right hand, put the empty cup mouth down on the table, show the bill in your hand, and put it in your pocket. When you lift the cup from the table, the crumpled dollar is back under it again.

You repeat the trick twice. Each time, you put the crumpled bill into your pocket, and it appears back under the cup. You give the bill back to the lender, but when he unrolls it he discovers that instead of a dollar bill, it has changed to worthless play money. After the joke, you take a real dollar from your wallet and give it to him to replace the one he loaned you.

Three variations of this trick also are explained below. In the first, before crumpling the bill into a ball, you have a spectator write down the serial number, and at the end it turns out the dollar you take from your own wallet to give him was the bill he originally let you borrow.

The second variation ends when a walnut appears under the cup. The borrowed bill is found inside the nut when it is cracked open. In the third, a lemon is found under the cup at the end, and when the lemon is cut open the lender's dollar is found inside it.

What you need

Two identical nine-ounce paper cups
A pair of small alnico magnets
Scissors, white craft glue, adhesive packaging tape
Two one-dollar bills
One play money bill, or any other sort of "joke" bill you prefer to use
A mat or soft small towel to put on your tabletop
Trousers with pockets, sports jacket
(Additional props needed for the variations will be explained later.)

The secret

The paper cup has a magnet concealed in a double bottom. You have a duplicate dollar bill in which a matching magnet is rolled, so the bill will cling inside the cup when the cup is turned mouth down. The play money bill is in your pocket, where it is switched for the borrowed bill. In the variations, either the walnut or the lemon is switched in your pocket for the bill.

How you fix it

Cut off one cup about 1/4" up from the bottom, so you have a piece that includes the bottom with a small attached collar around it. Trim the bottom piece evenly, and discard the rest of that cup.

Put one of the magnets at the center of the inside bottom of the second cup. Firmly fasten it with a strip of packaging tape. Coat the outside collar of the cut-off piece with white craft glue and push that false bottom down into the bottom of the whole cup. Press the sides to glue it in place and wipe away any excess glue.

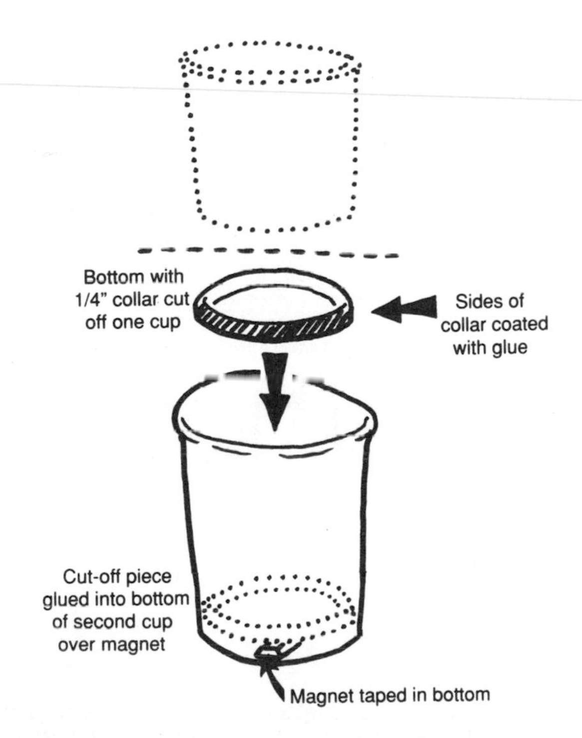

Press the cut-off bottom of one cup over the magnet in the other.

Place the magnet on the folded bill and crumple the bill into a ball.

Fold one of the dollar bills in half lengthwise. Place the other magnet on the folded bill and crumple the bill into a ball around it, so the magnet is covered by the double thickness of the bill.

When the glue is dry, try the cup. Put the mat or towel on the table. Drop the bill with the magnet in it into the cup. Turn the cup mouth down. If you lift the cup, no bill should appear under it because the bill clings to the inside bottom of the cup. But if you put the cup down rather sharply it will shake the bill loose, so that when you lift the cup again the bill will appear.

Crumple the play money bill into a ball and put that in the otherwise empty right-hand pocket of your trousers. Have the other real dollar bill in your wallet. The cup, with the magnet-bill in it, should be on your table beside the mat.

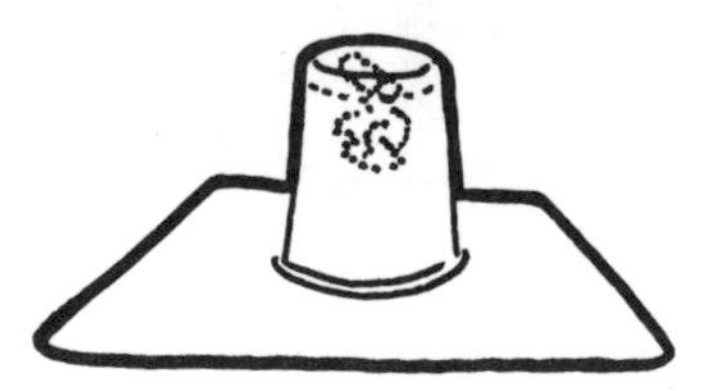

The cup stands mouth down with the magnet bill held inside it.

What you do

Borrow a dollar bill, crumple it into a ball, and drop it into the cup. Explain that this is a "little guessing game." Take the cup with your left hand, pour the borrowed bill out into your right hand, and rest the cup mouth down on the mat. Show the bill in your hand and put it in your pocket, pushing it to the top of your pocket so it won't get mixed up with the play money bill. Bring out your hand, and ask, "Where is the dollar?"

The answer will be that it is in your pocket. You say, "That's right. I wanted to be sure you were watching closely. I'll do it again."

Take the borrowed bill from your pocket. With your left hand, turn the cup mouth up, and drop the bill into the cup. Again pour the bill from the cup into your right hand. With your left hand, turn the cup mouth down on the mat, but a little more sharply so as to shake loose the magnet-bill hidden inside it.

Show the borrowed bill with your right hand and put your hand into your pocket as before. But this time bring your hand back out with the bill still hidden in your hand instead of leaving it in your pocket. Let your hand drop to your side.

Ask where the bill is. The answer will be that it is in your pocket. Say, "No. You're wrong. It's under the cup." With your left hand, lift the cup and show the bill that is there. Take the mouth-upward cup with your right hand at the top and secretly let the bill that was hidden in your hand drop into it. *At the same time*, reach with your left hand to pick up the other bill from the table and display it.

With your right hand, put the cup mouth down on the mat. The momentum will keep the bill in it as you turn it over. Transfer the visible bill from your left hand to your right hand. Put the bill into your pocket, but bring your hand out with the bill still hidden in it as before.

Lift the cup with your left hand to reveal the bill that appears on the mat. Transfer the cup to your right hand and secretly let the hidden bill fall into it from that hand. With your left hand, pick up the other bill from the mat, and with your right hand place the cup mouth down on the mat.

At this point, you are holding the crumpled borrowed bill with your left hand. The magnet-bill is clinging to the inside bottom of the cup that is mouth down on the mat.

Take the borrowed bill with your right hand and put that hand into your pocket. Inside your pocket, drop the borrowed bill, get the play money bill into your hand, and bring your hand out again as before, but with the play money bill hidden in it.

With your left hand, lift the cup to show nothing under it. Put it down again, but rather sharply so the magnet-bill drops from inside it to the mat. Ask again where the dollar is. Lift the cup and show that the dollar is under it and not in your pocket. Transfer the cup to your right hand, secretly dropping the play money bill into it. With your left hand, pick up the other bill and show it, and with your right hand put the cup mouth down on the mat.

The play money bill is now secretly under the cup. Take the magnet-bill in your right hand, put it into your pocket, leave it there, and bring out your empty hand. Lift the cup and reveal the play money bill.

Pick it up, give it to the lender, and say, "Thanks for letting me borrow it. That is your dollar, isn't it?" When he opens it out, he will discover that it is a fake bill. Joke about it and finally give him a dollar from your wallet for the one you borrowed.

His dollar in your wallet

In this version, you use the same routine, but when you borrow the dollar at the start you have the serial number written down. At the end, the dollar you take from your own wallet checks with that number and seems to be the bill you borrowed.

You will need a small stack of office index cards and a pencil. Ahead of time, write the serial number of a dollar on the back of the bottom card of this stack. Put that dollar in an otherwise empty wallet and put it in your hip pocket. Fasten a rubber band around the cards and have those, with the pencil, in your left jacket pocket.

Start the trick by saying, "I'd like to borrow ten thousand dollars from somebody," and pause before you add, "but I'll settle for a one-dollar bill." Borrow it, and say, "Maybe we should have a legal record of this, just in case something should happen to your money."

Take out the stack of cards and hand the top one to the lender along with the pencil. Turn the stack over as you put them back in your left hand. Rest his dollar on top of the cards, where you can see the numbers that you secretly wrote ahead of time.

Ask him to copy the serial number as you read it aloud. Look down as though reading the numbers from his bill, but really read the numbers from the card. Take back the pencil and put it away in your pocket with the rest of the cards.

Then crumple his bill into a ball, go through the routine with the cup, and after the play money joke at the end, you discover his "borrowed" bill in your own wallet. Have him check its serial number with the one he wrote on the card.

Bill in walnut

At the end of the cup and bill routine, instead of the play money bill, a walnut appears under the cup. You take out a nutcracker, crack open the walnut, and his "borrowed" bill is inside.

To fix it, split open a walnut at its center seam with a sharp-pointed knife. Scrape out all the nutmeat. Write the serial number of a dollar bill on the back of an index file card and roll the bill up into a tight ball. Coat the center edges of both walnut halves with glue, put the balled-up bill into the walnut, and glue the nut back together. Coat a little additional glue around the seam, and let it dry thoroughly.

Have a nutcracker in your inside jacket pocket, and put the walnut into the right pocket of your trousers. The stack of file cards for copying the serial number is in your left jacket pocket with a pencil.

Follow the same cup and bill routine, but at the end load the cup with the walnut instead of the play money. Lift the cup to reveal the nut, crack it open, remove the bill, and have the lender open it out and check it against the serial number.

Bill in lemon

In this version, instead of the walnut or play money bill, a lemon is found under the cup at the end, and when the lemon is cut open, the "borrowed" bill is discovered inside.

To fix it, carefully remove the pip from the end of a lemon that is small enough to fit easily inside the paper cup. With a sharp-pointed pencil, poke a hole down into the lemon. Write the serial number of a dollar bill on the back of an index card. Take a small piece of plastic wrap or wax paper, roll the bill into a tight cylinder, wrap the paper tightly around it, and push it all the way down inside the lemon. Glue the pip back into place and let it dry.

Put a sharp pocket knife in your jacket pocket. Have the lemon in your right trousers pocket, switch it for the last bill, and secretly load the lemon into the cup instead of the play money bill.

Lift the cup and reveal the lemon. With the pocket knife, cut the lemon halfway through all the way around. Take it apart, remove the wrapped dollar bill, and have it checked against the serial number.

You should have a small plate to cut the lemon on so the juice doesn't drip on the table. It is also a good idea to have a few facial tissues handy to wipe your fingers.

The Money Spell

How it looks

"I'm about to cast a spell," you say, as you show some cards with letters of the alphabet on them. Each card has one letter on the front and another on the back, and you spell them aloud as you show the letters, one at a time: "M-A-G-I-C, M-O-N-E-Y." Holding the cards stacked together in your hand, you say, "That spells 'magic money'—and here it is!"

You swing the stack of alphabet cards down to tap them against the palm of your other hand, and suddenly the cards all change into dollar bills. As you count the bills from hand to hand, showing both sides of them, you say, "M-A-G-I-C—and that spells 'magic'!"

What you need

Six play money bills
Two 5" by 8" unlined office file cards or other thin cardboard
White craft glue
A rubber band
Black felt tip pen, pencil, ruler, scissors

The secret

One alphabet card has a bill attached to its back, and the other bills are folded in that, hidden behind the card during the spelling.

How you fix it

The two file cards provide the cardboard for making six small cards, each the *exact* width of the bills and 3-3/4" long. It is easiest to cut one of the small cards first and use that as a pattern for marking out and cutting the others. Since play money bills vary somewhat in width according to the manufacture, measure the exact width of the bills you are using. Then take one of the file cards, and with the pencil and ruler mark off a section exactly that wide and 3-3/4" long. Cut out that small card and use it to mark around so you can cut five more the same size.

Turn one of the bills facedown with its narrow edges top and bottom. Coat one of the small cards with white craft glue and fasten that card to the bottom part of the bill so the edges match squarely at the bottom and both sides.

When the glue is dry, turn the bill faceup, with the attached card now underneath against the table. Trim off any tiny edges of card that may show beyond the edges of the bill. Fold the unfastened top part of the bill down against the face of it, toward the bottom, and crease the fold so the bill is flat.

Now turn the card side faceup. With the felt tip pen, print a big block letter "M" on it, filling the face of the card. (You may prefer to use a stencil or rub-on letters.) Take a second card and print a big "A" on its face and a "G" on its back. Print "I" on the face of the third one and "C" on its back. On the opposite sides of a fourth print "M" and "O", and on a fifth, "N" and "E". Print a "Y" on the last one and leave its back blank.

Turn the card with the attached bill so the bill is facing you and open out the top fold. Lay the five other bills evenly faceup on that one, with all edges matched, and fold them all down from the top together, inside the fold of the attached one. Again crease the fold.

Stack the cards in this order from the bottom up as the letters face you: first the bills, next the blank face, then E, O, C, G. Square them up, snap the rubber band around them, and put them in the empty left pocket of your trousers.

The first card has bills folded at the back of it.

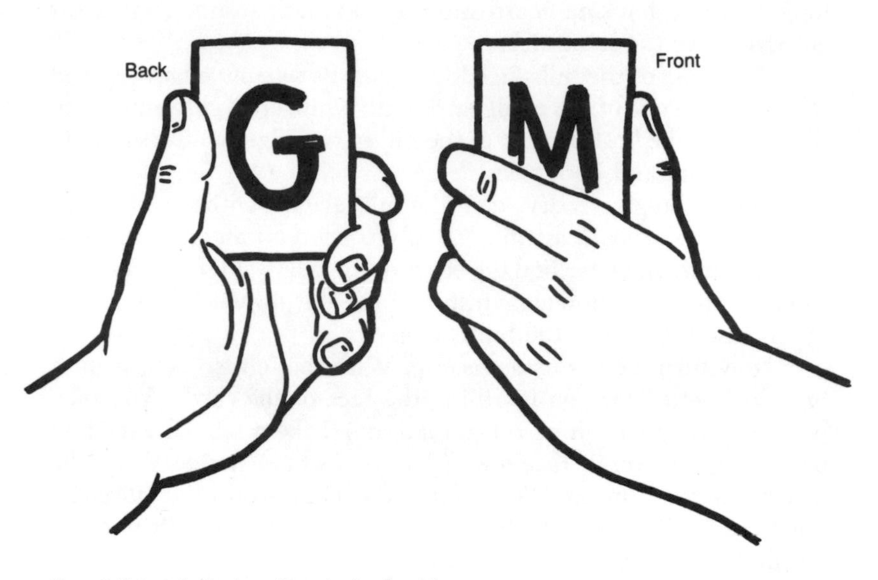

Your left hand displays the stack of cards.

What you do

As you say you are about to "cast a spell," take out the cards, remove and discard the rubber band, and hold the stack at its top edge between your right thumb and fingers so the face of the first card can be seen. Show the "M" at the face of it to the audience, and start spelling aloud, "M."

Leave the card where it is. Bring the palm of your left hand against the face of the stack to hold the cards with that hand, fingers across the front and thumb at the back. With your right hand, take the first card from the *back* of the stack. Hold that one up long enough for the audience to see the face of it, and spell aloud, "A." Turn that card around to show the back of it and spell, "G."

Now put the card at the *front* of the whole stack in your left hand and leave it there. Take the next one from the back, hold it up and slowly show the letters, first front and then back, as you spell, "I, C." Return it to the front of the stack, keeping the cards all squared up in your left hand.

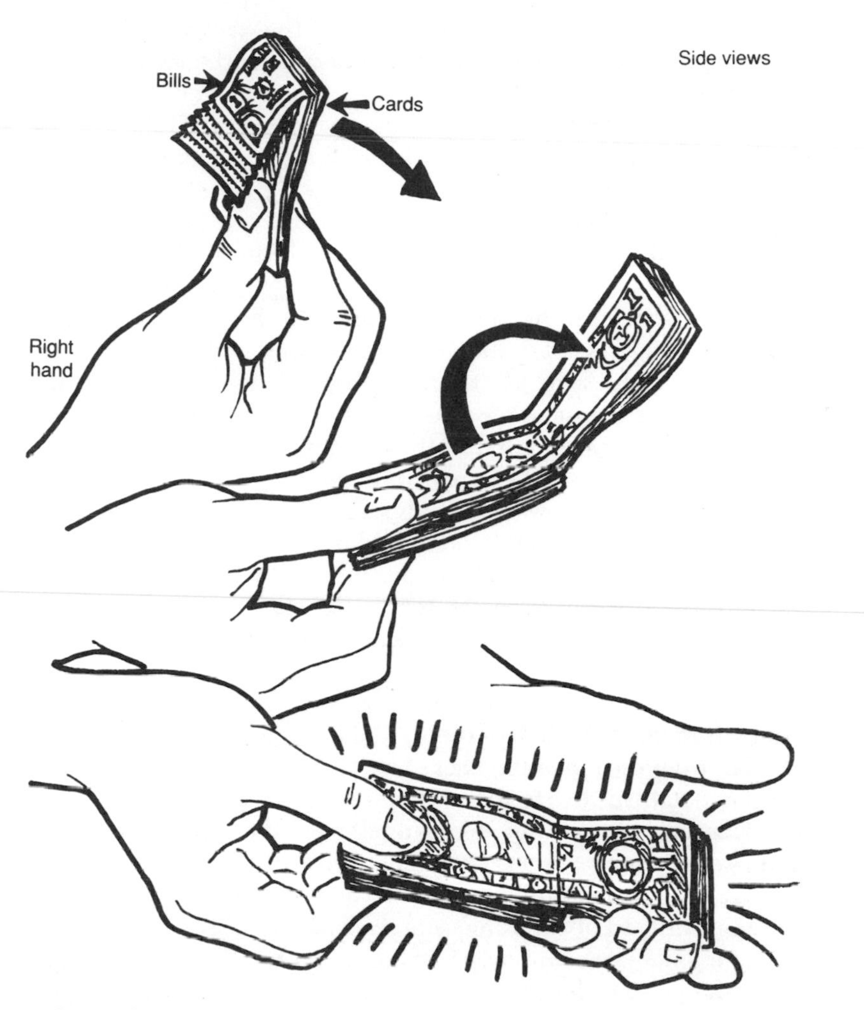

The folded bills snap open.

Pause a moment. Then in the same way—taking each card from the back, holding it up to show one side and then the other, and returning it to the front of the stack—spell out, "M-O-N-E-Y." With the last card, you show the "Y" at the face of it, turn it around to show that the back is blank, and return it to the front of the stack with the blank side still facing the audience.

The folded bills are now at the rear of the stack your left hand is holding. Bring your right hand to the bottom of the stack and take it with that hand, with your four fingers up in front of the bottom edge and thumb at the rear just *below* the edge of the folded-down bills. Hold the stack firmly and keep it upright so nobody glimpses the bills at the back.

Lower your left hand to below your waist, turn it palm up, and hold it out in front of you. Say, "That spells 'magic money'—and here it is!"

Bring your right hand straight down to the front so the stack lightly slaps against the palm of your left hand and the folded bills snap open. Close your left thumb across the top of the bills and close your fingers around the side edges to keep the bills fully opened out. Keep the cards squared in the palm of that hand beneath the bills, which now hide the cards from view, and tilt the hand forward so the front edges of the bills slant slightly toward the floor.

At this point your left hand is holding the stack and both hands are in front of you, down below your waist. With your right hand, separate the first bill from the top of the stack, making sure you have only one. Hold it up, show the audience the front and back of it, and say, "M."

Put that bill back under all the cards and bills in your left hand, sliding it in at the bottom of them, and leave it there. Separate the next bill from the top of the stack, hold it up to show both sides, and say, "A." Return that to the bottom of all the others.

Continue in that way, taking a bill from the top, showing both sides, saying aloud the next letter, and returning it to the bottom of the stack, as you naturally would if you were counting a stack of bills. But instead of counting, you spell aloud, "M-A-G-I-C."

(Actually you count only five bills from hand to hand, leaving the sixth one, which has the card glued to its underside, on top of the stack at the end. But the spelling aloud of the five-letter word *magic*, while showing a bill for each letter, leads the audience to believe you have shown both sides of all the bills. It also leaves the hidden cards sandwiched between the bills, so the cards are now covered top and bottom.)

The final spelling and counting off of the bills should be done quickly. As you finish the spelling, casually show both sides of the stack of bills in your left hand. As you fold down the tops of them to put them back into your pocket, say, "And that spells 'magic'!"

THREE

Magic with Paper

These tricks all use paper or things made of paper: a scratch pad, tissue, newspaper, cardboard, paper plates. With such inexpensive props, you easily can put them together, try them, change them about, practice with them—and any mistakes are the kind you can afford to throw away.

Some of the world's greatest magicians have featured tricks with newspapers, which have a special appeal because a newspaper is a common thing most people handle every day. It is something that doesn't look tricky, and its innocent appearance adds to the magical surprise.

Tissue paper tricks can bring a touch of the fabled mystery of the Orient to your magic show. They were first made popular by Chinese and Japanese magicians who toured the vaudeville theaters of Europe and America with their colorful acts of Oriental magic. Tissue offers bright colors, squeezes small so it is easy to hide, bulks large when opened out, and most tricks done with it have the charm of being simple and direct.

The Acrobatic Newspaper

How it looks

You have a newspaper in your hands, which you open out as though reading it, but everybody can see that you are holding it upside down. "I have a friend who always reads the paper while he is practicing his Yoga exercises—standing on his head," you say. "He claims the news makes more sense that way. But, of course, what is upside down to us would be right side up to him—if you see what I mean."

As you speak, you spread your hands apart and the opened-out newspaper seems to float in space for a moment as it does a forward somersault in midair. It flips itself over and turns right side up as you catch it between your hands again.

What you need

Two double pages from a small-sized (tabloid) newspaper or from a newspaper magazine section
Four pennies
Thin, lightweight cardboard like what you can cut from empty paper cartons
Strong black thread
White craft glue, transparent tape, scissors

The secret

The newspaper really is two sheets glued together, stiffened inside with cardboard, and weighted at the top with four pennies. A hidden black thread runs across inside the center, with large loops at each end that fit over your thumbs. When you release the paper from your fingers it hangs suspended on the thread, and the weight of the pennies tips it over forward to turn it right side up.

How you fix it

Open out one double newspaper sheet. Put it on a table with its long edges top and bottom and the printing turned *upside down*. Lay four pennies across just below the top edge, one near each corner and one at each side of the vertical center crease. Fasten the pennies to the paper with cross-strips of transparent tape.

You will need two pieces of thin, lightweight cardboard, each about two inches shorter than the page from top to bottom and about an inch wide. Place one piece close to the left edge of the double page, vertically beneath the penny at the top left corner, and the other piece close to the right edge, beneath the penny at that corner. Fasten those pieces to the paper with strips of tape at top, center, and bottom.

Cut four more pieces of cardboard, each an inch wide and slightly shorter than the distance from the attached side strips to the center crease of the paper. Place those across at right angles to the side strips and tape down their ends and centers.

Cut off a piece of thread about sixteen inches longer than the width of the double page. Lay it across the center of the paper, left to right, so there is an eight-inch end of thread beyond the paper's edge at each side. Fasten cross-strips of tape over the thread at the

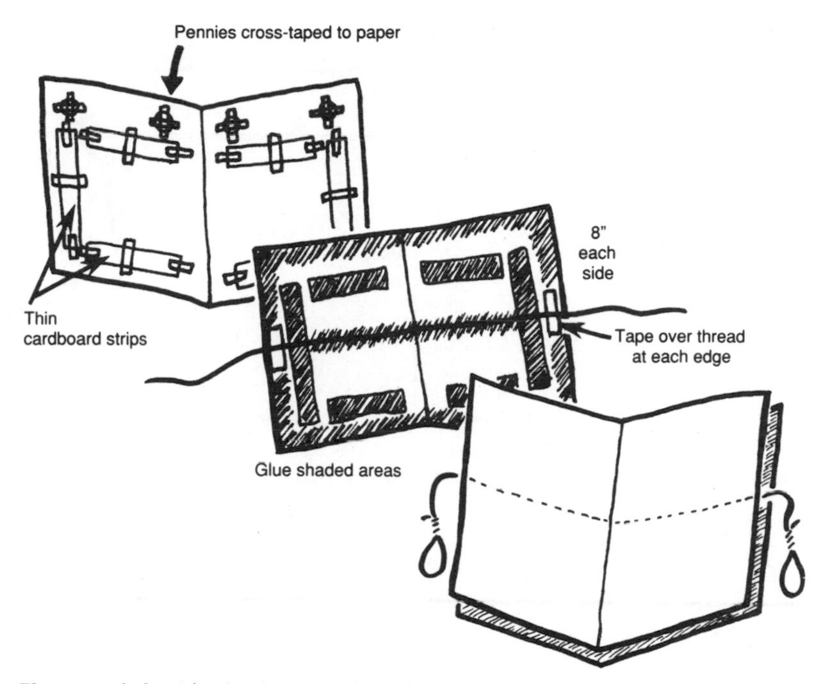

The second sheet is glued on top of the first. A large non-slip loop is tied at each end of the thread.

left and right edges of the paper. This will keep the thread from tearing through.

Spread a narrow band of white craft glue across the entire double page just above the thread, and a second band of glue across just below the thread. Then coat all the paper's edges and all the pieces of cardboard with glue.

Open out the second double sheet and turn it so its printing is *upside down*. Lay it squarely on top of the first sheet and glue the two together so their edges match. At each end of the thread, tie a non-slip loop about two inches long.

What you do

This trick has to be set up ahead of time out of sight of your audience. It should be performed as an opening trick, or as a "walk-on" bit between other acts.

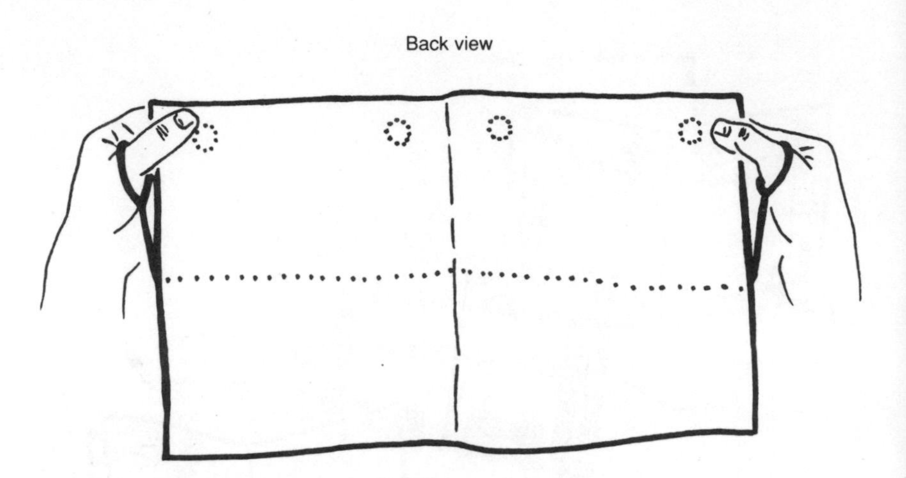

With loops over your thumbs, both of your hands drop the paper.

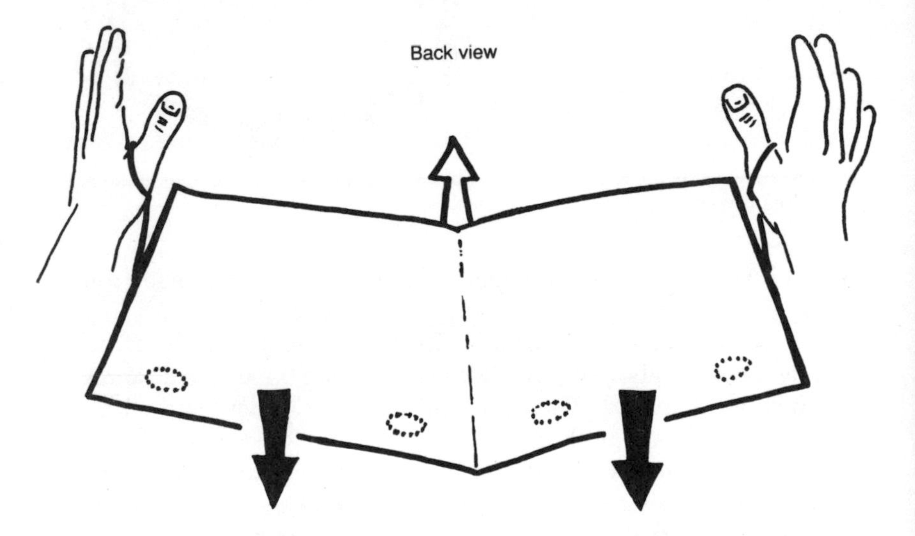

Turn your palms outward an instant as the paper flips right side up.

Slip the left loop of thread down over your left thumb and the right loop over your right thumb. Take the top left corner of the paper between your left thumb and fingers, palm toward you and with the fingers across the front of it and thumb behind. Hold the top right corner the same way between your right thumb and fingers.

Then bring your hands together to close the paper and hold it in front of you. That is how you will be holding it when you walk out to show the trick.

What follows should be done *slowly*; the effect will be lost if you do it too quickly. Open the paper between your hands and look down as though reading it. Give your audience time to realize it is upside down. Say, "I have a friend who always reads the paper while he is practicing his Yoga exercises—standing on his head."

Slowly move your arms straight forward in front of your waist, with the paper held open between your hands. "He claims the news makes more sense that way. But, of course, what is upside down to us would be right side up to him."

Now simply drop the two top corners of the paper from your hands, and *without moving your arms,* turn your hands palm outward for an instant and then quickly back again as they were, in order to catch the paper as it flips itself over and comes right side up. Catch it at the sides between your opened fingers, and then say, "If you see what I mean."

Hold it as it is for a moment and then close it partly, with your thumbs inside. Because the loops of thread are so large, you can very easily slide your thumbs out of them behind the paper as you turn to put it aside and go on with your next trick.

Yoo Hoo!

How it looks

"This is my magic telephone answering service," you say, as you show a small scratch pad. "All I need is a little piece of blank paper." You tear a sheet from the pad, show both sides of it blank, then tear that in half, and put the little torn-off piece on the table.

You ask a friend to place his hand over the scrap of paper. "Now let's pretend that your telephone rings when there's nobody home," you say. "Somebody's calling you and wants to leave a message. Instead of an answering machine, we'll just use magic."

You snap your fingers and ask the person to pick up the piece of paper and look at it. On what was the blank paper, a message has mysteriously appeared. Printed across it in pencil are the words, "YOO HOO!" You point to the message and say, "I knew there was somebody calling you."

What you need

A small scratch pad, about 3" by 5"
A pencil
Rubber cement
A shirt pocket

The secret

The paper that looks like a single blank sheet that you take from the pad really is two pieces of paper, partly cemented together with the message hidden between them. When you fold it to tear it in half, you tear off only the part with the message hidden at the back, and put it facedown on the table for the person to cover with his hand.

How you fix it

Turn back the top sheet of the scratch pad. On the *lower half of the second sheet,* using the pencil lightly so the marks won't show through, print "YOO HOO!" Coat the *upper half* of that second sheet with rubber cement and then close the top sheet evenly down over it to stick the two together.

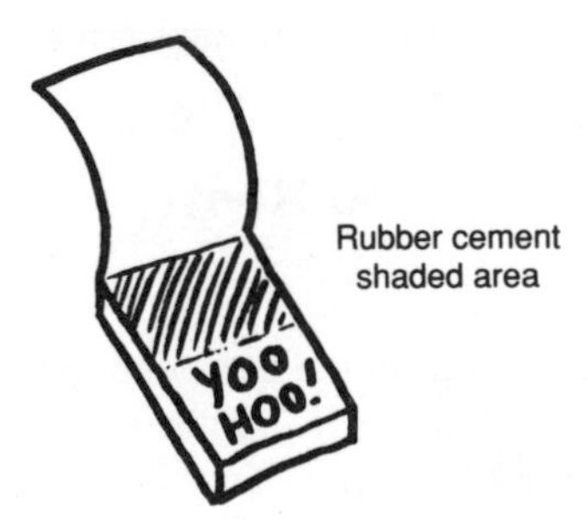

Stick the first sheet on top of the second sheet.

This gives you a double sheet still attached to the pad, with its top half fastened together and its bottom edges open. Hold the double bottom edges together and loosely roll them upward a few inches and let them spring free, so those bottom edges are slightly curled up away from the rest of the pad. Have the pad in your shirt pocket, with the face of the pad toward your body.

The double sheet on top is slightly curled up from the pad.

What you do

Take the pad from your pocket, show it, and rest it on your left palm. Put your right fingers under the curled bottom edges of the double sheet, grip the edges together between your right thumb and fingers, and tear the double sheet from the pad as if it were a single sheet.

With your left hand, slide the pad back into your shirt pocket and leave it there. Keep the double sheet held as it was between your right thumb and fingers, show both sides of it, and say, "All I need is a little piece of blank paper."

Turn it sideways, long edges top and bottom, fold it in half toward you from right to left, and crease it down the center. Separate the two edges at the left and open out *only the back sheet.* Tear it in half along the crease and put the torn-off half facedown on the table.

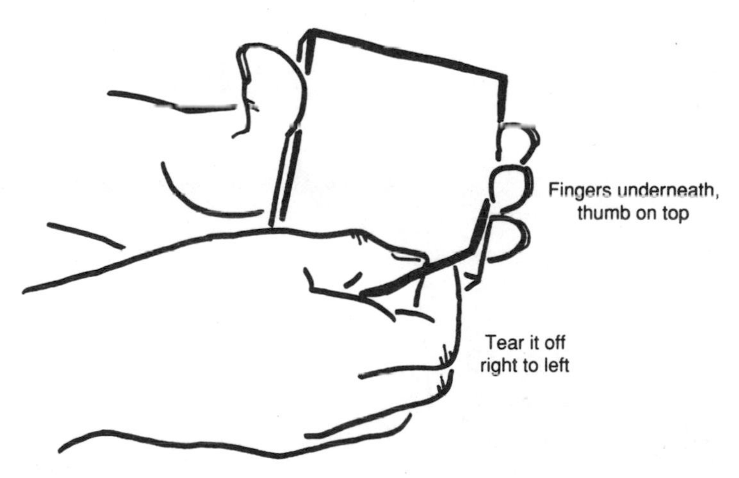

Your right hand tears the double sheet from the pad as if it were a single sheet.

This looks as if you simply folded the sheet from the pad and creased it, then opened it out again and tore it in half. But the hidden message is now on the piece on the table. Ask your friend to put his hand over it. While he is doing that, crumple up the rest of the sheet from the pad and discard it by putting it in your pocket.

Have him pretend the phone is ringing. "Somebody's calling and wants to leave a message," you say. "Instead of an answering machine, we'll just use magic." Snap your fingers, have him turn over the piece of paper he thinks is blank, and when he discovers the "YOO HOO!" message, tell him, "I knew there was somebody calling you."

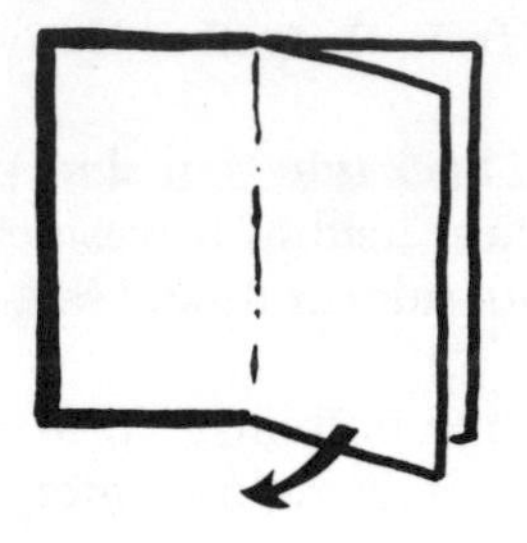

Fold it in half right to left.

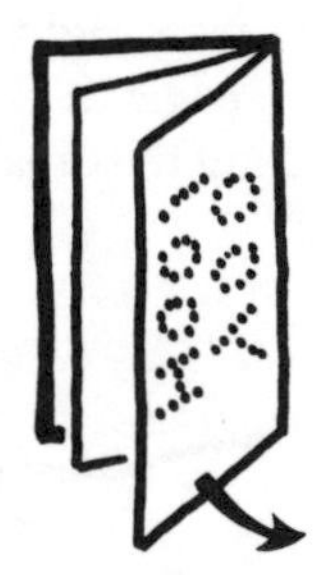

Open out only the single sheet at the back.

Tear it apart down center crease and put the torn-off piece facedown on the table.

The Third Hand

How it looks

"Do you remember the nursery rhyme about the cow that jumped over the moon and the dish that ran away with the spoon?" you ask, as you show a metal teaspoon. "I don't know whatever became of the cow and the dish—but this is the runaway spoon."

You hang a sheet of newspaper over your left arm and put the spoon up under it into your hand. Then you show your right hand empty, put that under the paper, and take out the left hand to show it empty. You claim that the spoon has run away again and disappeared, but it seems obvious you are just changing the spoon from hand to hand under the paper.

You lead your audience along with the joke and offer to show your "other hand." To everyone's surprise, you produce a "third hand," a cardboard cutout shaped like a hand. Finally you shake open the sheet of newspaper and show that both your own hands *are* empty and the spoon really has disappeared!

You crumple up the paper, toss it out to those watching, and reach down behind your knee and produce the missing spoon.

What you need

A double sheet of newspaper
A piece of thin white posterboard larger than your hand
A metal teaspoon
Transparent tape, pencil, scissors
A long-sleeved jacket

The secret

The spoon is pushed up your sleeve to hide it when you first put it up under the newspaper, but the byplay and comic production of the "third hand" help distract the audience from the very simple secret.

The "third hand" is taped inside the newspaper from the start. All the rest is acting to lead the audience along until you show that the spoon really has vanished. When you reach down behind your knee to produce it again, you just let it secretly slide down out of your sleeve into your hand.

How you fix it

To make the "third hand," place your own left hand flat on a piece of posterboard, thumb and fingers spread apart, mark around your hand with the pencil, and cut out the "hand."

Fold the open newspaper left to right on the crease between the pages. Lay the posterboard hand on the lower half, fingers pointing down, and fasten it there with a small strip of tape attached to the cuff so the hand will hang below the center cross-crease. Then fold the paper in half top to bottom to cover the hand.

Have the folded paper on your table with the spoon beside it. You will need to wear a long-sleeved jacket when you show the trick.

Lift straight up so the paper opens out.

What you do

Talk about the nursery rhyme, show the spoon, and put it aside on the table. With your right hand, take the top of the folded paper and lift it straight up so the center fold opens out. Bend your left arm across in front of you, fingertips to the right. Hang the center crease of the paper over the top of that arm, so the paper covers the left hand and end of the sleeve.

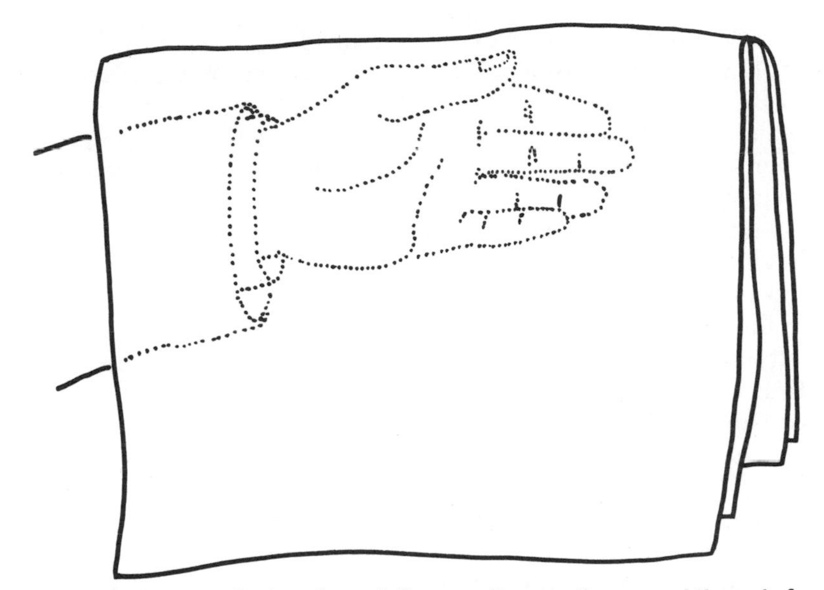

Hang the crease over the top of your left arm so it covers the arm and the end of the sleeve.

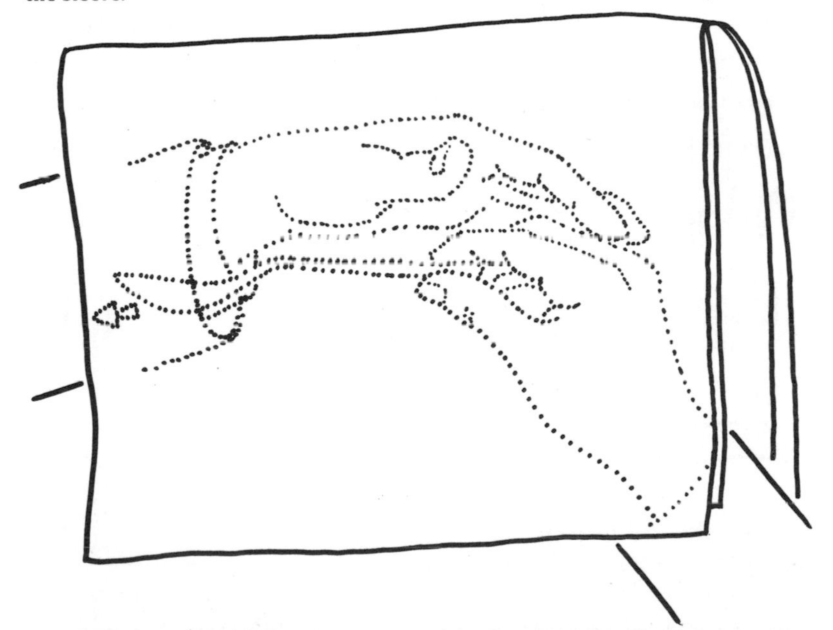

Your right hand pretends to put the spoon into the left hand under the paper but actually pushes it into the sleeve.

Pick up the spoon with your right hand, tap it on the table, and bring it up inside the paper that is hanging over your left arm, as though putting the spoon into your left hand under the paper. But push it up inside your left sleeve to hide it there. From now on, keep your left hand tilted upward slightly so the spoon doesn't fall out of your sleeve.

Immediately bring your right hand out of the paper again, hold its palm toward the audience to show it empty, and say, "The spoon isn't in this hand." Put your right hand back under the paper, as though taking the spoon from your left hand, and remove your left hand, leaving the paper hanging over your right arm and hand. Hold your left hand up to show it empty, and say, "And the spoon isn't in this hand."

Look at your left hand again, wiggle those fingers, and say, "If it isn't in this hand—" Put your left hand back under the paper as though taking the spoon from your right hand. Immediately bring your right hand out, leaving the paper hanging over your left arm and hand. Wiggle your empty right fingers and say, "And if it isn't in this hand, then it must be someplace else. And if it's someplace else, then it isn't here. It has run away again and disappeared."

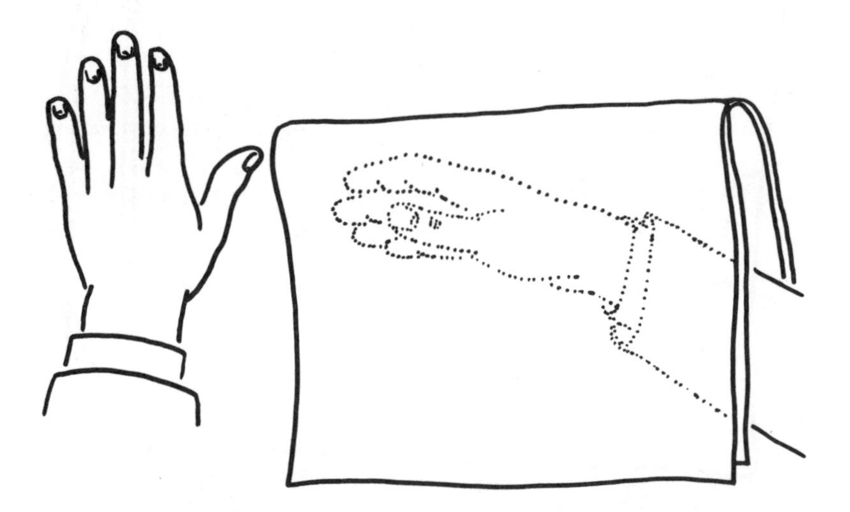

Show your left hand empty while the paper hangs over your right arm.

It seems to those watching as if you had simply transferred the spoon from hand to hand under the paper. They think it is just a joke. "Some of you seem to be suspicious," you say. "Would you like to see my other hand? All right." Hold up your right hand once more. "Here's one hand." Reach inside the paper with it, pull free the tape holding the "third hand," and bring that out with your right hand to hold it up and show it. "And here's another hand. Two hands. Both of them empty."

Wait for the laughter over the surprise production of the "third hand." Then put the posterboard hand aside on the table, shake your head, and say, "I wouldn't fool you—not that easily, I hope."

With your right hand, take the bottom front of the folded paper and lift the paper straight up off your left arm and hand. The paper falls open to reveal your empty left hand, which is held upright, palm toward the audience, fingers spread wide. "The spoon really has disappeared."

Keep both hands upright and crush the paper between them, bunching it roughly into a ball. With your right hand, toss the crumpled paper to the audience. Then say, "But the spoon didn't run away very far."

Bring your left hand down behind your left knee, so the hand and the end of the sleeve are covered from front view. As you lower your hand behind you, the spoon will slide from your sleeve into your left fingers. "Here it is again." Pretend to pull the spoon from behind your knee, hold it up high to show it, and say, "And that's what happened to the runaway spoon—when the cow jumped over the moon."

The Magician's Mistake

This routine, based on one of the classics of magic, has borrowed time-tested ideas from many performers. It has been shown to audiences large and small and of all ages for more than fifty years and is the author's favorite presentation of the torn and restored paper.

How it looks

You tell a story, illustrated with magic, about an ancient Chinese philosopher, and tear up a piece of colored tissue paper to restore it. But you make a "clumsy mistake" and drop the torn pieces, so that the audience discovers the secret of the trick. However, with the help of a little magic made by members of the audience themselves, all turns out right in the end. The paper is restored and the audience is mystified.

What you need

Three 7" squares of red tissue paper
Slacks with pockets

The secret

Instead of having two pieces of paper, as the audience believes, you really have three. There is a little sleight of hand involved, but it is very simple. The success of the trick depends almost entirely on how convincingly you act out the story.

How you fix it

Each square of tissue should be *loosely* crumpled into a small ball and all three put into the otherwise empty left pocket of your slacks.

What you do

"In ancient China, so I've been told, there once was an old philosopher and man of mystery who used to wander from village to village, talking to small crowds that gathered around him on the streets," you say. "His philosophy was that no matter how things *seemed* to change, they really stayed the same. He spoke of the way the sun draws water up out of the sea—that falls again as rain into the rivers that flow back to the sea. And he demonstrated by taking out a little ball of red tissue paper."

With your left hand, you reach into your pocket and gather up all three balls. You hold one between your thumb and first finger, and the other two are hidden by your fingers that are closed around them as you bring your hand into view. Showing the one ball, you say, "He opened it out." You do so, with the help of your right hand. "And then he tore it—north and south and east and west, until he had many torn pieces of paper."

You tear it as you speak, and crumple the torn pieces together. "He gathered them again into a ball. And he said that when the West Wind blew upon them three times—" You bring both hands

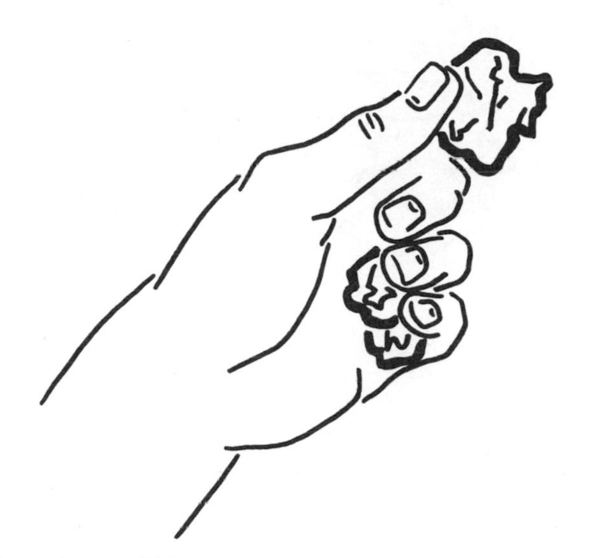

One is shown, two are hidden.

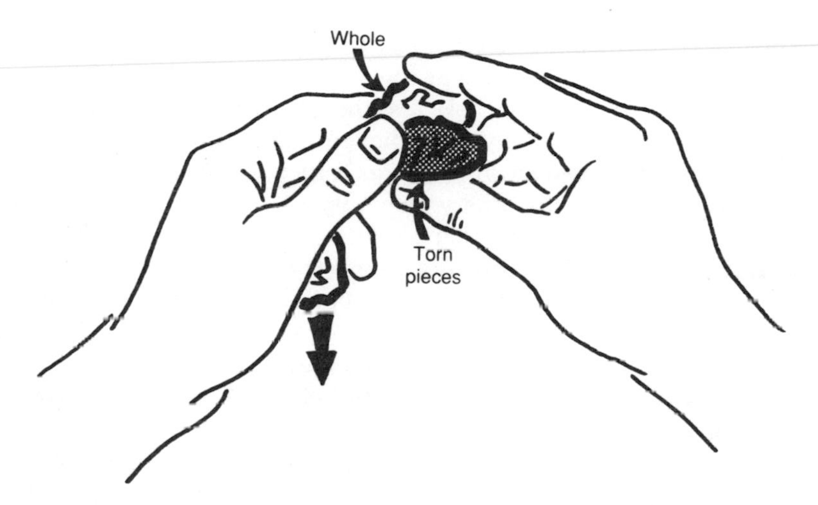

The other whole one drops to the floor.

together in front of your mouth and blow on the paper three times. But as you do, you press one of the duplicate balls of whole paper against the torn pieces and let the other duplicate ball of whole paper drop from your fingers and fall to the floor.

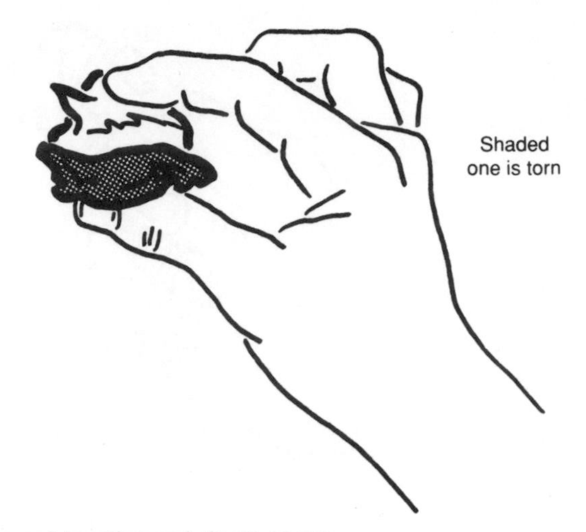

The two are squeezed together and shown as one.

Clearing your throat, you look a little nervous and embarrassed. You glance down at the ball that has dropped to the floor and make an attempt to cover it with your foot. The audience should get the idea that you've made a mistake and that the trick has gone wrong, but don't overact. Casually show the crumpled torn pieces and the duplicate ball pressed against them as if they were one. Let people see that your hands are otherwise empty.

Bring both hands together again in front of your mouth and secretly steal the torn pieces into your left hand. Close your lower fingers over the torn pieces and start to open out the duplicate whole piece between your hands.

"He said that when the West Wind blew upon the torn pieces," you repeat, "they all flowed back together again, just as the rivers flow back to the sea."

Show the opened-out whole piece of paper with your left hand. Drop your right hand to your side. Crumple up the whole piece with your left hand and put it into your pocket. Leave it there along with the torn pieces from your hand. Shake your head, look down at the ball of paper on the floor, and say, "That would have been a good trick if I hadn't dropped the torn pieces."

The audience will laugh. Smile good-naturedly, and say, "Well, those things happen." Still smiling, hold up both hands as if to halt the laughter. Let them see, without calling attention to the fact, that your hands are empty, and say, "But there's no use being a magician unless you can *do* something about it."

With the fingers of your empty right hand spread wide, reach down and pick up the ball from the floor. Transfer it to the fingertips of your open left hand. "I wonder if you'll all please help me," you say. "Will you all blow three times on the torn pieces, just as the West Wind would?" You blow on the paper ball yourself and coax them to do it with you. "Everybody, please."

Hold the ball high with your left hand and then bring it to the front of you and slowly begin to open it with both hands, as you say, "I don't think we have to go to *China* for our magic, because *you've* made magic—*right here*." Look out at the audience and open the paper ball more rapidly. "As the old Chinese philosopher said, when you blow upon the torn pieces three times, they always flow back together again."

Show the paper restored and toss it into the air to let it flutter down. Smile again, and say, "Just as the rivers flow back to the sea."

The Color Changing Plate

How it looks

"For fun, let's try a little air pollution test," you say, as you show an empty sheet of newspaper, fold it in half, and hold it in front of you. "As a testing screen, I'll use this white paper picnic plate." You show both sides of a paper plate and put that in the newspaper.

"We have to stir up a current of air and direct it against the plate," you explain. "Will you all take a deep breath, and when I count to three, just blow it out as hard as you can? Everybody, please. All together—one, two, three!"

When they have finished, you say, "Thank you. You really *blew* it!" You take what was the white plate from the otherwise empty newspaper. Magically the plate has changed color from white to blue! You show it blue on both sides, and say, "Look how hard you *blew*."

What you need

Two identical plain white paper picnic plates
A dark blue crayon
A double page of newspaper

The secret

When the two plates are nested, one inside the other, they look like a single plate. They are colored in a way that lets you secretly shift them in the paper, so you can show both sides of the double plate, first as white and later as blue.

How you fix it

Crayon the front of one plate solid blue except for the outer rim. Color the back of the other plate blue, again leaving the outer rim white. Put the one with the blue back inside the one with the blue front, nesting them evenly together. They now appear to be a single plate, white both sides. Have the plate on your table with the newspaper on top, folded on its natural creases, left to right and top to bottom.

What you do

Open out the paper, show it empty, and refold it. Hold it in front of you with your left hand, open edges at the top and the fold at the bottom, like a big bag. Slide your left first finger inside the top to keep it open.

Take up the double plate with your right hand. Hold it vertically and show that the front and back are white. Slide it down inside the paper and leave it there a moment.

As you explain that you want the audience to blow their breaths when you count to three, you casually seem to show the plate again. But what you really do is reach into the paper with your right hand, thumb the top edges of the nested plates apart, and lift out *only the front plate*.

Lift that up outside the paper a few inches, holding it close so only the white face is seen. Then immediately put it back into the paper, sliding it down *behind* the other plate hidden there.

This reverses the position of the plates in the paper, leaving them nested together with both sides now blue instead of white.

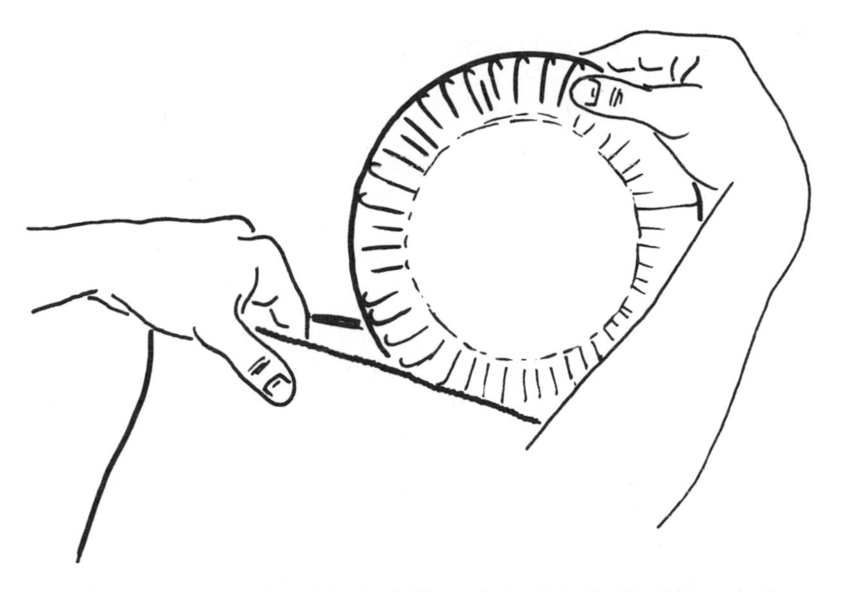

Nested together as one, the plates look like a single plate that is white on both sides.

Count aloud and when the audience has finished the breath-blowing, reach into the paper, make sure the plates are evenly nested together as one, and bring them out. Keep them held vertically, show that both front and back have changed to blue, and say, "You really *blew* it."

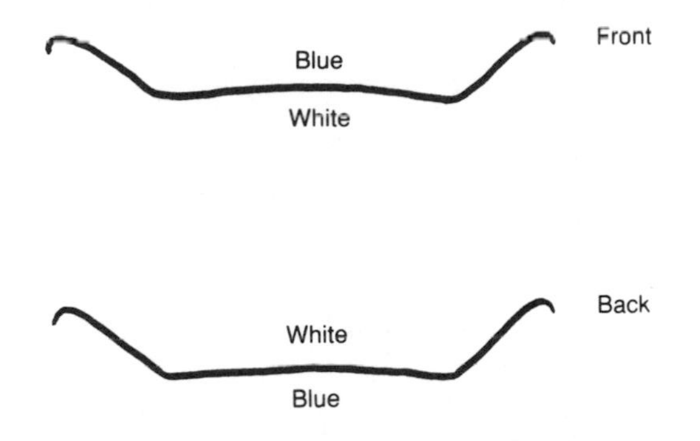

The plate changes to blue on both sides.

Release the top front edge of the paper from your left hand so the paper falls open wide and is seen to be empty. Hold the now all-blue plate high with your right hand, and say, "Look how hard you blew!"

Let's Go to the Fair

Discs of thin red cardboard are used instead of playing cards for this version of what magicians call *The Six Card Repeat.* The discs better fit the fairgrounds patter story and provide more colorful visibility while keeping the props so plain that the audience will realize only your personal skill is involved.

Actually a secret little push of the fingers accomplishes most of the trick, which depends on a simple false count that is not hard to learn.

How it looks

You tell of a visit to the fairgrounds, where you came upon a game of chance being played with six red circles. As you act out the story, you keep throwing away some of them, but six always remain. The story gains both its strength and its humor from repetition, and leads to a punch line that should bring laughter and applause.

What you need

Fifteen identical circles, about 3-1/2" in diameter, cut from thin red cardboard which has a smooth surface so the discs will slide easily during the counting

A compass, scissors, rubber bands

How you fix it

Set the compass for the proper diameter, make and cut out one circle, and use that as a pattern for the rest. The discs should be almost perfect circles so you can stack them neatly. Cross two rubber bands around them to keep them together until you use them.

How you use them

The false count makes use of a move magicians call *the glide,* but it is handled differently than with playing cards. Start by learning the position your hands will take for the counting.

Hold your left hand a little to the left of your body, with the back of it toward the audience, fingers to the left and thumb down. Put the edge of the stack of discs against the crotch of your left thumb and close your fingers and thumb around the rear of the discs to hold them. They should extend about halfway out the bottom of your hand. Hold them easily, not with an iron-tight grip.

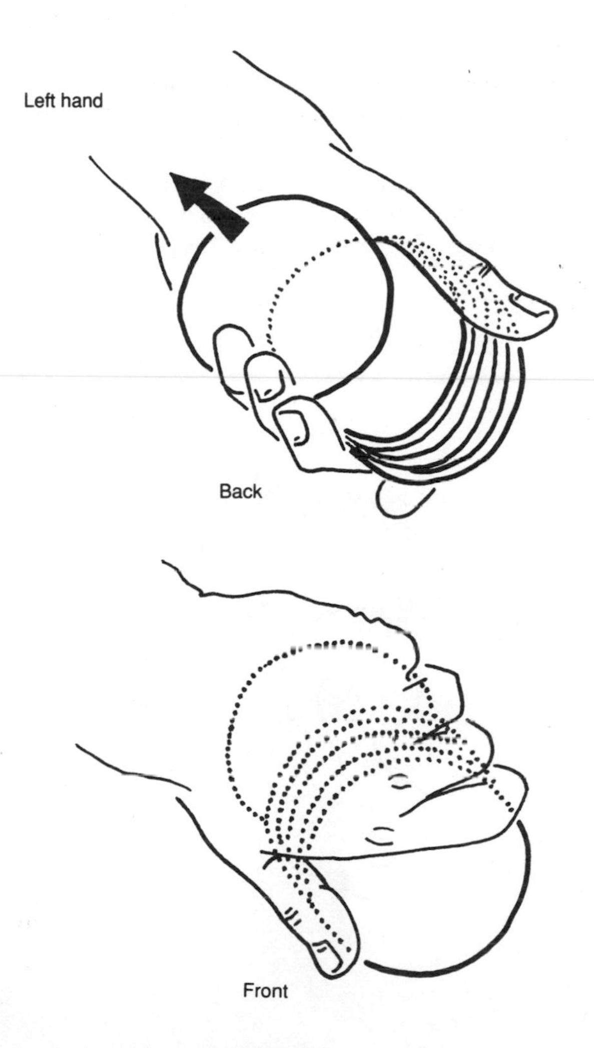

Slide the back disc up into your left hand.

Now bring your right hand up under the left one so that your right thumb rests on the front bottom edge of the stack and your fingers are at the back. With your fingers, secretly slide the back disc of the stack about halfway up inside your left hand. You are going to pretend to count fifteen discs as if there were only six.

With your right thumb, slide the top disc down off the stack and take it away between your thumb and fingers. Count off the second, third, and fourth ones the same way, by pulling them down off the top of the stack with your right thumb. But when you count the fifth one, take not just one disc but the whole remaining stack of them except for the last one, which stays for a moment in your left hand.

This is easy to do because the rear disc of the stack previously has been pushed up out of the way so you can grasp the bottom edge of the whole stack and take them all as if they were a single disc.

Counting them.

Then tap the discs in your right hand smartly against the one that remains in your left hand. Show both sides of that disc with your left hand and drop it on top of the ones in your right hand. Finally replace them all in your left hand as they were originally, so you can repeat the same count again.

You need not count rapidly, but you should do it smoothly. Practice counting aloud as you take the discs one at a time with your right hand until you can make the false count with an unbroken rhythm. It should look as if you were doing nothing but counting six discs from one hand to the other.

To set up for the trick, just stack the discs, cross the rubber bands around them, and put them in a pocket.

What you do

"I was out at the fairgrounds recently, out where they have all those games you bet on," you say. "The numbered wheels that spin around, the stuffed cats you knock over with baseballs, the saucers you try to pitch pennies into . . . but there was one fellow who had a game I had never seen before."

Take out the stack of discs and discard the rubber bands. "He had a table in front of him and a crowd was gathered around and he was taking bets on some little red circles he had in his hand. He kept moving them so you began to feel you were seeing spots before your eyes. It went something like this—"

You imitate the loud, glib monotone and brash, breezy manner of a carnival man addressing a crowd at a fair: "Step right up, folks! I'm going to show you the easiest way on the midway to make yourselves a little money. All you have to do is watch the little red spots and bet on how many of them I have in my hand—and I'm going to count them for you."

Put the stack of fifteen in your left hand, secretly pushing up the rear one, and count aloud, making the false count as practiced. Continue speaking as the carnival man: "I have one, two, three, four, five—and six." Put the stack back in your left hand as before. "Now I'm going to throw away three of these." Take three off the top of the stack, one at a time, and throw each to the table as you count. "One, two, three. It's the red that gets you, folks. It's what the per-fessors call psychological."

With your right hand, slap the remainder of the stack in your left hand, and continue imitating the carnival man: "How many have I got? How many have I got? Put up your money, folks! Put up your bets!" You pretend to hear someone in the crowd answer. "What did you say, ma'am? You said I have three? I'm sorry—I told you I had six."

Count them aloud, making the false count on the fifth to take all but one as a single disc, as before. "One, two, three, four, five—and six. Now I'm going to throw away—" Count off three, throwing each to the table as you pull them off the stack. "—one, two, three."

Slap the remainder of the stack with your right hand. "How many have I got? How many have I left? Put up your money, folks! Put up your bets! What did you say, bud? Three? I'm sorry—sorry. I told you I had six." Make the false count again. "One, two, three, four, five—and six."

You now drop your imitation of the carnival man and speak more quietly in your own voice, as if going on with the story of your visit to the fair: "He picked up the money and put it in his pocket." Make a gesture of picking up money from the table and putting it in your pocket. "Well, I waited until the crowd went away, and I went over to him. I told him it was a good trick. I said I was a magician and maybe we could swap a few ideas. I'd show him some of my tricks if he would show me how he worked the one with the little red spots. He said—"

Imitate the carnival man's voice again: "You're on, bud. You're a live one. Sure, I always like to learn new tricks."

Speak again in your own voice: "So I showed him a few tricks of mine and he seemed to like them. But then he started to walk away. I stopped him, and said, 'Hey, you were going to show me that one of yours with the red spots—remember?' He said—"

Imitate the carnival man's voice: "Sure, bud, sure. I'll show you exactly how it goes. First, you put your money down right here." Point to the table. "Then you count the little red spots." Put the stack in your left hand and make the false count. "I have one, two, three, four, five—and six. Now here's the tricky part, bud, the tricky part. So watch me closely. I'm going to throw away three of these." Count them off, throwing each to the table as you count. "One, two, three." Slap your right hand against the remaining stack. "How many have I left? How many have I left?"

You speak in your own voice: "Well, I thought a minute, and I said, 'Three from six leaves—'" Frown and count on your fingers, holding up your right fingers to tap with your left index finger. "'—one, two, *three*?' He said—"

Imitate the carnival man: "I'm sorry, bud, sorry. I told you I had—" Count them, letting each one fall singly from your hand to the table to emphasize the count. "—one, two, three, four, five—and six."

You speak quickly in your own voice: "And he picked up my money." Pretend to pick it up. "And put it in his pocket, and walked off, and—" Smile sadly and shake your head. "—I never *did* learn how that trick was done."

FOUR

Comedy Magic

Even when a magician is being serious he provides a sort of fun designed to amuse as well as amaze. He creates a sense of make-believe that gives his audience a chance to pretend with him that the laws of nature and common sense are to be forgotten for the moment. The situations and surprises his tricks produce are funny in themselves, because they almost always lead to completely unreasonable results.

But the tricks in this chapter are *designed* to be funny, not serious. They are the kind planned from the start to be played for laughs. Some depend on the acting out of jokes, others on visual humor—situations that carry things to the limit of the ridiculous. Although magical things seem to happen, their first purpose is comedy, not puzzlement.

Tomato Transit

How it looks

You show a tomato, cover it with a cardboard tube, and announce that you will make it disappear. But when you lift the tube, the tomato is still there. You try again, but it doesn't disappear.

"There's one sure way," you say. "I'll give it the double whammy." You wiggle your fingers over the tomato. "Now it will vanish as it falls down through the tube." You drop the tomato into the top and immediately lift away the tube. The tomato is gone, but in its place is a glass of tomato juice!

"Now, watch!" You hold up the glass. "The most marvelous vanishing trick in the world—the tomato juice will disappear before your very eyes." You *drink* the juice, put down the glass, brush your hands together, and say, "All gone."

Then you turn and look again at the tube. "I hope—" You lift the tube and the tomato is back again. "Oh, no. I quit!" You fold the tube flat and toss it aside. "That's one tomato that just won't disappear."

What you need

A tomato pincushion (This is a soft, stuffed cloth imitation tomato used to hold pins and needles, a traditional design available at sewing supply counters [Singer Company item 00256].)

A plastic juice glass about 3-1/2" high and smaller in diameter than the tomato

Four pieces of posterboard, 8" high and 1/16" wider than the diameter of the tomato

Self-stick cloth adhesive tape the same color as the posterboard

A small can of tomato juice

A tray and soft mat or towel (The tray makes it easy to carry the set-up props to your table, and the mat helps deaden the sound of the glass sliding down in the tube.)

The secret

The glass of juice is hidden in the tube at the start. When you cover the tomato with the tube, it pushes up the hidden glass, which is held inside because your fingers are squeezing the tube. Then when the tomato is dropped into the tube it falls down on top of the hidden glass, and your fingers again squeeze the tube to hold the tomato inside.

How you fix it

Form a square tube by fastening the four pieces of posterboard together with vertical strips of cloth tape connecting their side edges. Half-fill the glass with tomato juice. Put the mat on the tray and the glass at the right side of the tray. Cover the glass with the tube. Stand the tomato to the left of it.

What you do

"The world's greatest vanishing trick," you announce, with mock seriousness. "The last time I performed this, the audience showered me with gifts—eggs, fruit, vegetables. They threw them at me. I still have a tomato."

Hold it up, show it, and put it back on the tray next to the tube. Take the tube with your right hand around it, fingers in front and thumb at the back. Lift it up as if it were empty, by squeezing slightly to grip the glass through the tube so the glass remains hid-

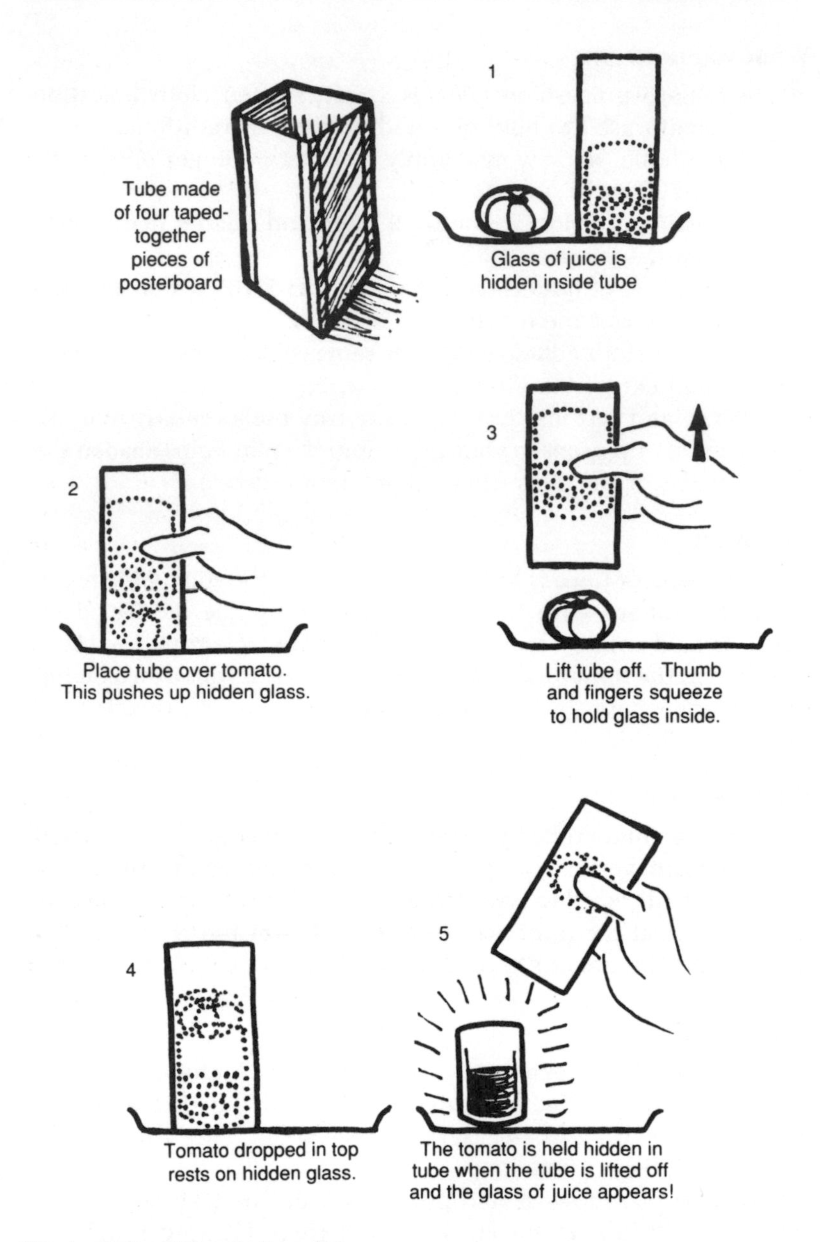

How to perform "Tomato Transit."

den inside. Casually put the tube down over the tomato. This automatically pushes the glass up inside the tube. Hold the tube in that position, covering the tomato.

"One, two, three!" Snap your left fingers. "And the tomato is—" As you speak, lift the tube with your right hand, secretly gripping the glass so it remains inside. Look at the tomato, registering disappointment, and admit that "the tomato is—still there."

Keeping the tube gripped in your right hand, immediately lower it over the tomato again. Loudly say, "Go!" and then in a pleading tone, "Please?" Lift the tube to reveal that the tomato still hasn't disappeared.

With your right hand, put the tube down next to the tomato, and as you do, gently release the pressure of your fingers so the hidden glass slides down inside the tube and comes to rest on the tray. (Guide the glass through the tube to let it slide down *very* slowly and as quietly as possible.) Take your right hand away and leave the tube standing by itself with the glass concealed inside.

At the same time, pick up the tomato with your left hand, and say, "There's one sure way. I'll give it the double whammy." Wiggle your fingers over it. "Now it will vanish as it falls down through the tube."

Take the tomato with your right hand. Hold it above the tube and drop it in so it falls down on top of the hidden glass inside. Immediately lift the tube with your right hand around it, squeezing your fingers to hold the tomato inside, and reveal the glass of tomato juice.

Put down the tube, releasing the hidden tomato so it secretly falls to the tray, remaining hidden in the tube. Pick up the glass of juice. "Now, watch! The most marvelous vanishing trick in the world—the tomato juice will disappear before your very eyes." Lift the glass to your mouth, drink the juice, and put the glass down. Brush your hands together. "All gone."

Wait a minute for the laughter. Then turn your head and look at the tube. "I hope—" Lift away the tube and stare at the tomato that has appeared again. "Oh, no. I quit!" Flatten the tube, slap it against your fingers, and drop it to the tray. Pick up the tomato, shake your head, and put it down. "That's one tomato that just won't disappear."

Musical Comb

How it looks

"Did you ever play a comb?" you ask, as you reach into your inside jacket pocket for one. "If you wrap tissue paper around it and sort of hum through your teeth against the paper, it makes music that sounds like a cross between a harmonica and a kazoo."

You take out a piece of tissue, wrap it around the comb, and give a demonstration. Then you admit, "I'm not a very good musician, am I? So instead of a *mus*-ician, I'll be a *mag*-ician—and make this comb disappear."

You suddenly crush the tissue paper, toss it out into the audience, and show your hands empty. The comb has vanished!

What you need

A 10" square of tissue paper
A pocket comb about 5" long
Elastic cord, two small safety pins, and cloth adhesive tape, preferably the same color as the comb
Sports jacket

The secret

As you wrap the comb in the tissue, an elastic cord attached to the comb pulls it out of sight under your jacket. But you pretend the comb is still inside the tissue until the moment when you show it has disappeared.

How you fix it

The exact length of elastic depends on the size of the person using it. Start with about two feet of it, rig it up, and adjust it to a length that works well for you.

Fasten one end of the elastic cord to the comb by tying it around the last large tooth at the right end of the comb. Push it up that end to the top, knot it twice to make sure it will hold, and trim off the end. Wind a small strip of cloth adhesive tape around the last two teeth of the comb to keep the elastic from slipping free.

Fasten the other end of the elastic cord to one of the small

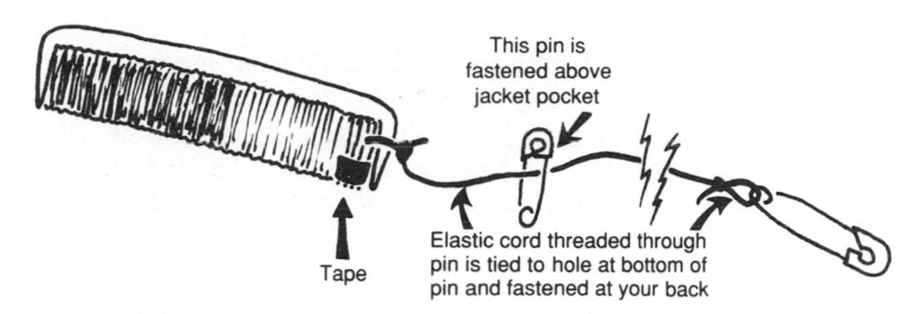

Comb prepared for "Musical Comb."

safety pins by tying it through the little hole at the bottom of the pin. Then push that pin through the center part of the second safety pin and thread the second pin onto the elastic. The elastic should slide freely through the second pin.

Lay your jacket on a table and open it to expose the inside right pocket. Put the comb in that pocket. Fasten the loose safety pin with elastic threaded through it to the jacket lining just at the inner edge of the pocket, near the armhole of the sleeve.

Now put on your jacket, reach up behind you, and take the end of the elastic cord. Draw it taut and fasten the pin at the end of the elastic to the center of your trousers at the waist, where your jacket will cover it.

It will be necessary to adjust the elastic to the proper tension. To try it, remove the comb from your pocket. Hold your right hand in front of your chest, a little away from your body, with the palm toward you. Take the right end of the comb in that hand so your fingers cover the knot and tape.

Without changing the position of your hand, release the comb. It should pull *through* your hand and be drawn in under your jacket until it hangs against the safety pin at the edge of your inside pocket. The comb should be hanging like this, *outside* your pocket, when you show the trick.

Fold the tissue paper in half left to right, again in half top to bottom, and put it in your inside jacket pocket. The paper remains folded that way when you use it to wrap the comb, so the comb won't show through the double thickness of paper.

What you do

Stand so you are leaning forward a little from the waist and your jacket hangs open freely. Take hold of your right lapel with your right hand to open your jacket slightly, and reach inside with your left hand to take the comb. Draw it out from the pin until it is at the edge of your jacket. (It appears as if you are taking the comb from your inside pocket.)

Just as you begin to bring the comb into view, transfer it to your right hand, which should be waiting to take it, and immediately reach back into your jacket with your left hand to take out the tissue paper.

Your right hand should hold the comb with your fingers covering the end tied to the hidden elastic, which runs through your cupped palm, behind your wrist, and in under your jacket. Display the comb that way with your right hand, as your left hand holds the tissue in front of your chest.

Bring your right hand over in front of the paper and place the comb against it. With your left hand, fold the paper forward and down over the comb. As the paper covers it, release the comb. The elastic will pull it through your right hand, which guides it, and draw it back under your jacket. Immediately use your right hand to help fold the paper, and continue to fold it as if the comb were still inside.

Put the folded paper against your lips, as if it held the comb, and hum against the paper. Pretend to play the "musical comb" and then admit, "I'm not a very good musician—so, instead of a *mus*-ician, I'll be a *mag*-ician and make this comb disappear."

Crush the paper suddenly between your hands and toss it high into the air and out into the audience. Show your empty hands. The comb has vanished!

Cans Full of Nothing

How it looks

"Some people puzzle me," you say, "the way they litter the highways with empty cans they throw away. But what puzzles me even more is why anybody would open a can at both ends. Everything would run out."

You pick up an old discarded vegetable can from your table. "I found this one in the road. Somebody had opened it from the top—and then opened the same can again from the bottom." Holding it up so everyone can look through it, you show that it has neither a top nor a bottom. "And then I found another one." You drop a second can through the first one and show that it is empty, too. "No top and no bottom."

Dropping the large can down over the smaller one, you lift them both together and a lemon rolls out of the empty cans onto the table. "That's what *really* puzzles me," you say, as you pick it up and show it. "Why would anybody want—canned whole lemons?"

What you need

Two empty and rather battered looking cans (The larger one may be the size that canned vegetables come in, and the smaller one a soup can. Any cans will do as long as one fits loosely inside the other and the smaller one will hold a lemon.)
A medium-sized lemon
A paper clip

The secret

The lemon is on a hook so it hangs hidden inside the smaller can. Passing the smaller can through the larger one transfers the hidden lemon from can to can, so you can show each can empty. When you nest the two cans together, you secretly push the lemon off the hook and it rolls out of the can onto the table.

How you fix it

Open each can at both ends with an opener that leaves the rims smooth. Wash the insides, but leave the labels on.

Open the paper clip so it makes a straight wire. Bend the top to make a hook, with one end longer than the other. Also bend the shorter end to give it a slight hook-like outward curve.

Push the long end of the wire into the lemon so it holds firmly. Hook the other end of the wire over the top edge of the smaller can so the lemon hangs hidden inside the can. Turn that can with the hook toward the rear. Have the larger, empty can on the table beside the smaller one.

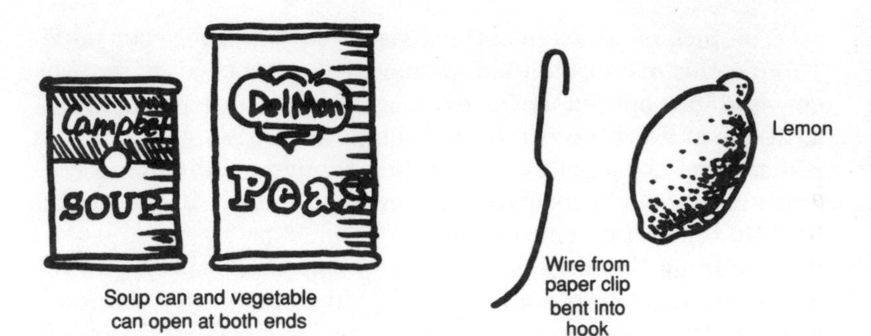

Props for "Cans Full of Nothing."

What you do

Show the larger can empty by holding it up so everybody can see through it. Turn it first with one end toward the front and then the other, and comment about the fact that it has neither top nor bottom. Rest it to the right side of the smaller can on the table.

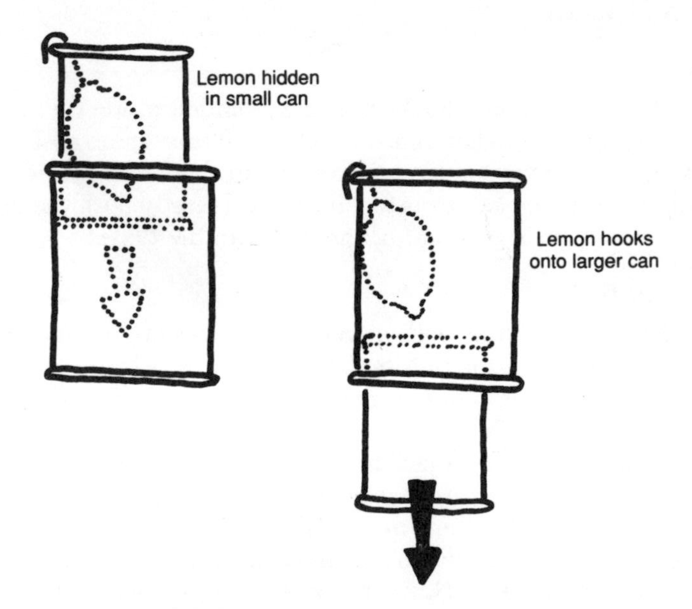

The small can is passed through larger can.

Drop the smaller can down inside the larger one, letting the hook catch on the rim of the large can. Immediately lift the large can off the small one, carrying away the hooked lemon, which is now hidden inside the large can.

Put the large can down on the table. Show that the small can also is empty and without a top or bottom. Put the small can on the table. Place the large can back over the small one so they are nested together.

When you lift them both, with your fingers inside the top, secretly push the lemon down off the wire hook so it rolls out the bottom of the cans to the table.

There is another, more casual, way to show the two cans empty and then produce the lemon, but it takes practice to do it smoothly. Start as before with the lemon hanging hidden on the hook inside the smaller can, which is beside the larger one on the table.

Pick up the large can and show it empty and without top and bottom. Hold it, with your left hand around it, about waist-high. With your right hand, take the smaller can and drop it right through the large one, catching it again with your right hand as it falls out the bottom of the large can. The hook, catching on the rim as one can passes through the other, transfers the lemon so it now hangs hidden within the large can.

With the small can still in your right hand, hold it up and show it empty. Then with your left hand, put the large can back down over the small one so they are nested together and held on the palm of your right hand. Holding the top rims with your left hand, secretly push the lemon free, and lift both cans to reveal the lemon on the palm of your right hand.

See Saw

How it looks

You invite the audience to play a game of "See Saw," but quickly explain you don't mean the kind of seesaw they rode up and down on when they were young. "This is called See Saw because you don't always *see* what you thought you *saw*," you say. "It is a game played with four white balls and a sheet of newspaper rolled into a tube."

You ask the audience to count aloud with you as you drop the balls singly into the top of the tube. Then you have everybody count again as the balls fall, one by one, from the bottom of the tube. Four are put into the top, but only three fall out the bottom. Then three are put into the top and only two drop out the bottom. Finally, two are put into the top and only one drops out the bottom. All the balls but one seem to have disappeared, vanishing one by one as they pass through the tube.

But you are holding the tube suspiciously, as if it still contained the missing balls. "I know what you're all thinking," you say. "But really—it isn't so!" Dramatically you crush the tube between your hands to show that it really is empty, and then throw the crushed wad of paper out into the audience.

What you need

Five white table tennis balls

A basket about 10" in diameter and 4" deep, tightly woven so its sides cannot be seen through

A tabloid size newspaper or a newspaper magazine section

Adhesive putty (Used instead of tacks or tape to put up posters, notes, or party decorations, this is available at stationery counters under such trade names as *Fun-Tak* and *Handi-Tak*.)

Transparent tape, sharp-pointed scissors

The secret

In addition to the four balls shown, there is a half-ball that looks like a whole one when you hold it facing front. Adhesive putty inside the bottom of the half-ball makes it cling to any whole ball that drops partway into it, so they look like one as they fall out of the tube together.

How you fix it

Cut one of the table tennis balls in half around its center seam. Take one of the halves and neatly trim another 3/16" off the center rim. Knead a piece of adhesive putty into a sticky ball about the size of a pea and fasten it to the inside bottom of the trimmed half-ball.

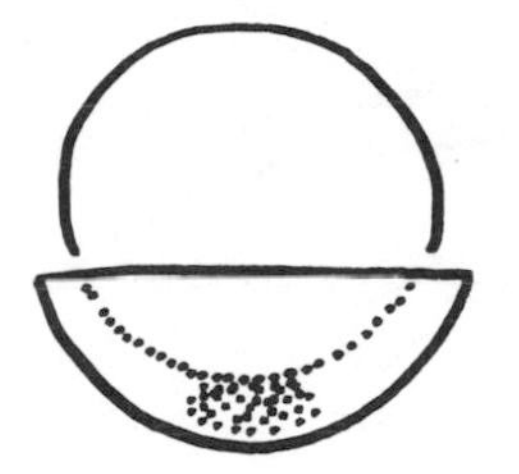

The whole ball fits partway into the half-ball, which clings to it because of sticky putty.

Roll a double sheet of the tabloid newspaper into a tube large enough in diameter for the balls to drop through freely. Fasten the tube with strips of tape near the top, center, and bottom.

To try it, put the half-ball rim upward in the basket with the four whole balls, and have the basket on a table. Hold the tube upright over the basket with your left hand. Your fingers should be around the tube near the bottom so you can put your little finger beneath the opening. Squeeze the bottom of the tube a little so that when the balls are dropped into it they won't fall on through until you want to release them, one by one.

With your right hand, pick up one of the balls from the basket, show it, drop it into the top of the upright tube, and let it fall down to where your fingers stop it at the bottom. Now reach into the basket with your right hand and pick up the half-ball, holding it by the rim between your four fingers at the top and thumb at the bottom. Hold it up with the ball part toward the front so it looks like a whole ball. Tilt the top of the tube back toward you slightly and drop the half-ball into the tube.

Pick up another ball and drop that into the tube on top of it. As they drop into the tube, one of the whole balls will go partway into the half-ball, which will cling to the whole one because of the adhesive. This happens automatically and is nothing you have to think about. Finally drop a third whole ball into the top of the tube.

Hold the tube about a foot above the basket. Squeezing slightly and feeling through the sides of the tube at the bottom with your thumb and fingers, release one ball so it drops out the bottom into the basket. Pausing a moment after each release, let the others

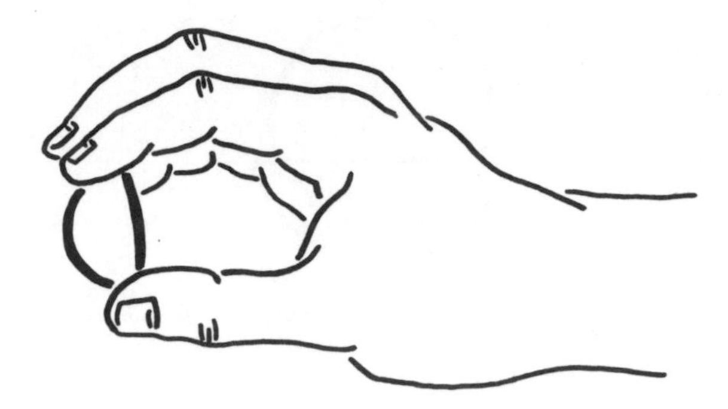

Side view showing how the half-ball looks whole from the front.

drop out the bottom, one at a time. You apparently have put four balls into the top of the tube, but because one has gone partway into the half-ball that clings to it, only three seem to fall out of the bottom.

To the audience, it seems that one ball has vanished in passing through the tube. If you put two in with the half-ball, only two will seem to drop out. Finally if you drop the half-ball into the tube and drop a whole ball in on top of it, only one will appear to drop out.

To set things up for the routine, put the basket on your table with the half-ball in it, rim upward, and the four whole balls beside it. Rest the paper tube in the basket.

What you do

"How would you all like to play See Saw?" you ask. "Oh, I don't mean the kind of seesaw we all played on when we were kids." You move your two hands up and down like a seesaw. "This game is called See Saw because—you don't always *see* what you thought you *saw*. It is a game played with four white balls."

Taking all four together from the basket, you drop them back into it one at a time. "And a sheet of newspaper, rolled into a tube." You hold that up to show it and keep it in your left hand, gripped near the bottom with your thumb and fingers around it, and the little finger under the bottom opening.

Reach into the basket with your right hand, pick up one of the balls and drop it into the top of the tube as your left hand tilts the tube backward slightly to receive it. The ball falls down inside until your fingers stop it at the bottom to keep it in the tube.

"One." You look out at the audience and coax them to count aloud. "Count with me, please." Your right hand reaches into the basket, takes the half-ball by its rim, holds it up to show it as if it were a whole ball, and drops that into the tube tilted to receive it. "Two."

You pick up another ball and drop it into the top of the tube the same way. "Three." Taking another, you drop that in. "Four. Now will everybody count the balls with me again as they come out the bottom of the tube? Everybody, please—out loud?"

Your left hand releases the balls so they drop one at a time from the bottom of the tube into the basket as everybody counts with you. Do it slowly, feeling through the paper to release only one ball for each count, pausing a moment after each.

"One—two—three?" You count the last one as if you were about to say "four," then look up at the audience questioningly when no more balls fall out the bottom of the tube. One seems to have disappeared. "Let's count them again."

As you count aloud, your right hand takes one ball from the basket and drops that into the top of the tube. You then take the half-ball, showing it as a full ball, and drop that in. Then take another and drop it in. "One—two—three—Count with me again as they come from the bottom of the tube." Your left hand releases them, one at a time and pausing after each, and you count as they drop out into the basket. "One—two?"

You pause, look at the audience, and wait for a second for the disappearance to register. Reach into the basket with your right hand, pick up the half-ball, show it as a full ball, and drop that into the top, then pick up another ball and drop that in. "One—two in the top." Your left fingers at the bottom release the ball and clinging half-ball as one, which drops into the basket. "One?"

Looking out at the audience, you walk forward, holding the upright tube in your left hand, fingers squeezing it slightly at the bottom as if the missing balls might be inside it. "I know what you're all thinking—" You glance at the tube and then at the audience. "But really—it isn't so!"

You crush the paper tube between your hands, crumple it up and smile, hold it a moment, and then throw the empty wad of paper out into the audience.

The Little Black Bag

How it looks

You start by introducing what you say is "one of the oldest tricks in magic," with a little black bag and a little white ball. The ball vanishes from the bag and spectators think they see you hide it under your arm, but they are wrong. It again vanishes from the bag and appears in your pocket, vanishes from your pocket and appears in the bag. People suspect you may be using two white balls instead of one, and you surprise them by producing *four!*

This routine is based on the classic known to magicians as *The Egg Bag*, because it usually is done with an egg instead of a ball. It has strong audience appeal in the direct simplicity of its magical plot, and this version has an added surprise ending that carries the original theme to a logical climax.

What you need

Four white table tennis balls
Three pieces of heavy black rayon lining material, each piece 9-1/2" by 11"
Someone to machine-sew the pieces of cloth into a bag
Double-faced transparent tape (sticky both sides)
A small metal tray
Trousers with pockets

The secret

The bag is a double one, so that when it is turned inside out it seems empty although the balls are hidden in one side. Part of the secret depends on the use of table tennis balls, light in weight and easily concealed in the double bag, a section of which is kept closed by a strip of tape.

Although the trick looks like difficult sleight of hand, it is easy to do as far as the magic is concerned. But its success depends on smoothness, pace, and—most importantly—rehearsed acting and facial expression.

How you fix it

When the bag is finished the narrow edges will be at the top and bottom. Separately hem the tops of the three pieces and then

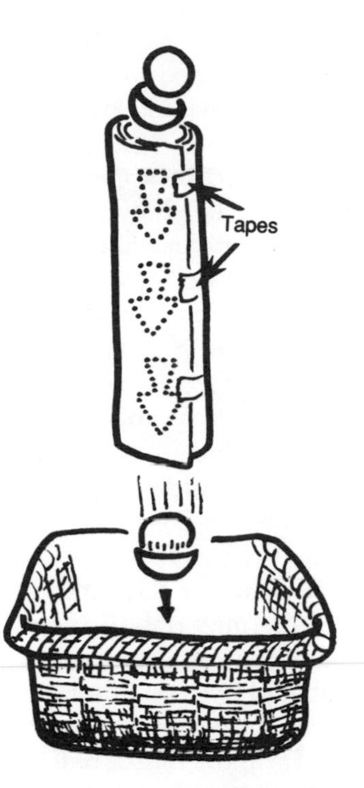

Falling through the newspaper tube into the basket, the whole ball and half-ball cling together as one.

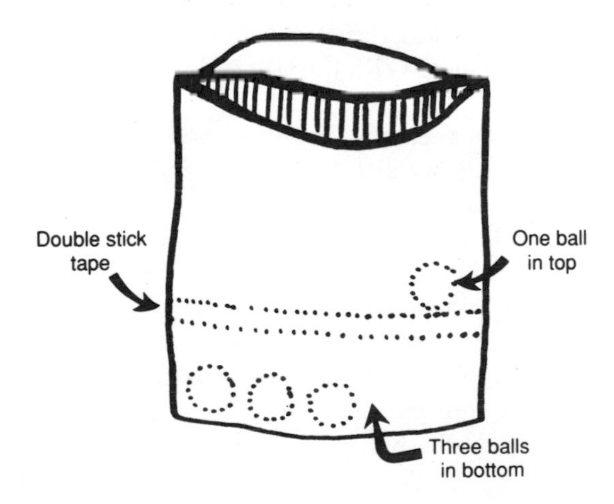

Double bag.

sew all three together with a French seam down the sides and across the bottom. The seams are turned to the inside. The result should be a bag divided inside into two sections by a piece of material in the middle.

To see how it works, start by apparently vanishing one of the white balls in it. With your left hand, pick up the bag by its left corner and hold it in front of you. Show the ball with your right hand and put it into the *rear* section of the bag. Now hold the bag between both hands by its top corners so that your two thumbs are in the *front* section. By keeping your hands that way and gathering the material up into your fingers, you can turn the bag inside out and the ball will seem to have disappeared.

To fix the bag so as to hide the other three balls in it: Start by turning the *rear* section of it inside out, and with the bag flat on a table run a strip of the double-faced tape straight across horizontally, about 2-3/4" from the bottom of the bag. Turn the bag right side out again, drop three of the balls into that section, and press the tape so it sticks to the material all the way across inside that part of the bag.

The three balls should now be in a hidden pocket at the bottom of the *rear* section of the bag, with the strip of tape closing them into that pocket. Drop the fourth ball into that same *rear* section, where it rests above the taped part.

Handling the bag as you did when only one ball was being used, put your two thumbs into the top of the *front* section, gather up the material, and turn the bag inside out. It still looks empty with the four balls concealed in it. With the bag inside out, you can show all sides of it.

Gather it up between the fingers of both hands once more to turn the bag right side out again. Put your right hand into the rear section and spread your fingers wide as you reach the bottom, so the sticky tape pulls away from the material and the secret pocket at the bottom is open. Apparently you have shown the bag empty and you can now produce the four balls from it, one at a time.

Here is how you seem to make one of the white balls vanish from the bag and appear in the pocket of your trousers: Start with the right pocket of your trousers empty and one of the white balls in the *front* section of the bag and a second ball in the *rear* section of it.

Take the ball out of the front part of the bag, show it, and put it into your pocket. Turn the front section of the bag inside out to show it empty and then turn it right side out again. Gather the top of the bag together and hold it with your left hand. Push your right hand into your pocket and push the ball that is there to the top inner corner of your pocket with your thumb as you pull the pocket lining inside out. The ball seems to have vanished from your pocket.

Push the pocket lining back in, show your hand empty, and reach into the bag and take out the duplicate ball. It appears as if the ball flew from your pocket into the black bag. You can now make it seem to fly from the bag back to your pocket. Show the ball and put it into the *rear* section of the bag. Wave your hand over the bag and then gather up the material between your hands as before to turn the *front* section inside out and show the bag empty. Reach into your pocket and produce the other ball that was there, so it magically seems to have gone back to your pocket again.

To set things up for the routine: Put three balls into the *rear* section of the bag and press the sticky tape so they are pocketed in the bottom of it. Place the fourth ball in the *front* section of the bag. Rest the bag on the small metal tray, which you will have on your table, and have your right pocket empty.

(The sticky tape can be used several times while practicing, but a new strip should be used for each public performance. It peels easily from the material for replacement.)

What you do

"I'd like to show you one of the oldest tricks in magic," you say, as you pick up the bag by its left corner with your left hand and display it. "It involves a little black bag—" With your right hand, you reach into the front section of the bag, bring out the ball to show it, and drop it to the metal tray on the table. "—and a little white ball."

Both hands hold the bag between them, thumbs in the front section, and your fingers gather up the material to turn the bag inside out. "This is one of the first tricks I ever saw a magician do. It's still one of my favorites." You show both sides of the bag and gather it up between your hands to turn it right side out again.

"The idea is that you put the little ball into the bag—" Your right hand picks up the ball from the tray, shows it, and slowly puts it into the rear section of the bag. Then you withdraw your hand, casually show it empty, and drop it to your side. Your left hand bunches the top of the bag together and holds the bag high. "—and you cast a magic spell over it that makes the ball invisible."

Wiggling your right fingers, you cast a "spell" on the bag. Both hands take the bag between them, thumbs in the front section, and your fingers slowly gather up the material and turn the bag inside out and show both sides of it. "Naturally the little ball is very hard to see when it's invisible."

With both hands, you turn the bag right side out again, and your left hand bunches the top and holds the bag high. "But if you take away the magic—" You wave your right hand at the bag, which lets the audience see your hand is empty, and then you reach into the rear section of the bag with that hand and slowly remove the ball and show it. "Then the little ball becomes visible again—"

"Let's try it once more." You place the ball into the rear section of the bag with your right hand, but bring that hand out closed as if it were concealing the ball in it. Moving that closed hand swiftly to your left armpit, you pretend to tuck the ball up under your arm to hide it there, then quickly bring your hand away. Your left upper arm stays tightly pressed to its side while your left fingers bunch up the top of the bag. You wave your right hand to cast a "spell" on the bag. "A little magic to make it invisible—"

Some of the audience may shout that the ball is under your arm, but you pay no attention and go right on with the trick, whether there is shouting or not. Taking the bag between your hands, thumbs in the front section, you gather up the material in your fingers, turn the bag inside out, and show it empty. "And it's gone once more."

You turn the bag right side out. Holding it in front of you, you lift both elbows high while displaying it, revealing in a subtle way, without making a deliberate gesture to show there is nothing under your arm, that the ball is not hidden there. "It goes and it comes." Your right hand reaches into the rear section, takes the ball from the bag, and drops it to the metal tray. "A little white ball—and a little black bag."

Putting the ball into the rear section of the bag with your right hand, you spread your fingers wide so the sticky tape pulls free and the bottom part of the bag is open to the other three balls that have

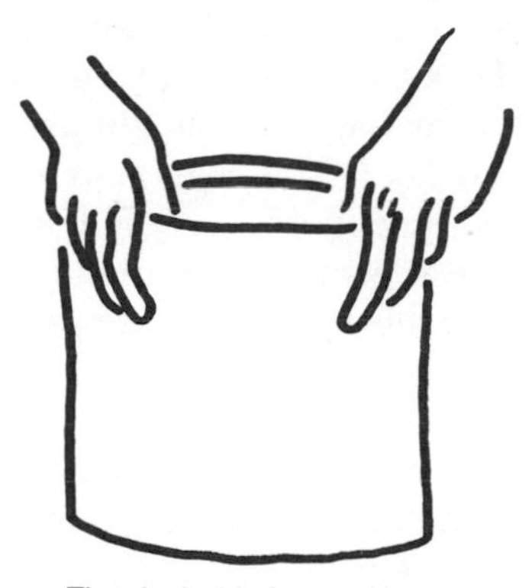

Thumbs inside front section

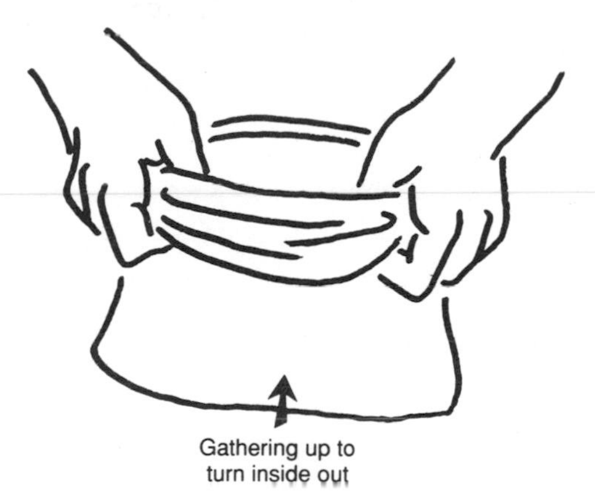

Gathering up to
turn inside out

been hidden there all the while. With your left hand, you hold up the bag.

With your right hand, you take any ball from the bag, show it, turn your right side slightly so the audience has a clear view, and put the ball in the right pocket of your trousers. "This time, we'll make it fly through the air." Snapping your right finger and thumb in front of your pocket, you reach into the pocket, thumb the ball to the top corner of it, and pull out the lining to show the pocket empty. You push the pocket lining back in, withdraw your hand, casually show it empty, and snap your thumb and fingers above the top of the bag.

"Did you see it go? Well, it did." Reaching into the rear section of the bag, you take out any ball, hold it up to show it, and put it back into the rear of the bag. "We might as well use the other half of the round-trip ticket." You snap your right fingers above the top of the bag, then quickly snap them again in front of your pocket. Reaching into your pocket, you produce the ball and hold it up to show it. "It took the express—no stops along the way—

"Some of you seem a bit suspicious. I heard what you just whispered to your friend—" Pointing toward someone in the audience, you speak as if at first denying it, then smile as you finish speaking. "You said that I had more than one little white ball. Well, you were absolutely—*right!*"

With your right hand, you reach into the bag, produce the balls, one at a time, and drop each of them to the metal tray. "I have—one—two—three—four!"

FIVE

Magic with Handkerchiefs

The brightly colored silk handkerchiefs or scarves that are so much a part of modern magical entertainment were things magicians seldom thought of using for tricks until almost the start of the 20th Century. The now obvious advantages of being able to compress large silk squares into small and hidden spaces from which they can be instantly expanded to full size again were ignored.

It was in the late 1800s that French magician Buatier de Kolta helped to create a whole new dimension in magic by his use of silk handkerchiefs. As a boy he had learned a lot about Chinese silk from his father, a silk importer, and he later put the knowledge to use when he took up magic as a hobby.

Gaining fame as a professional magician, he produced, multiplied, and vanished handkerchiefs from his bare hands and created many of the handkerchief tricks that were to become classics of magic. He was appearing as a vaudeville headliner in the United States when he died in New Orleans in 1903. By then, magicians everywhere were doing handkerchief tricks.

Basic handkerchief tricks and their variations have grown to fill three large volumes of an encyclopedia solely devoted to the subject. Probably the most enduring of all the classics, introduced before the turn of the century, came to be known as *The Twentieth Century Handkerchief Trick*. There have been at least a thousand published routines for it, one of which you will find in this chapter, and the trick is such an audience-pleaser that magicians are likely to go on performing it for another few centuries.

Molten Rainbow

How it looks

You pour clear water from a large paper cup into a small glass pitcher, and you shake the cup upside down to show it has been drained empty. You then pour the water back into the cup.

Picking up a small glass, you fill it from the cup, but it pours out red. You fill a second glass with green liquid from the cup, a third glass with yellow, a fourth with blue. Then you empty all four colored liquids back into the cup, and pull out a string of red, green, yellow, and blue handkerchiefs, all perfectly dry.

What you need

A paper drinking cup
A larger paper cup, about twice as high as the smaller one and at least 1" wider in diameter
Four small juice glasses
A small glass pitcher or clear drinking glass
Four 18" square silk handkerchiefs: red, green, yellow, blue (You may prefer to use a linked-together chain of colored ribbons.)
Food coloring, such as that used in cake icings or desserts
White cloth adhesive tape, scissors, and enough water to half-fill each of the glasses

The secret

The large cup has a rimless smaller cup fastened inside it, into which the water pours. The handkerchiefs are tucked down into the bottom of the larger cup, where they stay hidden until you pull them out dry. A drop of food coloring in each glass changes the water to colored liquids.

How you fix it

Cut the rim from the smaller cup. Put the smaller one down inside the larger cup, about an inch below the top rim of that. Fasten it there by holding it against the inside wall of the large cup and by running a vertical strip of adhesive tape from the inside top of the large cup down inside the smaller one and across the inside bottom of it. Add a second strip of tape slightly overlapping the first, then a third strip overlapping the second. Make sure that all are firmly stuck.

Tie the handkerchiefs diagonally end to end in an order that will match the colored liquids. Starting with the end of the string, push them down past the side of the inner small cup into the bottom of the large cup. Leave the end of the last handkerchief stick-

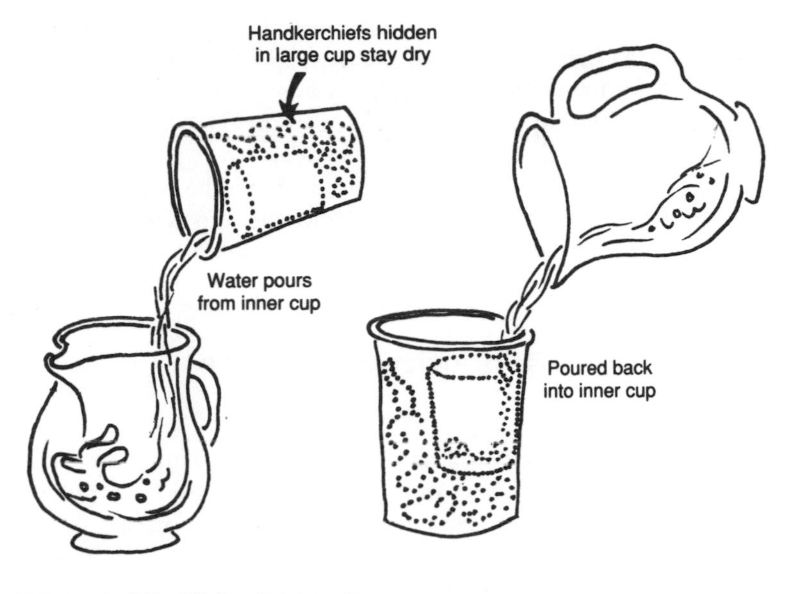

The secret of the "Molten Rainbow."

ing up at the side of the small cup so you can reach it easily. Put a drop or two of food coloring in the bottom of each glass. This can be done far ahead of time since the coloring still works after it has dried.

To set up the trick: Fill the inner paper cup with enough water to half-fill each of the four glasses. Line the glasses in a row on the table, or on a tray, and have the glass pitcher next to them. Turn the large cup so you can pour water out of the fastened side of its inner cup.

What you do

Stand behind your table. Pick up the cup with your left hand and pour it to the right to spill the water into the pitcher. Turn the cup upside down over the pitcher and shake it gently to show you have drained the cup empty. Turn it upright again and put it on the table.

Take the pitcher with your right hand and hold it well above the cup. Pour the water down into the smaller inside cup. Empty the pitcher and put it down. Now take the cup with your left hand and half-fill the first glass. Put down the cup and hold up the glass long enough for the audience to realize you apparently have poured red liquid from the cup. Repeat with the other three glasses, seeming to pour green, yellow, and blue liquids.

Then take each glass in turn, hold it above the cup, and spill its liquid down into the inner cup. Hold the cup with your left hand, reach into it with your right, and pull out the string of colored handkerchiefs.

The Hypnotized Audience

How it looks

You remove a yellow silk handkerchief from your pocket and show your hands otherwise empty. "People ask me if magicians ever try to hypnotize their audiences to fool them," you say. "They *don't,* of course. You know very well there is no way I could hypnotize you to make you believe this yellow handkerchief in my hand is blue."

You jokingly wiggle your fingers and make a gesture of casting a "hypnotic" spell over the audience. As you push the yellow handkerchief into the top of your hand and draw it from the bottom, it gradually does turn blue.

"But you know very well that it isn't blue," you say. "Because you know it's yellow, don't you?" Suddenly the yellow handkerchief appears again at your fingertips, hanging beside the blue one. You hold up one and then the other, and ask, "Is it yellow—or is it blue? Or *were* you hypnotized?"

You snap your fingers as if removing the spell. "Anyhow, when you put yellow and blue together," you say, "you always get—green." As you speak, a green handkerchief appears, stretched out in your hands between the other two.

What you need

Three lightweight silk handkerchiefs, yellow, blue, and green, each 12" square

A hollow plastic ball, such as a toy golf ball or a round fishing float, about 1-1/2" in diameter at its center

Sharp-pointed scissors
Flesh-colored adhesive tape
Sports jacket

The secret

The blue and green handkerchiefs are hidden inside the hollow ball, which is secretly transferred from hand to hand as the yellow one seems to become blue and then multiplies from one to three.

How you fix it

Cut away the top of the hollow ball to make a round opening 3/4" in diameter and then cut a hole the same size in the bottom, so the two holes are directly opposite. Wrap flesh-colored adhesive tape around the ball, but leave the holes open.

Take the blue handkerchief by one corner and tuck it down into the ball, folding the handkerchief upon itself until all of it is inside. In the same way, stuff the green handkerchief inside the ball on top of the blue one. Then turn the ball over and pull out just a tiny tip of the blue handkerchief.

Put the yellow handkerchief down into the outer breast pocket of your jacket and the ball into the same pocket, so it is out of sight just below the top edge of the pocket. The side with the blue handkerchief should be at the bottom of the ball.

Hollow ball with holes top and bottom.

What you do

Because they are explained in great detail, so they will be easy to follow with the props in hand, these moves take far longer to describe than they do to perform. Actually the trick is a rather quick one, and there is nothing difficult about it, although you will need practice to do it smoothly.

With your left hand, reach to your breast pocket, put your first two fingers inside, get the ball hidden in your hand, and pull out the yellow handkerchief. Open it out with the help of your right hand, and hold it stretched between your hands to show it, with the backs of both hands toward the audience. The top left corner of the handkerchief should be held between the thumb and first finger of the left hand and the right corner between the thumb and first finger of the right hand.

You now want to show first one hand empty and then the other. Drop the right-hand corner so the handkerchief hangs from the left hand, and show the right hand empty. Now bring your right hand, palm toward you, to the bottom of your left hand so the two hands touch. Close your right hand around the handkerchief and run your hand down the length of it.

Bring your right hand up as if to repeat that. But as your hands meet, steal the hidden ball from your left hand with the help of your right thumb and keep it concealed in your right hand as it strokes down the length of the handkerchief again. When your right hand gets to the bottom, grip that end with your finger and thumb. Release the handkerchief from your left hand and show the left hand empty.

The next step is to change the color of the handkerchief. At this point, the ball is hidden in your right hand, with the handkerchief held between your finger and thumb and hanging down over the back of that hand. You first want to transfer the ball secretly to your left hand.

Bring the bottom of your right hand to the top of your left hand so they meet and the handkerchief is hanging in front of both hands momentarily. Cup the fingers of your left hand and let the ball drop down into them from your right hand. Then grip the top end of the handkerchief between your left first finger and thumb, and take your empty right hand away.

Start tucking the yellow handkerchief down into the ball in your left fist with the first finger of your right hand. When you get some of it inside the ball, pull a little of the blue handkerchief out from the bottom of your left fist. It seems to be changing color as it is gradually pushed through your hand. Continue that until all the

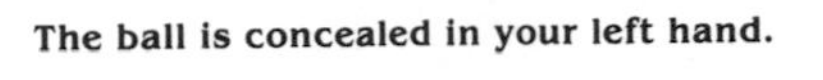

The ball is concealed in your left hand.

Your right hand steals the ball.

yellow handkerchief has been tucked into the ball from the top and you have pulled almost all the blue handkerchief out of the ball from the bottom.

Now hook your right first finger down into the hole at the top of the ball and pull that finger back against the palm of the hand, so as to steal the ball away from the left hand with the right. Immediately bring your right hand, concealing the ball, down to the bottom end of the handkerchief. Take that end with the right hand, release the top of the handkerchief from your left hand, and hold it up with your right hand to display it. Turn your left hand palm toward the audience, open the fingers wide, and show that hand clearly empty.

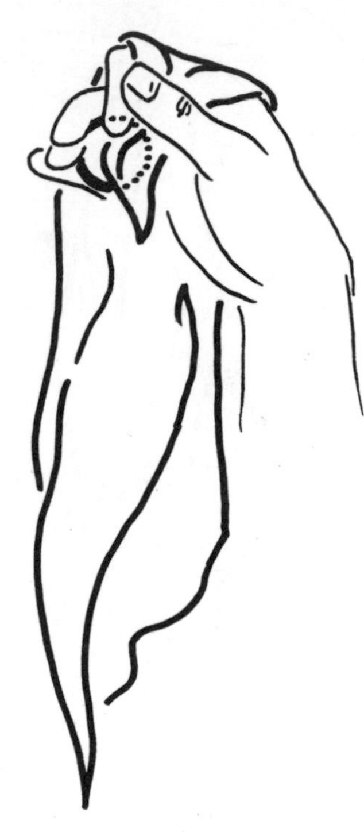

The ball is concealed in your right hand.

The ball is concealed in your left hand.

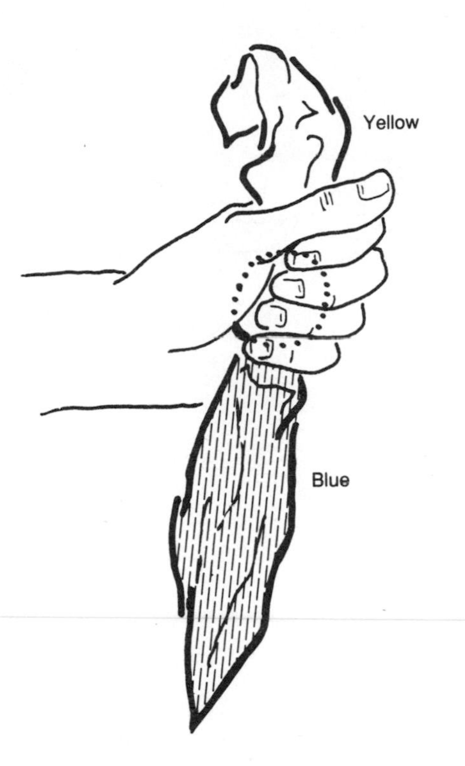

The handkerchief changes color.

The color change is complete and you apparently have only one blue handkerchief. Next you want to make the yellow one suddenly appear again, so you can show both yellow and blue. With the left hand, take the blue handkerchief again from the right hand. Do that by bringing the left thumb under the top end of it and holding that end in the crotch of the thumb. Turn the left hand palm toward the audience, with the handkerchief hanging down across the palm.

Stroke the blue handkerchief once or twice with the right hand by running that hand down the length of it. Then bring the right hand up in front of the left again. With the left first finger and thumb, grip the tip of the yellow handkerchief in the ball. Bring the right hand straight down once more and the yellow handker-

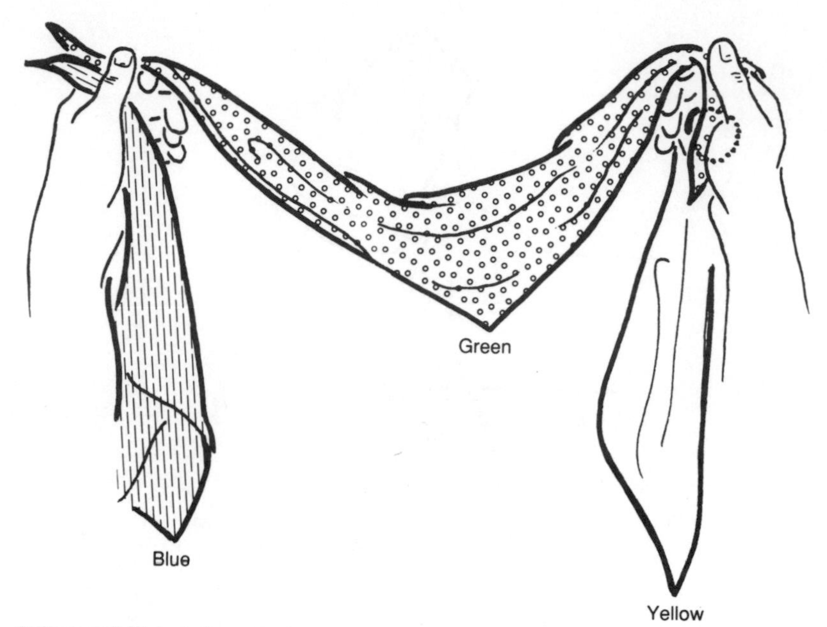

Yellow and blue make green!

chief will pull out of the ball, to make its sudden appearance in the left hand with the blue one.

Finally take the yellow one from the left hand with the thumb and first finger of your right hand. Hold the blue in the left hand, the yellow in the right, backs of both hands toward the audience. The blue one is still clipped under your left thumb.

Bring both hands together in front of you, with the left hand nearer your body. With the first finger of your left hand, pull a little of the green handkerchief out of the ball that is hidden in the right hand. Get the corner of it and draw the hands apart, so it pulls through the right hand and is brought into view.

Show the blue hanging down from your left hand, the yellow hanging down from your right, and the green stretched horizontally between both hands. Hold them that way a moment. Then gather all three handkerchiefs into your right hand and put them away in your jacket pocket, dropping the hollow ball into the pocket with them.

The What-Knot

How it looks

"This is a what-knot," you say, as you show a black paper tube. "It's used for solving knotty problems." You unroll it, show it empty, roll it up again, and put it on your table. "When you were very young, did you ever get your shoelace jammed in such a knot that no matter how you pulled and pulled, you couldn't pull it free?"

You take a blue handkerchief and a green one from your pocket, tie their ends together, and tug to show that the knot is tightly tied. "Or did you ever get a package in the mail with the string so tightly tied around it that there wasn't any way to untie it, and you had to hunt all over the house for a pair of scissors to cut the string?" You take out a yellow handkerchief, tie that to the green, and again tug the knot. "Well, if you've ever had such a problem, what you needed was one of these little what-knots."

You pick up the tube and push the string of three tied-together handkerchiefs into it. "With a what-knot," you explain, "you just push the *knots*—up into the *what*. Then you say the magic words: 'what knot—what knot—what knot'—and all the knots disappear."

As you speak, you pull the three handkerchiefs from the other end of the tube, and they come out unknotted. You open out the tube to show it empty and roll it up again.

"But the knots don't really disappear," you say, as you push the three separate handkerchiefs back into the tube. "They just become slightly invisible. As a matter of fact, I've been thinking of putting these invisible knots on the market. I could sell them to Boy Scouts for their knot tying sessions. And they'd come in handy for couples who are engaged—and anxious to tie the knot."

You tap the tube. "All of this may seem slightly *knots* to you. But really it isn't. Because—if the magic has worked—the blue one has tied itself once again to the green, and the green has tied itself to the yellow—"

Lifting the tube high, you reach into the end and pull out the handkerchiefs knotted together again in a string that hangs down from your hand. "And so they have!"

What you need

Six lightweight silk handkerchiefs, each 18" square, two blue, two green, and two yellow
An 18" by 24" sheet of flexible black construction paper
Black cotton binding tape
Craft glue, a ruler, a pencil, and scissors
Sports jacket

The secret

The audience thinks only three handkerchiefs are used, but the tube is made to conceal the duplicate set so that the knotted ones can be switched for the singles, and the other way around.

How you fix it

Cut two pieces from the black construction paper, one 9" by 17" and the other 7" by 7". Fold the larger piece in half left to right, like a book, so the two edges exactly meet, and crease the fold flat.

The smaller piece will form a hidden tube within the larger one. Coat the left edge of that small piece with a band of glue about an inch wide. Turn it over and glue it firmly to the center of the folded edge of the large piece.

When it is thoroughly dry, coat another inch-wide band of glue down the left edge of the attached small piece. Roll it up from right to left to form a tube about 1-1/2" in diameter, sticking it together firmly as it rolls onto the glue. The result should be a tube glued to the center of the folded edge of the large piece.

Cut two slits in opposite sides of the small tube at its center. Thread the black cotton tape through one slit, straight across, and out the other slit. (An easy way to do it is to nip the end of the tape with the scissors and use them to pull it through.)

Adjust the threaded tape so there is an equal length at each side of the small tube. Then push the center of the tape all the way down inside the tube to the bottom. Bend down the outer ends of the tape and glue them to the sides of the tube.

Tightly *roll* the folded large sheet from left to right into a tube with the attached small tube inside it. Work your hands around the outside until the paper naturally curls into a tube. To help give it a permanent curling, snap some rubber bands around it and keep it rolled up when not in use.

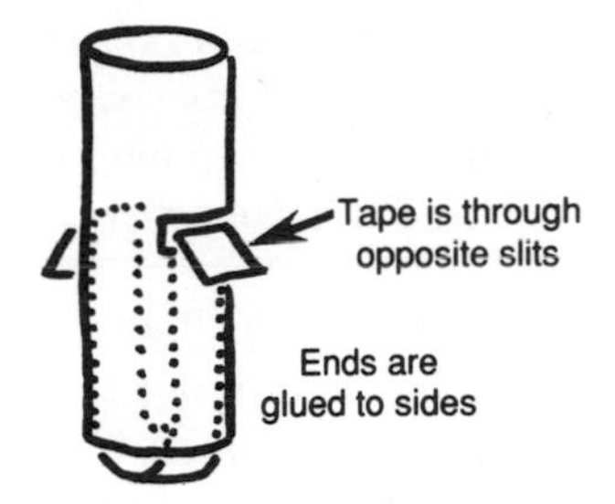

Hidden inner tube.

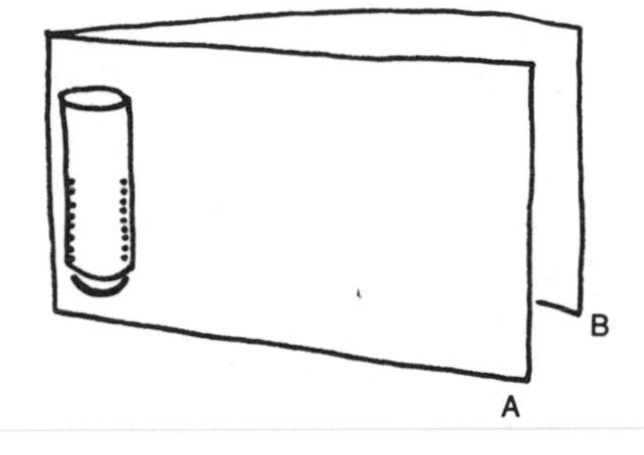

The tube is glued to the left folded edge.

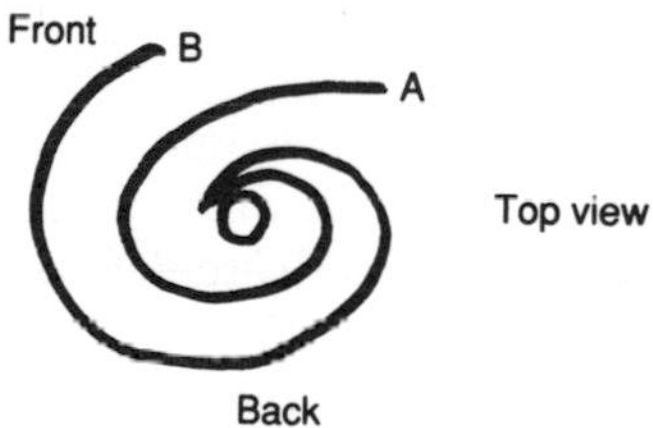

The hidden tube curls within the large tube.

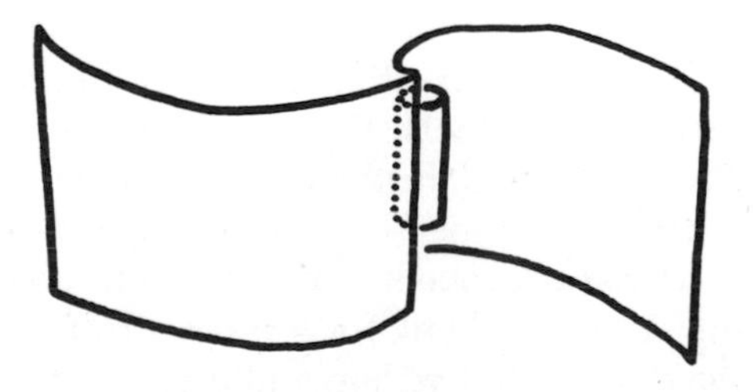

Back view when opened.

To understand how the trick works, remove the rubber bands and hold the tube upright with the two open edges of the paper toward the right. Take one edge with the thumb and first finger of the left hand, and the other edge with thumb and first finger of the right hand.

Simply draw both hands wide apart, out toward the left and right, to uncurl the tube and show it empty. The secret inner tube automatically stays hidden at the rear. Bring your hands back together and the tube rolls itself up again so the small tube is hidden inside.

When you are performing, the upright tube should be held chest-high and close to your body so nobody can see the back.

To set it up for the trick, turn the tube horizontally. Push a yellow handkerchief, then a green, and finally a blue into the *left* end and into the inside hidden tube. Make sure the last one is well inside so its end doesn't pop out. Put the duplicate yellow handkerchief in the bottom of your right jacket pocket, then the green, and the blue. Have the rolled-up tube on your table.

What you do

Pick up the tube and unroll it to show it empty. Close it again and stand it upright on your table, with the open edges toward the front.

Take the blue and green handkerchiefs from your pocket, tie them end to end, and tug at the knot as you talk about a shoelace knot getting jammed. Take out the yellow handkerchief, tie it to the green, and again tug at the knot.

Hold the tube horizontally and push the three tied-together handkerchiefs into the right end and into the hidden tube, one at a time, displaying each knot as you come to it. The patter allows time to do this slowly, which adds to the effect.

Take the tube with your right hand, reach into the left end with your left first finger and thumb, and pull out each of the untied handkerchiefs. Hang each one over your arm as you show it. Then gather up the three, drop them onto your table, turn the tube upright, and open it out to show it empty.

Rest the rolled-up tube upright on the table, empty end at the top, while you talk for a moment. Then pick it up with your left hand and hold it horizontally. With your right hand push the separate yellow, green, and blue handkerchiefs, one at a time, into the right end and into the inside hidden tube. Transfer the tube to your right hand and lift it high.

Reach into the left end with your first finger and thumb and grip the yellow end of the tied-together handkerchiefs. Give them a sudden sweeping pull to draw all three from the tube and hold them high so they hang down in a string from your hand.

Another Century

How it looks

"I'm about to show you something that happens so fast that if you blink your eyes you'll miss it completely," you say. "Two red handkerchiefs that I'm going to tie together by their tails." You show them separately and tie them together. "I have a little folder to put them in."

The folder, which you show front and back, is a narrow one so that when you put the two red handkerchiefs in they hang down at each side and remain in view. You pick up a black handkerchief, toss it in the air, and catch it. "This separate black one goes in on top." You push the black one into the folder. "Now watch! One—two—two and a half—"

You take an end of one of the red handkerchiefs and whip it into the air as the folder drops open empty. The separate black handkerchief is now knotted between the two red ones. You hold them up and say, "Tied between!"

What you need

Three red silk handkerchiefs and two black silk handkerchiefs, each 18" square
Someone with a sewing machine to sew them
Three pieces of white posterboard, each 4-1/2" by 7"
Red plastic adhesive tape, 1/2" wide
A small tray, slightly larger than the pieces of cardboard

The secret

This is a self-contained and trouble-free version of the *Twentieth Century Handkerchief Trick*, which preserves the simple and direct magical plot of the original. Despite its simplicity, it has a

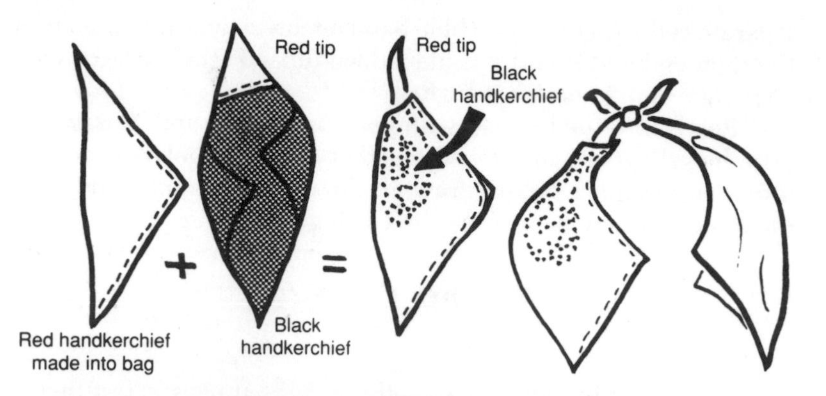

Preparing the handkerchiefs for "Another Century."

strong visual effect. It is based on a combination of long-tested methods: a handkerchief sewn into a bag to conceal another, and a double-sided folder to permit the disappearance of the separate black one.

How you fix it

One of the red handkerchiefs is made into a bag. This is done by folding it diagonally so its edges meet, and by then machine-sewing the edges together except for a 2" space left open at the top diagonal corner.

One of the black handkerchiefs has a red corner. This is how it is made: Lay the black handkerchief squarely on a table. From the top right corner, measure 3-1/2" down the right side and make a tiny cut at that point with scissors. From the same corner, measure in 3-1/2" across the top, and make another tiny cut. Now cut off that corner diagonally, from one scissor-cut to the other. Discard the cut-off corner and keep the rest of the black handkerchief.

Next you need a diagonal 4" corner from a red handkerchief. Cut that off as you did the black one, save the red corner, and discard the remainder of the red handkerchief.

Fold back the extra 1/2" at the cut diagonal corner of the black handkerchief, machine-sew the red corner to it there, sewing it tightly so it will hold against strong pulling, and then trim away the excess black material. You should now have a black handkerchief with a 4" red right corner.

Take the other red handkerchief that has been sewn into a bag and hold it at the corner where the opening is so the handkerchief hangs down from your hand. Now take the corner of the prepared black handkerchief that is diagonally opposite to its red tip, and tie that plain black corner to the corner of the red handkerchief you are holding. Tuck the black handkerchief down inside the red one until only the extra red tip is still outside the bag.

If you hold your right hand loosely around the handkerchief to cover the place where the tip comes out of the bag, you will see that the whole thing looks like one red handkerchief from the front.

To try it out, hold it that way in your right hand and show it as one red handkerchief. With your left hand, pick up the second red handkerchief and use both hands to tie one corner of that to the exposed corner of the other. Take the bottom corner of the plain red handkerchief and whip them all out into the air, and the black handkerchief suddenly will appear tied between the two reds.

The posterboard folder is made in sections and then hinged together with the red tape so it will open out flat. The red tape also is used to make decorative borders around the edges to hide the double thickness of the folder.

To make it, start by putting one piece of posterboard vertically on top of a second piece so all edges exactly meet. Run a strip of the tape down the left side of the two so that you can fold half of the width of the tape over to the back, to hold the two pieces together at that side. Now tape the two together the same way at the bottom and at the right side, leaving the top open.

Put your fingers between the two pieces at the top to hold them apart, and run a strip of tape across the top of *only the front piece* of posterboard, folding half the width of the tape back *inside* along that edge. Do the same thing with the top edge of the second piece of posterboard. The result should be what looks like a single piece of posterboard, edged all the way around with a narrow red border, but open at the top so there is a pocket between the two pieces.

With the tape, put a decorative edging around all the edges of the third piece of posterboard. Use a horizontal strip of tape to hinge the bottom edge of the double piece to the top edge of the single piece, so as to form a folder that will open out flat. Allow a small space between the pieces when doing this so that the tape

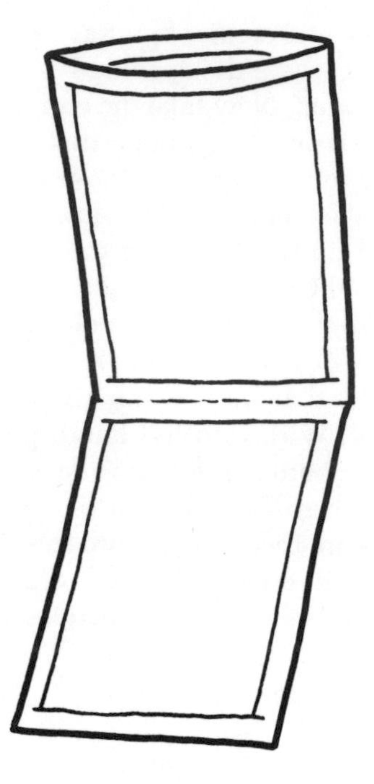

The posterboard folder is hinged with red tape.

hinge will work freely. Reinforce the hinge by running a final strip of tape all the way around it, front and back.

To set up the trick: Put the plain black handkerchief on the tray with one corner hanging over the back end. Put the folder on top of the handkerchief, with the double side upward and the hinged edge toward the front. Tuck the red-tipped black handkerchief down inside the red bag handkerchief it is tied to until only the tip is out of the opening. Put that on top of the folder with the trick end of the handkerchief hanging over the back of the tray. Lay the plain red handkerchief beside it.

(For packing, you can fold in the ends of the handkerchiefs, put a piece of cardboard on top of the tray, snap a few rubber bands around it, and everything will hold in order so the trick will be all set up when you later unpack things for your show.)

What you do

Pick up the bag handkerchief with your right hand so your fingers cover the opening, then pick up the plain red handkerchief with your left hand. Use both hands to tie the corner of the plain one to the tip of the bagged one. Then hold them just below the knot, so the bag opening is concealed and they hang from your right hand.

With your left hand, open the folder a little, while it is still on the tray, by putting your fingers on the back of it and bending it up with your thumb. Then pick it up and let it fall open, with its back toward the audience, and turn your hand to show the front of it.

Bring your right hand over and put the knot of the tied handkerchiefs against the hinged part at the center of the folder, so the ends of the handkerchiefs hang out at each side. Close the folder and hold it with your left hand.

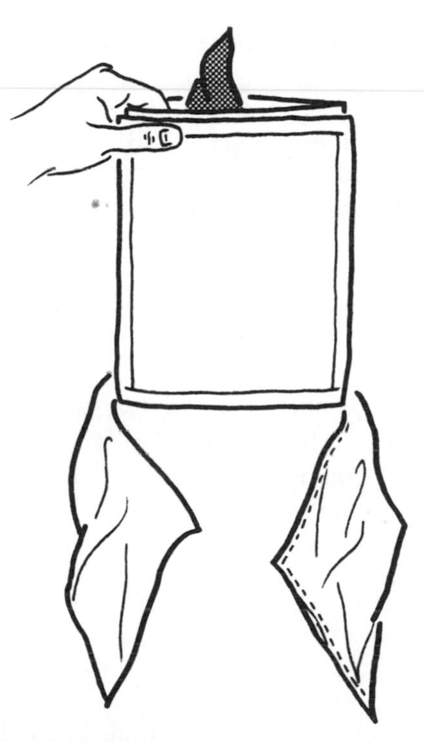

Black handkerchief in hidden pocket.

The chain of handkerchiefs.

With your right hand, pick up the black handkerchief, toss it in the air and catch it, and then tuck it all the way down inside the secret pocket of the folder. Take your right hand away and hold the folder high with your left hand.

Count, "One—two—two and a half—" Reach suddenly with your right hand, firmly grasp the corner of the nearest handkerchief, and whip the chain of three into the air with that hand as your left hand lets the folder fall open. With your left hand, turn the folder to show the back of it, as your right hand holds the string of handkerchiefs high and you say, "Tied between!"

It's a Corker

How it looks

"All of us have trouble at times seeing things that are invisible," you say. "Like air pollution. You know it's there, but you can't always see it." You show a cardboard tube, which is standing upright in a drinking glass. "This is a portable pollution particle perceptor. (Pause.) Some of you apparently don't believe me. I don't blame you, because I don't believe me either. But if it *isn't* a portable pollution particle perceptor, then it must be something else—and I don't know what else it could be."

Holding the glass, you invite someone from the audience to remove the tube. "Would you care to have a look at it—so you can give us all a scientific report on what you find? You'll notice that it is tightly closed by a cork at each end. Would you remove the corks, look inside, and tell everyone what you see?—Nothing at all? Just good clean air? Thank you. Would you replace the corks so it is tightly sealed again and put the tube back into the glass to isolate it?"

You put the glass with the re-corked tube in it on your table. "I have here some pollution," you say, taking out a white handkerchief that is covered with black spots. "It was scientifically collected—by hanging this handkerchief out on the line."

You pick up a tube of rolled black paper, unroll it to show it empty, and let it roll up again. "This one is not a portable pollution particle perceptor, of course. It's just a piece of paper." You push the spotted handkerchief into the black paper tube. "I'll collect the pollution in this and then spread it out into the air—"

Putting the paper tube to your lips, you blow through it. Then you open it and show that the spotted handkerchief has vanished. "The pollution is out there somewhere. You may not see it." You take a deep breath and cough. "But it's there."

You put the black paper tube aside and pick up the glass containing the other tube that was tightly corked by the spectator who examined it and found it empty.

"And now, if the portable pollution particle perceptor works—" You take the corked tube in your hand, clearly show your hands are otherwise empty, remove the cork from the top of the tube, and with just your finger and thumb pull out the spotted handkerchief that disappeared. "I haven't the slightest idea how the thing works," you say. "But it does."

What you need

A cardboard tube about 1-1/4" in diameter, such as the one inside a roll of paper towels or plastic wrap (Exact diameter is unimportant, as long as you can close your thumb and fingers around it.)

Three large tapered corks, like those sold for vacuum bottles, that tightly fit the ends of the tube

An 8" by 15" piece of black construction paper

A clear drinking glass, about 5" high

Flesh-colored cloth adhesive tape, 1-1/2" wide

Two duplicate lightweight silk handkerchiefs 18" square, white with black polka dots (If you wish, you can use plain white silk handkerchiefs and spot them with a black marking pen, but both should look alike.)

Scissors, a craft knife, white craft glue, a ruler, sandpaper

Sports jacket

The secret

In addition to the tube that is examined and corked by the spectator, there is a separate small length of tubing with a cork in the top, and a duplicate handkerchief is concealed in that. When the extra piece is held in the hand with the corked tube, it looks like the top end of the tube itself.

The other black paper tube for vanishing the handkerchief has a smaller tube attached and is hidden in your hand when the paper is unrolled to show it empty.

How you fix it

Cut off two pieces of the tube, one 6" long, the other 1-1/2" long, and discard the rest of the tube. The ends of both pieces should be cut evenly.

Fasten a strip of cloth tape across the bottom of the short piece, to close off the bottom so you have a little topless round box. It should be firmly fastened, but so that not more than 1/4" of tape covers the sides of the tube. From another piece of tape, cut a circle that will fit inside the bottom, sticking it to the inner surface of the first tape, so the inner bottom of the short tube is not sticky.

Fit one of the corks into the top of the short piece, and lightly pencil-mark the side of the cork at the point where it wedges into the tube. Remove the cork and cut off the bottom of it a fraction of an inch below the pencil mark. This should give you a shortened cork that will tightly fit the tube. (It must be shortened to allow as much room as possible for the handkerchief.) Cut the other corks to a length that matches the first one, and smooth off the bottoms of all three with sandpaper.

Stuff one of the handkerchiefs into the small tube and fit the cork in the top. Fit the other corks in the ends of the longer tube.

Now, to see how deceptive it looks when the two are held together, hold the small piece by its cork in the crotch of your left thumb, and close your thumb and first finger around it so their tips touch. Close the other fingers into a half-fist with your palm toward you.

Corked sections of tube. A handkerchief is in a separate corked section.

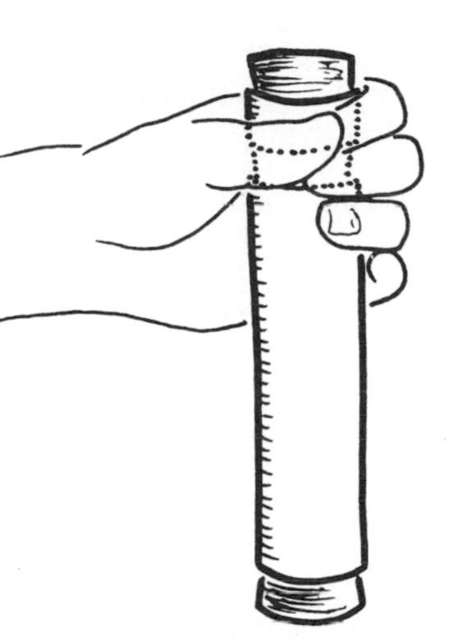

When held together the two parts look like one tube.

With your right hand, bring the longer piece of corked tubing against the palm of your left hand so its top cork is directly beneath the bottom of the smaller piece. Push the two up together until the cork top of the smaller piece is pushed above the top of your left fist and your thumb covers where the two tubes touch. Close the rest of your left fingers around the bottom tube and hold the tubes together in your hand that way.

You now can show your left hand front and back and it looks as if you are holding one tube, the top corked end of which extends a little above your fist. If you remove the cork with your right hand, you can pull out the handkerchief and it looks as if you are pulling it out of the single tube. The slight additional length of the tube will not be noticed.

Next, to make the paper tube from which the duplicate handkerchief vanishes, put the black construction paper on a table with its wider part lengthwise. From the top right corner, measure off and cut away a piece 5" by 5", and discard it. From the bottom right corner, cut away and discard another piece 1" by 5". You are left with an 8" by 10" sheet of paper that has a 2" by 5" extension at the right.

Coat that extending 2" by 5" piece with white craft glue and roll it upon itself from right to left, sticking it as you roll it, until

The construction paper is cut to form an extension.

The extension is rolled up to form a small tube.

you have a small tube about 1-1/4" in diameter. When the glue has dried, put a strip of cloth tape across the top end to close the tube off. Then roll the whole paper tightly from right to left, working around it with your hands until it curls that way naturally, with the smaller tube inside.

To try it, push a handkerchief up into the bottom end of the rolled paper, so it goes into the smaller inner tube. Then hold the rolled paper upright in your left hand, against your palm, and with your fingers partly closed around it near the bottom.

With your right hand, pull it open. As it unrolls, the little tube will come directly under your left fingers so they conceal it, and you can hold the paper open to show it empty. Then let it roll up again into your left hand.

Set up the trick by putting the small section of the corked tube, loaded with one of the handkerchiefs, in your left jacket pocket. Have the other handkerchief and the rolled paper tube upright in the same pocket. Stand the large corked tube in the drinking glass and have that on your table.

What you do

Pick up the glass and corked tube. Have the spectator take the tube from the glass, examine the tube to make sure it is empty, re-cork the two ends, and put it back in the glass. Carry the glass to your table and leave it in full view with the corked tube standing upright.

Stand to the left of the table. Take the black-spotted handkerchief from your pocket, display it held out between your hands, and take it with your right hand. With your left hand, remove the rolled paper from your pocket, open it out, and then roll it up again.

Hold it in your left hand and push the handkerchief up inside the bottom end of it and into the secret tube, making sure it is tucked well within the small tube. Take the rolled paper with your right hand, hold it to your mouth, and blow through it. Hold it with your left hand again and unroll it to show that it is empty and the handkerchief has vanished.

Let it roll up, and put it in your pocket with your left hand. With that hand inside the pocket, get the small section of corked tube into your fingers, so you are holding it with the corked top in the crotch of your thumb. Bring your hand out and let it fall to your side. Pretend to breathe in the "polluted" air and cough.

Turn your body a little to the right and reach toward the table with your left hand. Bring your hand down over the corked tube

Roll the paper with the small tube inside.

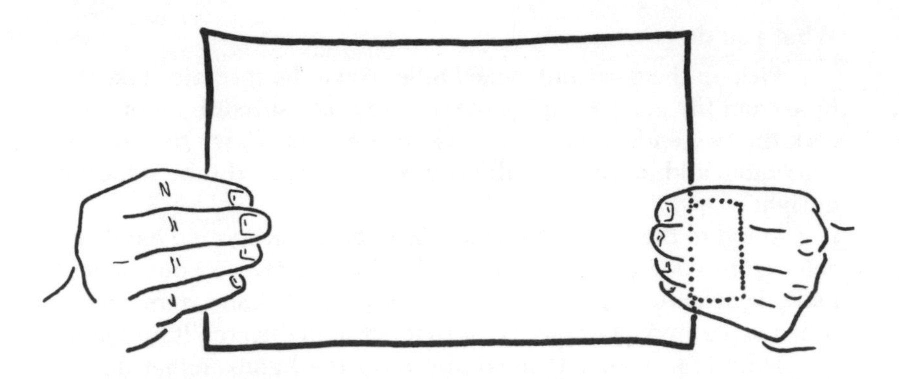

The small tube is concealed by your left hand.

that is standing upright in the glass, so the bottom of the small section of tube in your hand comes right on top of it. Slide your fist down a little around the tube to grip it. This pushes the top section up in your hand so your thumb and finger cover where the two come together.

Lift them from the glass together that way, as one. Face front and hold your left hand out to the left of your body. Clearly show that your right hand is empty. With your fingers spread apart so everyone has a clear view, slowly remove the cork and take the handkerchief out of the tube. (Really out of the small top section.) Then replace the cork.

Hold the handkerchief with your right hand. With your left hand put the corked tube, top first, into your pocket, dropping the extra section into your pocket with it. Hold out the handkerchief between both hands to show it. Then, after a moment, take the corked tube from your pocket, remove the top cork, tuck the handkerchief into the tube, and say, "I haven't the slightest idea how the thing works. But it does."

SIX

Magic with Rope and String

Magicians usually do their rope tricks with soft white cotton clothesline. It should be unglazed and have no chemical stiffening. If you shop around in variety stores you usually can find soft rope that is suitable. Dealers in supplies for magicians sell clothesline specially designed for rope tricks. If no soft rope is available, glazed clothesline may be boiled to remove the stiffening and then hung to dry.

Almost any ordinary clothesline of the type that has a braided outer jacket and an inner core of string or plastic cord can be made soft and pliable if you remove the core. Just push back the outer braiding a little at one end, grip the core, and gradually strip the outer braiding free by bunching it and working it down a few inches at a time. This leaves an outer "shell" of braiding that looks like clothesline. Discard the inner core.

Quick and Easy Cut Rope

How it looks

"There is one trick I'm not going to do," you say, "because most of you probably have seen it. I mean the one where the magician shows a piece of rope such as this and doubles it to find the exact center. Then he takes out a pair of scissors and cuts the rope in half so he has two pieces. He cuts each of the ends a few times to trim them off evenly—"

As you explain what you're *not* going to do, you actually do it. You show the rope, hold its center, take the scissors from your pocket, seem to cut the rope in two, and trim off the ends.

"Then he taps the rope once—twice, like this—and behold, a miracle! The rope is fully restored in one piece." Taking one end you flip it out and show it whole. You hold it a moment, look at the audience, and smile. "That's one I promise I won't do. But I would like to show you another trick with this rope. It's one I call . . ." You then go on with another rope trick.

What you need

A four-foot piece of soft clothesline
A four-inch piece of the same rope
White thread
Scissors small enough to fit in a jacket pocket
Sports jacket

The secret

This is the cut rope in its simplest form, but effective because it is quick, amusing, and right to the point. Instead of cutting the real center of the rope, you cut through a small extra loop that you secretly get in your hand when you reach in your pocket for the scissors.

How you fix it

Bend the two ends of the small piece to form a loop. Bind the ends tightly together by winding the thread around several times. Tie the thread and snip off any extra. Put that piece in your left jacket pocket, loop toward the front, and the scissors in the same pocket with their handles toward the front.

What you do

Show the rope, let it be seen that your hands are otherwise empty, and double it to hold the center in your right hand, loop against your palm and long ends hanging toward the floor.

Reach into your pocket with your left hand. Take the scissors so their blades are against your fingers and the handles stick out of your fingers toward the front. Close your fingers around the extra rope loop, so it is hidden in them, lying against the blades of the scissors.

Bring out the scissors. Move your right hand, which holds the rope, over to your left hand. Place the real center loop of the rope into your left palm directly *on top of the fake loop hidden there,* keeping the palm tipped up toward you. Take the scissors by their handles with your right hand and pull them out of your left hand. Show them and click the blades with a snipping motion.

Now with your right thumb and fingers pull the center of the fake loop up into view above the top of your left hand. Press your left thumb against the tied ends of the fake loop and top of the real loop, covering where they meet in your palm. You can now turn your left hand outward to show the palm. It should look as if you are just holding the doubled rope with its center loop sticking up above the top of your hand.

Turn your left palm toward you again and cut through the center of the fake loop with the scissors. Pull the cut ends slightly apart to show them. Then cut several small pieces off each of the ends, cutting them alternately, and let the pieces fall to the floor. With the last cut, nip the remaining pieces of fake loop between the blades, pull that away from your hand, and let it drop like the others.

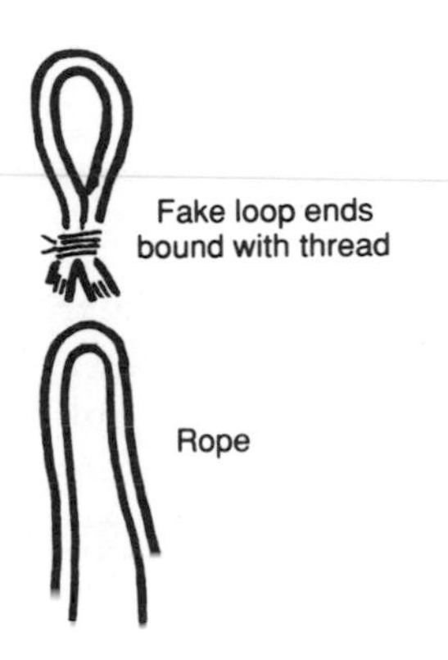

Preparing the rope for "Quick and Easy Cut Rope."

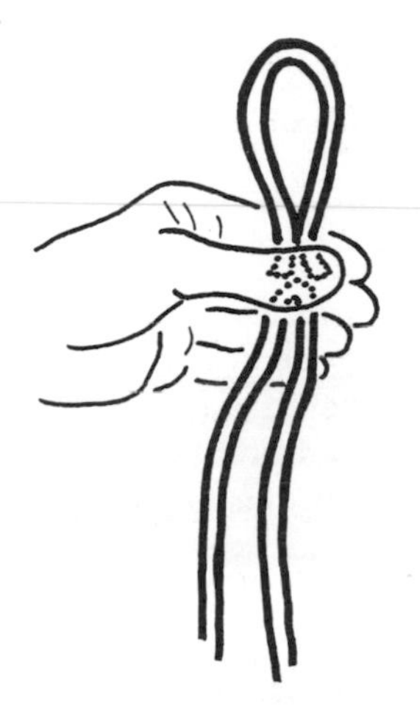

The combination looks like one rope.

Close your left fist. Tap the top of it twice with the scissors. Reach down below your left fist with your right hand and take one of the hanging ends of the rope. Release the rope from your left hand and flip it out into the air with your right, holding the end. Take the rope between both hands, give it a couple of tugs, and smile at the audience as you say, "That's one I promise I won't do."

Coffee, Tea, or Magic

How it looks

You drape the center of a rope over your hand so the two ends hang to the bottom. Then you pick up a coffee cup and hold it by its handle with the same hand. "I call this one 'Coffee, Tea, or Magic,'" you say. "I'm sorry there's no coffee or tea to offer you. But there is—*magic*!"

You grip the cup with your other hand and quickly pull it down to leave it hanging at the center of the rope, magically linked to the rope by its handle. Tilting the rope up and down, you slide the linked cup back and forth on it. "At least, it's a new way to dry the dishes," you say. "Just hang them out on the line."

What you need

A 3-foot length of soft clothesline
A coffee mug with a large handle

The secret

As you place the cup in your hand at the start of the trick, you secretly push a small loop of the rope through the handle and hook it over the tip of the thumb holding the cup. When you pull the cup down it automatically draws one of the rope's ends through the handle, but this happens so quickly that spectators will be convinced the two ends were never out of sight.

How you fix it

There is nothing to prepare. Just have the cup and rope on your table.

What you do

Show the rope and hold it at the center with your right hand so the two ends hang down. Hold your left hand out to the side of your body, fingertips to the left and palm toward the audience. Hang the center of the rope over the top of the left fingers, with the part that comes down the front of the hand lying against the fingers' middle joints.

Pick up the cup by holding the front of it, leaving the handle free, and bring it to the held-out left hand. As your hands come together, the cup and right hand partly hide the left hand from view, which covers the one secret move you have to make. There's no need to hurry, but it should look as though you were merely taking the cup from your right hand with your left. Here, in detail, is what you do:

With your right hand, touch the back of the cup's handle against the two middle left fingers close to where they join the palm. Draw back the left middle finger and with the tip of it push a little loop of the rope through the handle toward you. Stick your left thumb up through that loop and hook it well over the tip of the thumb. Then close the left thumb and fingers against the sides of the handle to hold the cup, and remove your right hand.

Holding your fingers that way, you can show the cup and rope quite freely, since the secret loop is hidden behind the cup. Now turn your left hand in toward you, with its back to the audience,

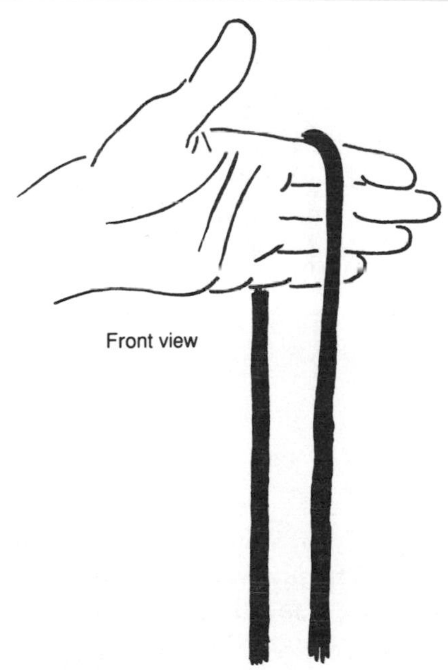

The rope lies over the middle joints.

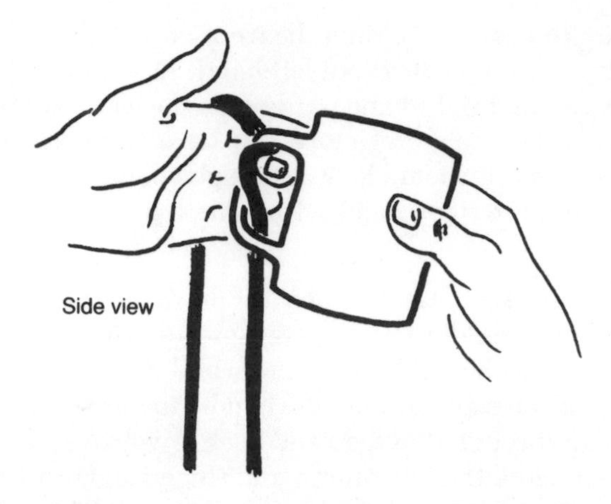

Your right hand puts the cup into your left, and your left middle finger pushes the loop through the handle.

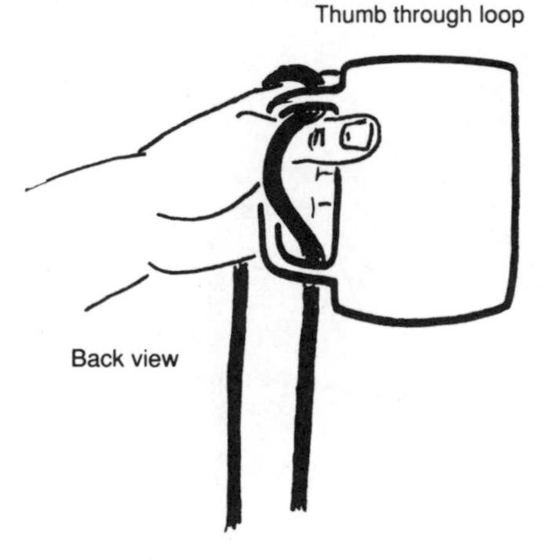

Your left hand holds the cup and the rope.

and hold it high in front of you. When you are ready to link the cup to the rope, grasp the cup firmly with your right hand around the outside of it, fingers in front and thumb at the back.

Quickly pull the cup straight down toward the floor, closing your left hand around the two ends of the rope to hold them as they are drawn up to the top of the hand and the center loop is pulled to

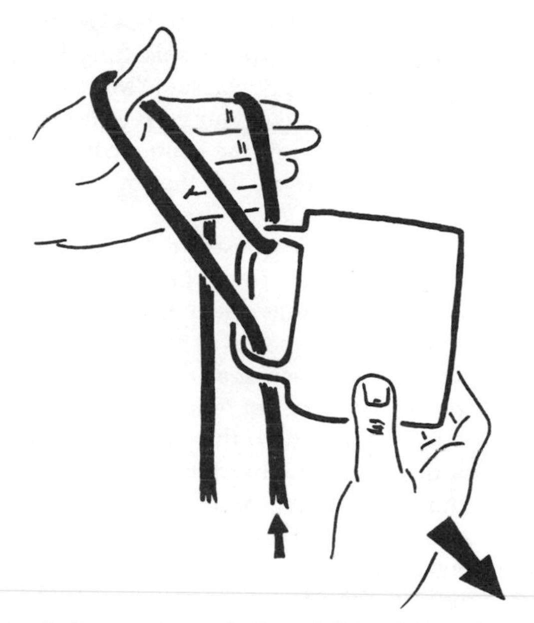

Your right hand pulls the cup down out of your left hand. The center loop goes down and the end of the rope pulls up through the handle.

the bottom. Pulling the cup down that way automatically draws the rope through the cup's handle.

Take your right hand away and leave the cup hanging at the bottom of the loop. Then bring your right hand up, take one end of the rope from your left hand, and spread your hands apart. Tilt your hands up and down so the cup slides back and forth on the rope outstretched between them.

Soap and Rope

How it looks

"We come now to the educational part of this program," you say. "Here's a household hint that can save you a little money—and make it safer to take a shower."

You hold up a large bar of soap that has a rope threaded through a hole cut in its center. The rope is tied in a loop, and you untie it and remove the soap.

"You all know what shower soap is—the kind you hang round your neck so that when the water is splashing in your face you don't have to grope for the soap," you say. "Most shower soap is expensive, but you can easily make your own at home. Just take any cake of soap, cut a hole through the center with a kitchen paring knife, and string it up on a rope. Tie the rope through twice, like this."

As you explain, you demonstrate by threading the rope through the soap, and again tying it into a loop, which you put over your head so the soap hangs down in front of you. "There you are. You've got your own inexpensive shower soap in your favorite brand." You hold up the roped soap. "But there is one problem with shower soap. When you've got it hanging around your neck like this, how do you reach down with the soap to wash your toes?"

You awkwardly show how hard it would be to reach down to your feet with the soap roped around your neck. "Of course, you could untie it from the rope," you say. "But there's a simpler way. You just use magic—and pull the soap right through the rope!" Suddenly you pull the soap free from the rope that hangs around your neck. "There it goes—and now you can wash your toes!"

What you need

A five-foot length of soft clothesline
A large (bath size) unwrapped bar of soap
A sharp-pointed kitchen paring knife
A penny
White cloth adhesive tape
A ruler

The secret

The ends of the rope are switched during their threading through the soap, secretly doubling the rope upon itself and forming a small loop. The loop is drawn inside the hole where it jams into a position that keeps the soap on the rope until you are ready to release it.

How you fix it

With the ruler, find the center of the soap, front and back. Press the penny against the soap, first one side and then the other, to mark a circle around those centers. Cut and scrape a hole the size of the penny through the soap with the knife.

Bind each end of the rope with a short strip of white tape to prevent fraying and to make it easier to thread the rope through the hole in the soap.

Put one end through the hole from back to front. Draw out half the length of the rope, bring it around the bottom of the soap, and then put *that same end* through the hole from back to front again. Bring both ends to the top and tie them in a loose square knot, so the soap hangs at the bottom of the long loop.

The soap is now really tied on the rope and that is the way you first show it to the audience, so they can watch you untie it, which helps convince them that the later retying is genuine.

What you do

Start by showing the soap tied on the rope. Untie the top knot, unloop the rope, and remove the soap. After explaining about the "shower soap," what you seem to do is tie it back on the rope as it was tied before. The following moves should be practiced until you can do them smoothly and deliberately, without hesitation:

Hold the soap upright with your left hand, fingers at the front around the left edge and thumb at the back just above the center hole. Take one end of the rope with your right hand and push it through the hole from back to front. Draw the rope out until the two ends hang even at the bottom. Move your right hand, with its palm toward you, down about two inches below the bottom of the soap. Bring that hand around *both parts* of the hanging rope, so they hang down through your fingers.

Grip the part of the rope that hangs down from the *front* of the soap between your right thumb and first finger and move your right hand straight up against the back of the soap to just above the center hole. This forms a little loop across the top of your right first finger. Put that loop under the tip of your left thumb and hold it with that thumb against the back of the soap.

Leave that part of the rope hanging and slide your right hand back toward you along the *other part* of the rope to the end of it. Take that other end around the loop and push that end from back to front through the left side of the hole in the soap. Pull the end out through the hole to the front until it draws the little loop into

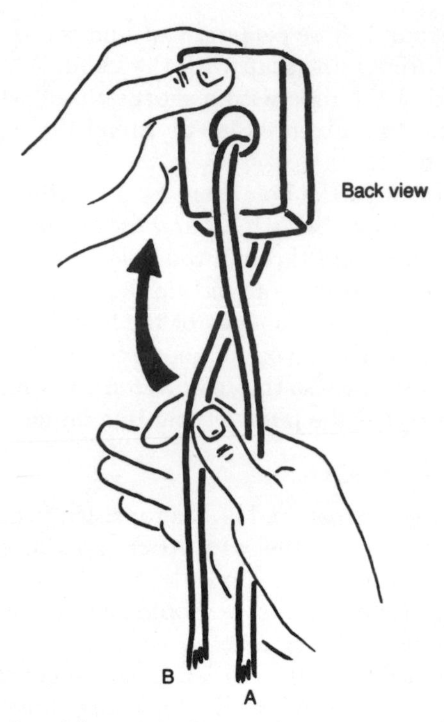

Your right thumb and finger take the part that hangs to the front and your hand moves up to the back of the soap.

the hole. Continue to pull that end *gently* forward until the little loop is jammed inside the hole.

Bring both ends of the rope to the top, tie them with a square knot, and put the loop over your head so the soap hangs on the rope in front of you. Joke about the problem of trying to wash your toes while the soap is tied around your neck.

"Of course, you could untie it from the rope," you say. "But there's a simpler way." Take the bar in your right hand. "You just use magic—and pull the soap right through the rope!" As you speak, pull the bar *out toward the right,* away from the rope, and it will come free, leaving the tied loop still hanging around your neck. "There it goes—and now you can wash your toes!"

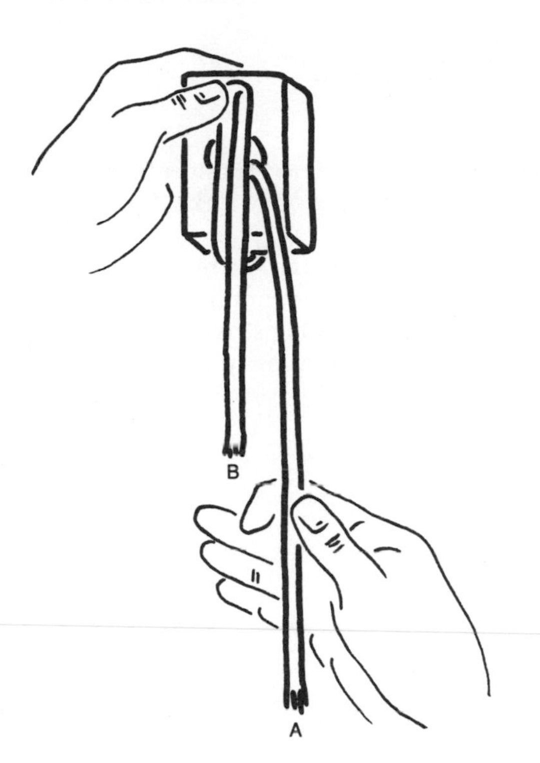

The loop is held by your left hand while your right hand moves back to take the other end.

After the back end has been put through the left side of the hole.

Magic Spaghetti

How it looks

"I was in such a hurry to get here, I didn't finish eating," you say, as you reach into your pocket and take out a fork. "I was having a spaghetti dinner."

You show each hand empty and then tap the top of your left hand three times with the fork. Dipping the fork into your hand, you magically produce what looks like a long string of spaghetti, which you wind in loops on the fork as you slowly draw it out between your hands.

What you need

A fork
A ball of soft white string
Scissors
Sports jacket

The secret

A long piece of string, used to look like spaghetti, is wound in a special way around the fork handle. When you transfer the fork from hand to hand, showing each hand empty, you secretly hide the string.

How you fix it

Cut off one yard of string and tie a small loop at one end. Turn the fork handle to the right. Place the little loop horizontally against it, with the top of the loop to the left and about an inch from the end of the handle.

Wind the string vertically once around the handle and up over the right end of the loop to hold the loop there. Continue to wind the rest of the string rather loosely around the handle to form a ball.

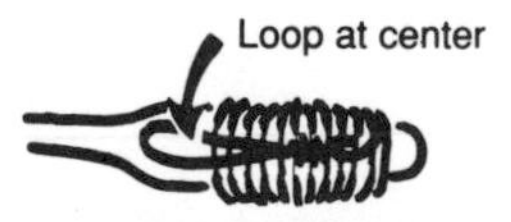

The string is wound around the loop and handle.

When you come to the opposite end of the string, tuck that in under the top strand of the ball with the point of the scissors to hold the ball together.

The little loop should now stick out to the left against the handle, at the center of the ball. It is fixed that way so when you do the trick the loop will be at the top of your left hand where you can find it quickly to draw the string out without tangling it. Gently slide the ball back and forth a little on the handle to make sure it holds together but will slide off easily. Put the fork in your right jacket pocket, handle toward the rear.

What you do

Put your right hand in your pocket, close your fingers loosely around the string and handle, and bring the fork out with the back of your hand toward those watching. Hold it with its pointed end upright and show it.

Show your left hand empty and bring that hand down, palm toward you, to take the fork. As your hands come together, with the left hand in front of the right, swing the handle into your left palm to transfer the fork to that hand. Take it away in your left hand and immediately show your right hand empty.

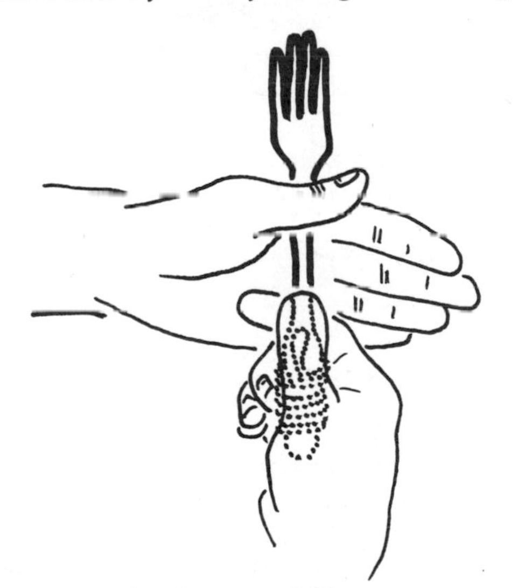

Your left hand takes the fork from your right.

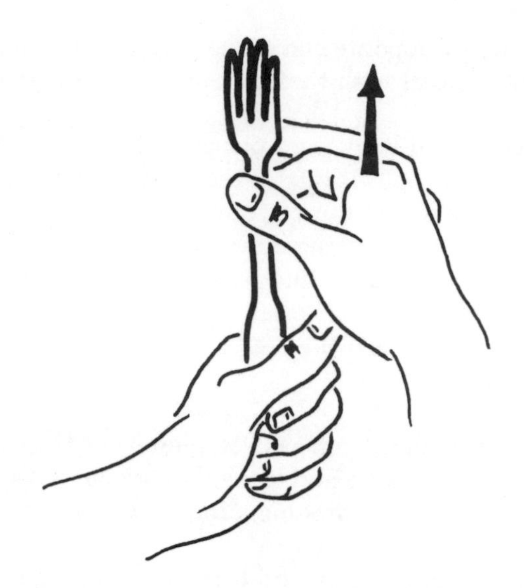

Your right hand pulls it up out of your left. The string slides off and stays in your left.

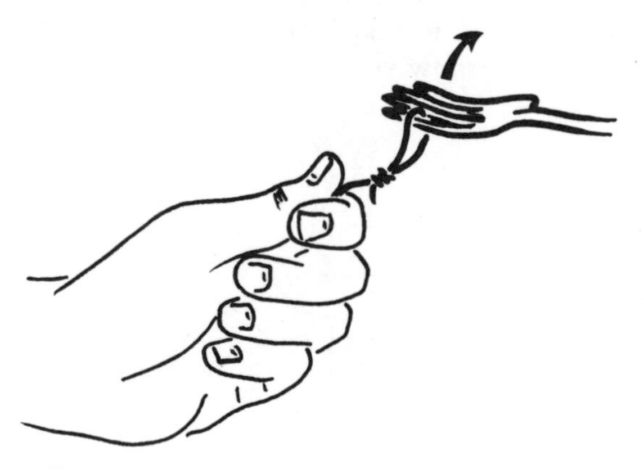

The fork goes through the loop and starts to draw out the string.

You are now holding the upright fork in your left hand. Take it again with your right hand, by simply drawing it straight up out of the left hand so that the balled string slides off the handle and stays hidden in your fisted left hand. With your right hand, tap the fork three times against the top of your left hand, as if casting a magic spell.

Open your left fist enough so you can see the little loop that sticks up from the center of the hidden ball of string. Slide one of the points of the fork through that loop, and *slowly* start to pull out the string, a few inches at a time, twisting the fork to wind a little of the string on it. As you gradually spread your hands apart, catch up the string in larger loops to make it look like a big forkful of spaghetti.

String and Envelope

How it looks

You show an envelope with a small hole at its center and thread a string through the hole so the two ends hang down outside in full view. Then you pull the center of the string up out of the envelope and cut the string in half.

Without touching the top cut ends, you slowly draw them back down inside the envelope by pulling the bottom ends of the strings. Suddenly you pull the string free of the envelope. It is whole again, magically restored to one piece!

What you need

A two-foot length of string
A four-inch length of the same string
An envelope
Transparent tape
Scissors small enough to carry in a jacket pocket
Sports jacket

The secret

The short piece of string is made into a loop and it is the extra loop that is cut, not the string itself. What makes the trick convincingly puzzling is the way the extra loop is secretly positioned inside the envelope so the hanging ends of the long string move with it. Because of that you seem to be really cutting the center of the long string.

How you fix it

Tie the short piece into a loop and trim the knot close. Turn the envelope with its narrow ends top and bottom, its back toward you and flap to the right. Cut a small hole through the back and front of the envelope at its center. It should be just big enough to thread the long string through without fumbling.

Take a 1-1/2" length of transparent tape. Bend down about 1/2" so it sticks to itself, leaving 1/2" uncovered and still sticky. Open the envelope and fasten the sticky part of the tape inside just above the center hole. The tab of tape that now sticks up above the hole serves as a "hook" on which to hang the extra loop of string.

Hang unknotted part of the extra loop over the tape so the hole in the envelope is about at the center of the loop. Close the envelope, seal it, and cut about 1/4" off the top end to leave that open. Wind the long string around the envelope and have it in one of your pockets with the scissors.

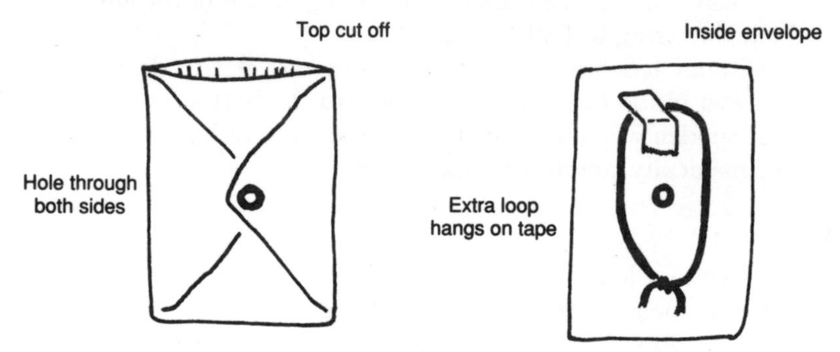

Fixing the envelope for "String and Envelope."

(Once you have made up the props, the only thing needed each time you show the trick is a little loop of string to hang over the tape "hook" inside the envelope.)

What you do

Unwind the long string, show it, and thread one end through the hole in the envelope. Draw it out until the two ends hang down even at the bottom. This puts the string through the center of the hidden extra loop.

Hold the envelope upright with your left hand near the top and squeeze the sides so the top billows open and you can look down into it. Reach into the envelope with your right fingers, take the

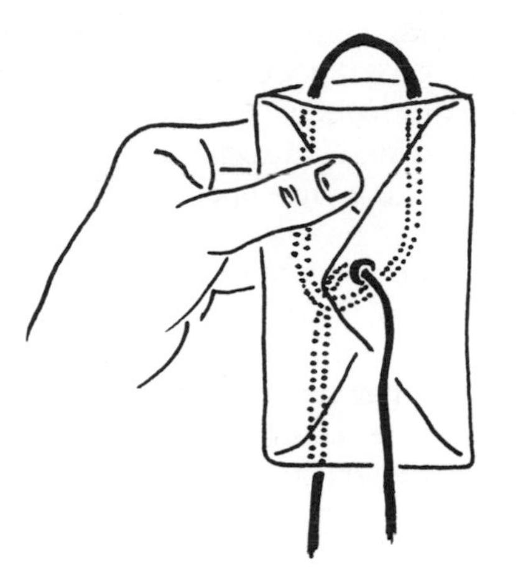

Your thumb presses to hold the loop for cutting.

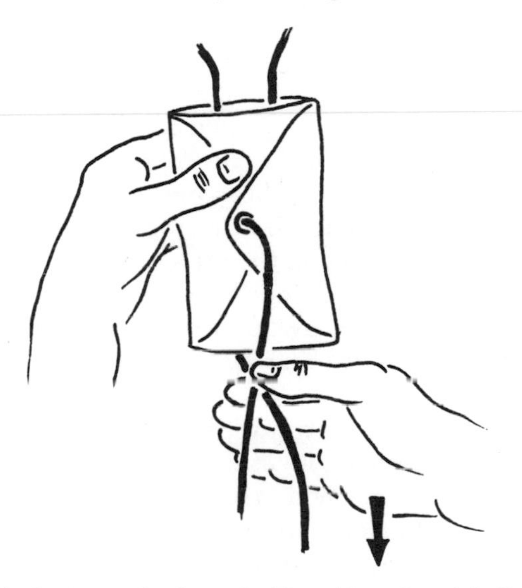

Pulling down the bottom ends also pulls the cut loop down into the envelope.

loop, and draw about half of it up out of the top of the envelope. As you pull the loop up it will pull up the hanging ends of the long string, so you seem to be really pulling up the center of the string itself.

Press your left thumb against the outside of the envelope to hold the loop in place. Take the scissors with your right hand and cut through the loop; this looks as if you are cutting the string in two. Use the point of the scissors to separate the two cut ends that stick up above the top of the envelope, and then put the scissors aside.

Bring your right hand down to the two free ends that hang at the bottom of the envelope. Take them together and *very slowly* pull them down. This draws the two cut ends at the top down inside the envelope, where they remain hidden so there is nothing to conceal in your hands at the end of the trick. Finally, take one end of the string, pull the string out through the hole in the envelope, and show that it is whole again, restored to one piece.

The Magic Baseball Game

How it looks

"I'd like to show you what I call a magic game of baseball," you say, as you show a piece of rope and coil it up around your left hand. "Instead of a ball, we'll use this rope. And instead of three bases, this game has only one—this paper bag." With your right hand, you pick up a paper bag, show it empty, and drop the coiled rope inside. You put the bag on the table.

"We need some players for our team," you say, as you pick up a second piece of rope and show it. "Are there any ball players in the audience? Please raise your hands. No need to leave your seats—I'll play out to the field."

As you speak, you tie a large overhand knot and hold the rope by its two ends so all can see it.

"How about you?" You nod to someone in the audience. "Will you be our catcher? Just hold up your hands as though you were going to catch a ball and I'll throw you this knot."

You flick the rope forward, still holding both ends, and the big knot visibly vanishes. "Did you catch it?" you ask. "Good—just hold it for a minute. Now we need a pitcher for our team."

You tie another large knot in the center of the rope and nod to someone else, "Will you be our pitcher? Hold up your hands and I'll throw you this one." Again you make the knot vanish while seeming to throw it in his direction.

"And now, a shortstop." As a third person holds up his hands to catch the vanishing knot, you add a little comedy by saying, "Oh, I'm sorry—you dropped it. That was my fault. Would you mind picking it up? It fell next to your chair." You point. "Right down there. These knots are awfully hard to see when they're invisible."

You put aside that rope and pick up the paper bag, which contains the other coiled-up rope. Turning toward the first person, who is supposed to be holding an invisible knot, you say, "Would you please throw yours back?"

As he makes a throwing motion, you move the bag as though catching the knot, and the sound of the knot landing inside the bag is heard. You do the same with the other two players, "catching" the knots in the bag as they are thrown, and each time the sound is heard.

"Now let's see how you've done," you say. You lift out the rope that has been in the bag and show that three knots have become tied in it. "Say, you're pretty good ball players!"

What you need

Two five-foot lengths of soft white clothesline
White cloth adhesive tape, 3/4" wide
A brown paper lunch bag

The secret

The fun of this routine depends on the way the audience takes part in the make-believe ball game. The knots that vanish are formed with a simply prepared rope, and you make noise by secretly snapping a finger against the back of the bag as each knot is "caught." The way the other rope is coiled up as it is put into the bag at the start of the trick produces the three knots that appear.

How you fix it

Take a 1-1/2" length of cloth adhesive tape, turn it *sticky side out*, and wind it *tightly* around the center of one rope. (From a short distance the little band of sticky white tape cannot be seen on the white rope.) The other rope needs no preparation. Put the prepared rope on a table, the flat paper bag on top of it, and the unprepared rope on top of that.

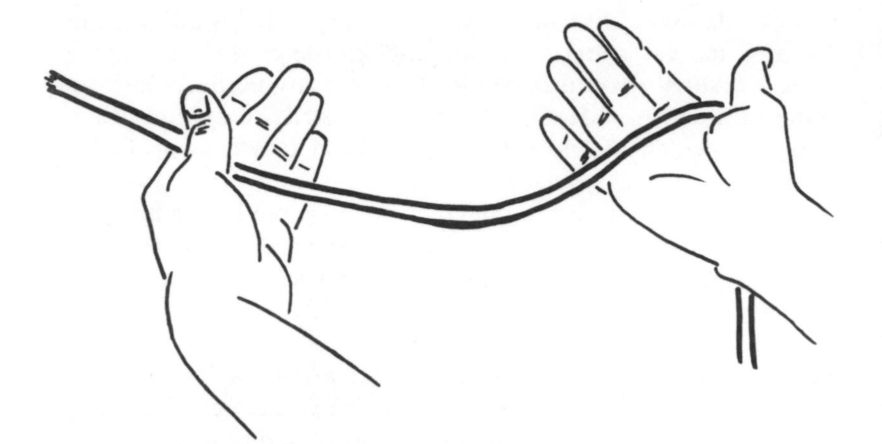

The rope should lie across both palms.

What you do

Since the plot already has been given in detail so you can follow it easily, we will deal here only with the actual moves that are made.

The unprepared rope is shown and coiled three times around the left hand so you can secretly make three knots in this way:

Start by clipping one end of the rope under your left thumb. Turn your palm up. Put your right hand, palm up, under the rope so the little fingers of both hands are about three inches apart. The rope should now lie across the palms of both hands and be held by the two thumbs.

Close the right fingers to make a fist. Turn your fisted right hand to the left to bring it palm down. A loop of rope now runs through your right fingers. Hang this loop over the outstretched fingers of your left hand.

Turn the right palm up again and move it along the rope to where you can make a second loop. Turn the right hand over and put the second loop on the left hand. Make one more loop the same way and hang that over your left hand. All of this should look as if you were merely coiling up the rope in a casual way.

Hold the coils in the left hand and pick up the paper bag with the right hand. Shake out the bag and show that it is empty. Now, as you are asking whether there are any ball players in the au-

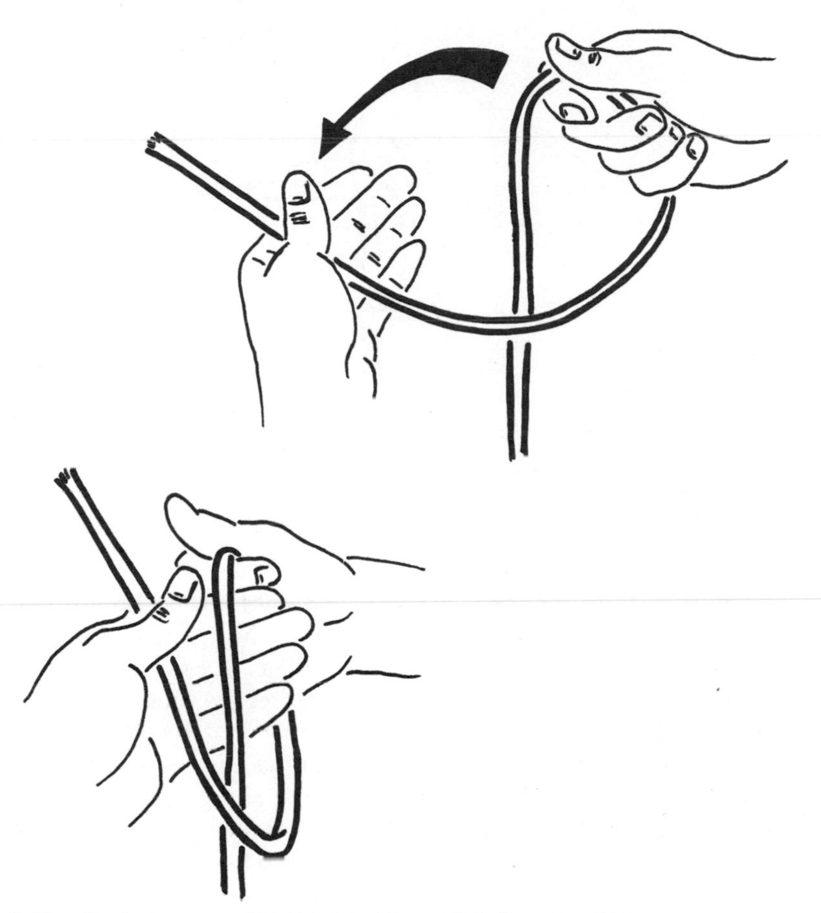

Coiling the first rope around your hand to put it in the paper bag.

dience, pass your right hand *through* all the loops that are hanging over your left hand, and with the right hand grip the end of the rope that is under your left thumb. Pull that end out to the right, through the coils.

Hold the end and the coiled rope with your right hand and put the rope in the bag. Keep the end pressed against the inside top of the bag with your fingers as you put the bag on the table, *on its side,* and with the bag opening toward the rear. If you keep the end of the rope at the top of the bag you won't have to fumble for it later.

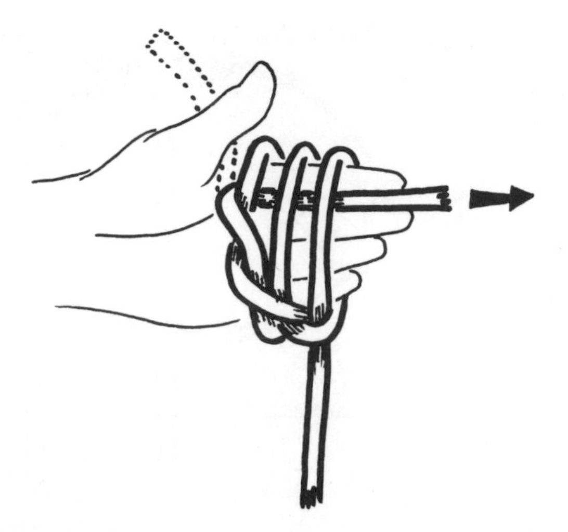

From under your thumb, pull the end of the rope through the loops.

Next pick up the prepared rope and hold it with both hands near the center. The hands should be palm down, with the rope held between the thumb and first two fingers of each hand. Slide your hands apart along the rope until you feel the sticky tape with your left fingers.

Hold the sticky tape with your left thumb and fingers and continue to slide your right hand about a foot along the rope to the right. Grip the rope there and move your right hand forward toward the audience and then over to the left to form a loop by sticking the part in your right hand to the tape. Give it a little squeeze with your left thumb and fingers so it sticks tightly.

Now slide your right thumb and fingers along the rope toward the right end. Take that end and put it through the loop from the front, pointing toward yourself, as if you were tying a knot. Gently slide both hands out to the ends of the rope. The fake knot will hold its large loop in the center. If you give the rope a quick forward jerk, the knot will vanish instantly, because the loop comes unstuck and the rope becomes a straight length.

"Throw" the three knots to the persons who are supposed to catch them, one to the right, a second in the center, and the third on the left. Each of them in turn pretends to catch a knot.

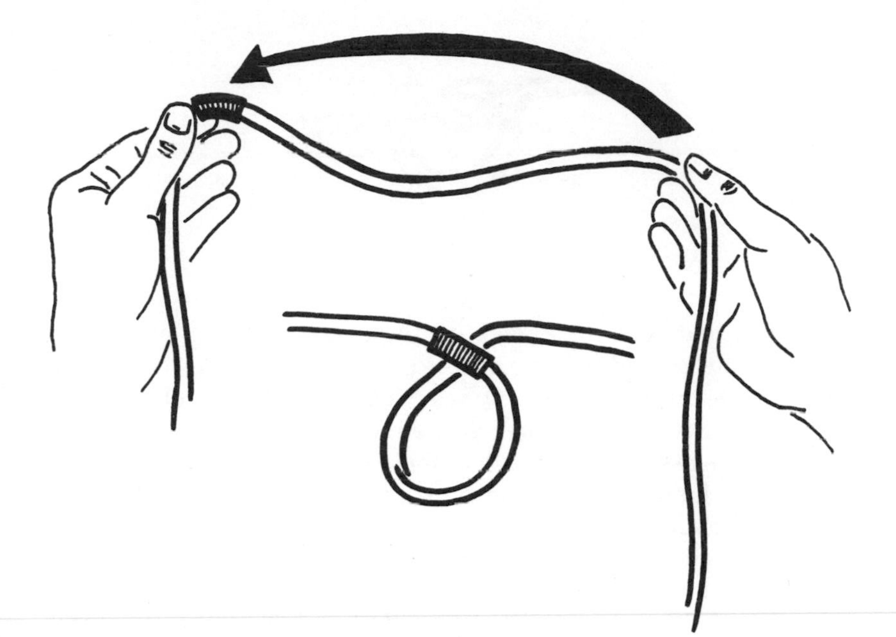

Make a loop by sticking the rope to the tape.

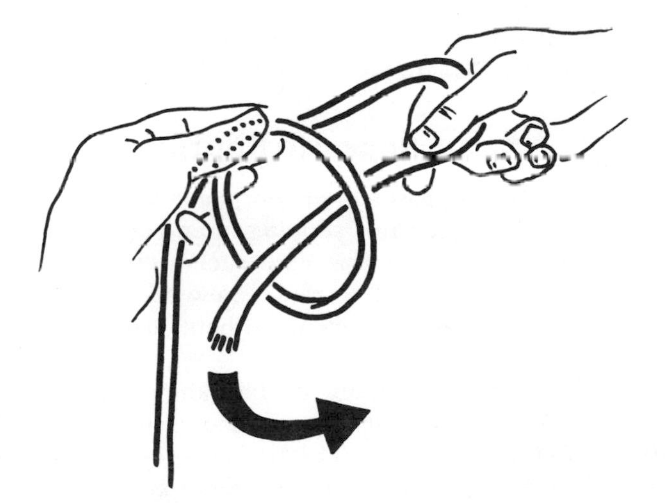

Put the end through to tie the fake knot.

Fake knot.

Put that rope aside. Pick up the paper bag with your right hand. Your second finger goes inside the bag and holds the end of the rope against the inside top rear. The other fingers of the right hand remain outside the bag at the rear.

As the players throw each of their knots back, make the sound of a knot landing in the bag by snapping your right first finger sharply against the rear of the bag with your thumb. After you have "caught" all three knots, transfer the bag to your left hand, holding the end of rope inside the top with your left fingers.

Reach into the bag with your right hand. Take the end of the rope and give it a few shakes inside the bag as you remove it, so the knots will fall into place. Hold the rope high to show that the three thrown knots have been "caught." Toss aside the paper bag and give the audience a cue for applause by nodding to the players as you tell them: "Say, you're pretty good ball players!"

Kellar Rope Tie Routine

Famous magicians, past and present, have featured many versions of an instant rope escape, slipping in and out of a rope that binds their wrists. They do this with such startling speed that the effect is comic as well as puzzling. Few other tricks provide so much stage-filling entertainment without elaborate props or equipment.

The Kellar Rope Tie is among the best-known methods for accomplishing the trick. Basically this method in its simplest form is used in the following routine. The trickery depends on nothing more than learning one simple twist of the rope.

The entertainment depends, not on the method, but almost entirely on the story and the way the performer presents it. Here then is not something new, but something old—a practical and detailed routine that plays for about five minutes and can be shown almost anywhere to an audience of almost any size.

What you need

A five-foot length of soft clothesline
Sharp scissors small enough to be carried in your breast pocket
Sports jacket

The secret

A twist in the rope allows slack so that your hand easily can be slipped in and out, although your arms seem to be tightly bound behind your back.

How you fix it

There is nothing to fix, except to have the rope on a table and the scissors, with their points down, in your breast pocket.

What you do

To learn this trick, you will need someone's help in tying you. Have that person hold the rope stretched out between his hands. Place your left wrist, with the palm of your hand down, on the center of the rope. Have him take the two ends and tie a *tight* knot on top of your wrist and then drop the ends.

The two ends of rope now hang freely, one at each side of your wrist, from the knot on top. Lower your hand slightly and grasp the right side of the rope between your first and second fingers. Twist your wrist to lift that end out to the left, so your fingers pass in *front* of the end of the rope that is hanging from the left side of your wrist. Hold the rope in that position and bring your left arm around behind you against the small of your back. Your palm now faces toward the rear, with the end of the rope still grasped between your fingers.

This has all been done with only your left hand. Now bring your right hand behind your back, palm outward and fingertips toward the left, and put it *between* the two hanging ends of rope. Hold your wrists pressed together against your back, and turn your back toward the person who is helping you. Have him tie the ends *tightly* around your right wrist.

If you go through this several times, you will see that it really involves only a lift of the fingers to position the rope. You should

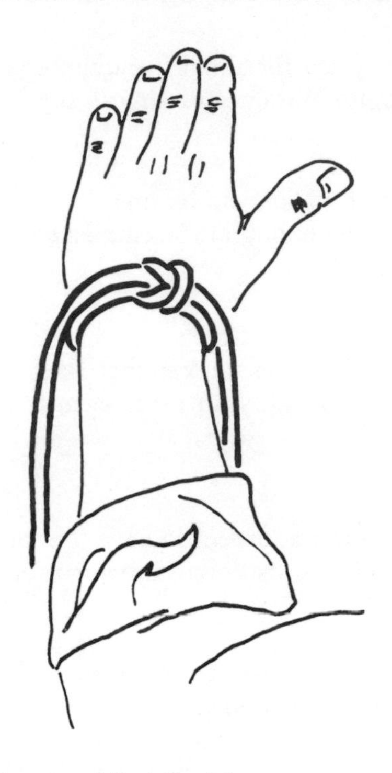

The first knot is tied on top of the left wrist.

learn to do it smoothly so it seems that you are merely placing your hands behind your back and turning to have the final knot tied. There is no need to hurry. The movements are natural and nothing about them looks tricky.

The release from the rope is easy. With your hands tied behind your back, face front again. Simply lower both hands until their fingertips point toward the floor, and slip your right hand out of the loop.

Keep your left hand behind your back and wave your right hand high in the air. Bring your right hand behind your back again, palm outward, and slip it into the loop. Lift the right hand with fingertips toward the left until the rope again is twisted tight around the right wrist. Hold both arms together against the small of your back as they were before.

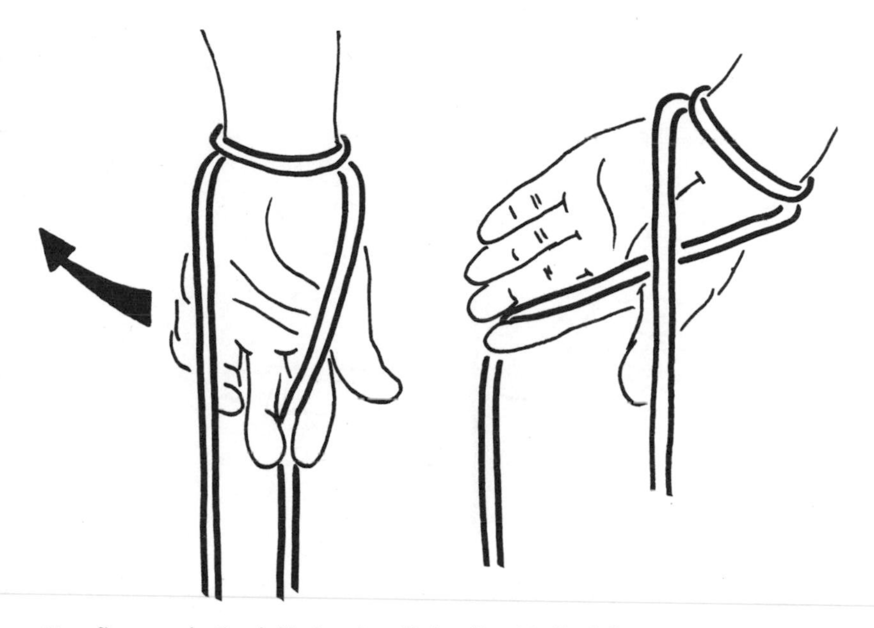

Your fingers grip the right strand and bring it out to the left.

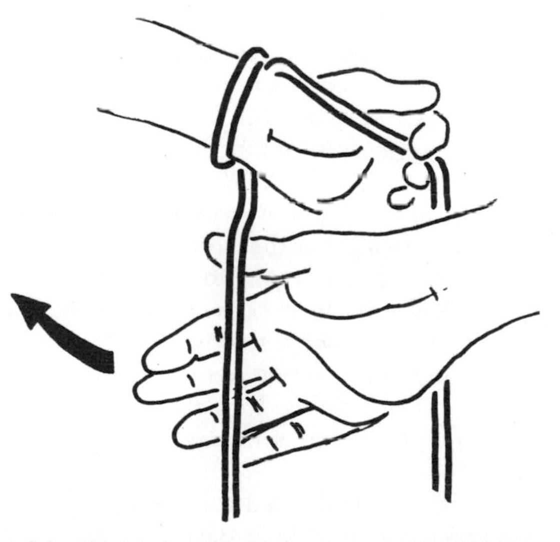

Bring the left hand behind your back and put the right hand between the two hanging ends of rope.

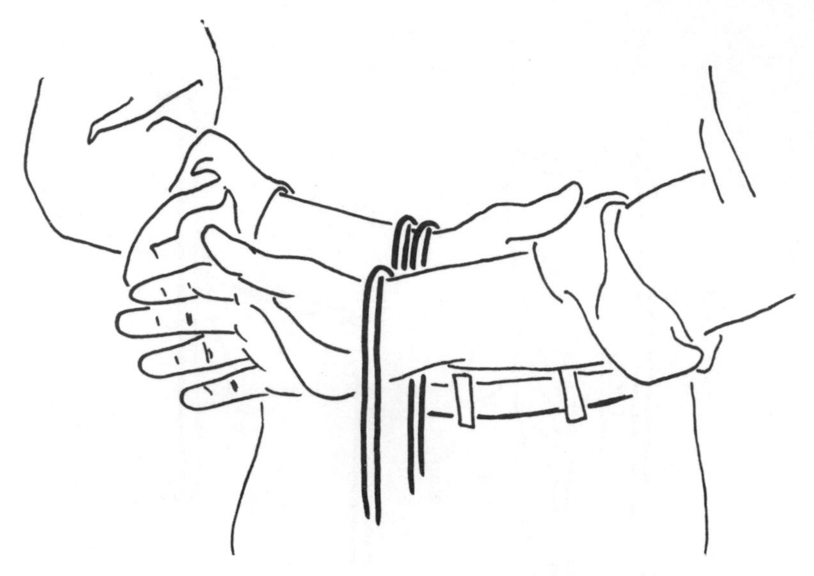

Draw your wrists together up against back for tying of the second knot.

Quickly turn around to show that your arms are still tied. With your arms in this position, the knots can be examined. By lowering your right hand, you can free your hand as often as you wish when your back is turned, then almost immediately swing around to show that your arms are still firmly bound.

Here is the full routine, written in the form of a script for a play. Rehearse it as you would if you were acting a part in a play:

MAGICIAN: *(Speaks slowly and seriously.)* More than a hundred years ago, newspapers all over the world were filled with headlines, columns, whole pages, devoted to a serious discussion of whether two upstate New York farm boys, known as the Davenport Brothers, could bring back to earth the spirits of the dead.

(Picks up rope, and as he continues to talk, slowly unbuttons the cuffs of his shirt. Then he pulls back the sleeves of his jacket, first one and then the other, and turns his shirtsleeves up, so his forearms are bare.)

The Davenport Brothers allowed themselves to be tied with rope—their hands bound behind their backs.

(Puts his hands behind him and turns his side to show them. Then faces front again and continues to roll up his sleeves.)

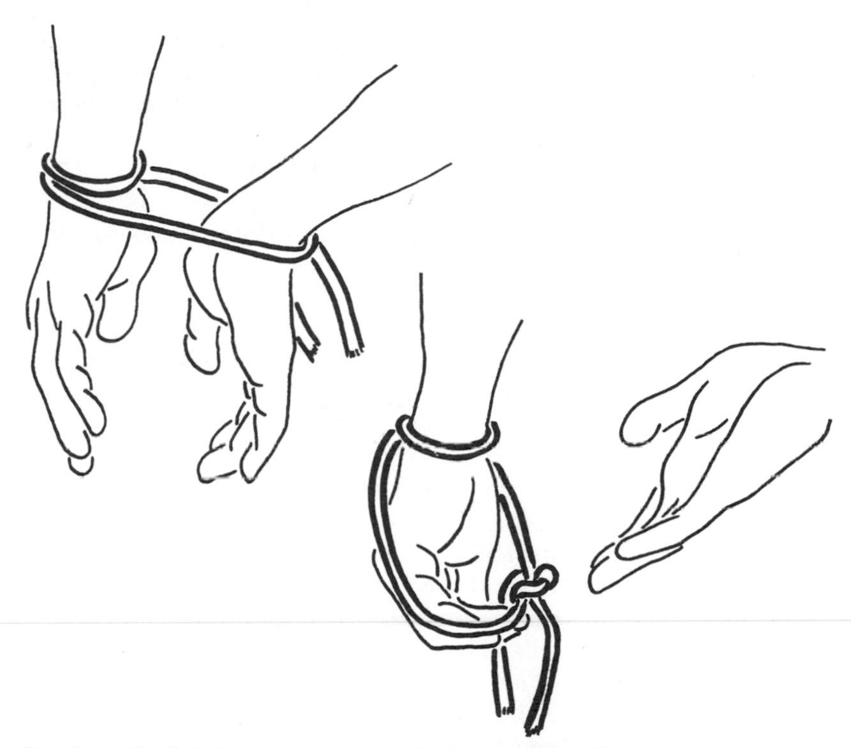

To release the right hand, turn both hands downward and slip the right hand out of the loop—keeping the left hand behind your back. Reverse the moves to tighten the rope around your wrists again.

They were placed in a cabinet, along with horns, bells, and musical instruments—and the cabinet doors were shut. When the horns began to blow—

(Briefly lifts fingers to mouth as though he held a horn.)

—the bells began to ring—

(Briefly shakes hand as though ringing a bell.)

—and the musical instruments began to play—

(Briefly strums an imaginary banjo with his fingers.)

—with the brothers tied in the cabinet like that—

(Briefly turns his side, puts hands behind back, faces front again. Completes rolling up sleeves during following remarks.)

—many people were convinced that the spirits had returned. The Davenports had an assistant, later their business manager, who left them and went on to become one of the greatest magicians the world has ever known. His name was—Harry Kellar. His early success depended a great deal on his ability to reproduce some of the ghostly illusions of the Davenport Brothers—by pure trickery, just for fun.

(Holds rope between his hands and snaps it taut.)

Tonight, if I may, I'd like to show you my version of the famous spirit escape—as performed by the great Harry Kellar—a century ago.

(While talking, he mentally has picked out two men to help him. They are seated close to each other and near the front, so he will have no delay in getting them up front. He walks directly to the first of the men he has chosen.)

Will you take this rope, sir?

(Gives it to him. Turns to the other man.)

I'll need your help, too. Right up here, please.

(Leads them up front.)

Will you stand to my left . . . and you to my right. Thank you.

(Turns and introduces himself to man on left, giving own first name, and repeating man's name clearly when it is given to him.)

My name's Bill—what's yours? Joe? I'm glad to meet you, Joe.

(Shakes his hand, then turns to man on right.)

And you're—? Fred? I'm glad to know you, Fred. *(Shakes hand.)* Are you two gentlemen acquainted? Joe, this is Fred—Fred, this is Joe. Shake hands—shake hands, but don't come out fighting.

(The audience may be only slightly amused by this somewhat silly bit of byplay, but the real reason for it is to put both helpers in a relaxed and friendly mood, so they will be good sports, will follow instructions, and will join in the fun.)

Will you take one end of the rope, Fred—

(Gives him one end.)

—and stretch it out between you and have a little tug of war? That's enough. I just wanted you to be sure it's a good strong piece of rope.

(Stands behind the stretched rope, at its center and slightly back from it. Puts his left wrist on top of the center of the rope, with palm of his hand down.)

Now, Fred, will you please give your end of the rope to Joe—and Joe, will you tie a good tight knot right here on top of my wrist where everybody can see it?

(Points with right index finger to top of left wrist to show where he wants the knot tied.)

Thank you. You can let go of it now.

(Holds out left wrist so everyone can see the knot. With his left fingers, grips right side of hanging rope in the way practiced. Brings left arm behind his back and then brings right arm into proper position against it. Immediately turns his back to audience.)

I hope you'll excuse me for turning my back. Fred, will you please tie the two ends together.

(Turns back slightly toward helper.)

A good tight knot, please.

(When the helper has finished tying the knot, the magician turns his back slightly toward the other helper.)

Joe, will you examine the knot? Are my hands tightly bound? Thank you.

(Faces front again and steps back a few feet so the two helpers can't see behind him. Releases right hand from rope, but keeps it behind his back a moment.)

At this point, Mr. Kellar used to say, "Gentlemen, if you are convinced that my two hands are tightly tied, then nature must have royally endowed me—

(Raises right hand high in air and waves it.)

"—with a third hand!"

(Puts his right hand behind his back again, slips it into the loop, lifts his arms against his back to tighten the tie, and instantly swings around so his back is toward the audience.)

But almost immediately, he would show that, in fact, his two hands were still firmly tied. Will you try the knot, Joe?

(Turns his back slightly so helper can examine knot. When he has, the magician turns so other helper can make the same examination.)

Is the knot still tied tightly? Thank you. Now will you gentlemen please move in a little closer to me?

(Facing front, he stands between them, so their shoulders are almost touching his.)

Right up close on this side, Fred—and, Joe, right up close on this side.

(Secretly slips right hand out of loop, but keeps hand behind back. Turns his head to helper on right.)

Do you believe in ghosts? No?

(Turns head to helper on left.)

Do you believe there are spirits hovering around us and that—?

(As he speaks to man on left, taps his right hand on shoulder of man on right. Lets audience see hand, then immediately drops it behind his back, slips it into loop, holds arms up tightly against back. He has abruptly interrupted what he was saying and swings head toward man on right, showing surprise.)

What was that? A ghost? It must have been—

(Swings around so his back is toward audience.)

—because my two hands are still tightly tied.

(Faces front, moves back a few steps, and secretly releases right hand. Brings it out and points to floor in front of him, then out toward audience, as if pointing out a moving ghost.)

But I do believe I saw a ghost! There he goes! Right out into the audience—did you see him go?

(Brings hand behind back, slips it into loop, draws arms tight against back, and immediately swings around so back is toward audience, showing that his hands are tied. After a moment, faces front again, and turns slightly toward helper on left.)

In my breast pocket, there is a pair of scissors. Would you remove them, please?

(Moves close so helper can take scissors from pocket. Then turns his back to helper, so his side is toward audience.)

And will you cut the rope from my wrists—*(Winks to audience)*—so as to free me? Be careful to cut just the rope, please, not my wrist.

(When helper has cut the top loop, so he can free his right hand, magician brings both arms to the front, takes the scissors from the helper, and cuts the remaining rope from the left wrist. He snips the rope in half and drops scissors back into his breast pocket. Gives one piece of rope to helper on left and other piece to helper on right.)

Thank you. Here's a piece for you, Joe, and a piece for you, Fred. Souvenirs of your visit with the spirits. Thank you both for helping me. *(Turns to audience.)* Let's give them both a hand for being such good sports.

(Claps hands to lead applause for them as helpers return to seats. Bows to encourage applause for himself.)

SEVEN

Magic in Mind

The magician who pulls a rabbit from a hat deceives the eye. But the mental magician deceives the mind. He creates the illusion that he is able to read minds, that he can transfer thoughts from his mind to the minds of others, predict future happenings, and perform other demonstrations of psychic phenomena.

What he does is no part of the serious scientific and psychological research into such things. Whether performing for a few friends or for a larger audience, he is an actor playing the role of a mentalist, an entertainer presenting a rehearsed show of mental magic.

The mental magician doesn't say it is all a trick, any more than the magician who takes a rabbit from a hat would break into a performance to explain that there is no real magic in what he does. He claims no supernatural powers, but he suggests the possibility that they may exist for some people, demonstrates what might be accomplished if someone did possess such powers—and leaves it to the audience to decide how it is done.

Most of the secrets of mental magic are simple ones, far simpler than the audience imagines. Some of the props are tricked, of course, but seldom in an elaborate manner. The mentalist relies more on subtlety than on apparatus. Because everything must be made to look as innocent as possible, the less there is to hide, the better.

Simple, bold, direct methods allow him to concentrate on the presentation, and that is what counts—not the trick as a magical puzzle designed to fool the spectators, but the illusion he can build around it in their minds.

Silent Commercial

How it looks

Showing a folded slip of paper, you ask a spectator who is standing beside you, "May I put this in your pocket?" Tucking it into the top of his breast pocket, you say, "We are about to conduct a marketing survey. But first, we'll have to take time out for a commercial."

You stand silent for a moment with your eyes closed, and then open them and say: "There—the commercial's finished. You didn't hear it because it was a silent commercial. There were no pictures to watch because it was an invisible commercial. It was in my mind—and perhaps it is now in your mind, too, even though you may not be aware that you heard any commercial message at all."

From your pocket, you take four metal-rimmed cardboard discs and explain that on each of them you have written the name of a breakfast cereal. You ask the spectator to take them and read them aloud, and he reads: "Flakes, Crackles, Toasties, Crunchers."

"My sponsor is the manufacturer of one of those four brands," you say, "and our survey is to test whether silent commercials work—whether you have been mentally influenced to buy that brand instead of one of the others—so that you reach for my brand by some blind impulse."

You drop all the discs into the side pocket of your jacket and hold it open wide as you invite the spectator to dip his hand in and take one of them. "Mix them up. Don't take the first one you touch—unless you want to. You have one? Will you please read the name on it aloud?"

He reads: "Toasties." You then ask him to remove the slip of paper that you put in his breast pocket at the start and to read that aloud. He reads: "Thank you for listening to my silent commercial. My sponsor will be pleased that you bought—Toasties."

What you need

- Eight round metal-rimmed blank cardboard tags, 1-3/4" in diameter, with their strings removed
- A sheet of paper from a small scratch pad
- Black felt tip marking pen
- A jacket with a small "ticket pocket" inside the top of the right hand pocket (Most men's jackets are made with such a pocket.)

The secret

There are four duplicate tags, all with the same name on them, in the bottom of your right-hand jacket pocket. The other four, with various names on them, are shown to the spectator and then are dropped into the little "ticket pocket" inside the top of your right-hand pocket. You hold your hand over the "ticket pocket" as you spread the rest of your pocket wide so that he may dip his hand into it. He is forced to "choose" one of the four duplicates from the bottom of the pocket, and what he chooses, of course, bears the name that was written on the slip of paper given to him at the start.

How you fix it

Print the four breakfast cereal names, or any other product names you may wish to use, on four of the tags. Then print one of those four names—Toasties, for example—on all four of the other tags. Write the prediction note, worded as explained, and fold it.

Drop the four duplicate tags, all with the same name on them (Toasties), into the bottom of your right-hand pocket. Put the other four, all with different names on them, into the little "ticket pocket" along with the folded slip of paper.

What you do

Have the spectator stand to your right. Remove the prediction slip from your pocket. Show it without opening it and ask if you may put it in his pocket. Tuck it into the top of his breast pocket so part of it remains in view.

Say that you are about to conduct a marketing survey, "but first—we'll have to take time out for a commercial." Stand with your eyes closed and silently count to twenty. Then open your eyes and explain that he didn't see it or hear it because it was a silent and invisible commercial—"in my mind—and perhaps it is now in your mind, too."

Remove the bunch of four different tags from your "ticket pocket." Show him what is on them, give them to him, and ask him to read each of the names aloud. Take them back, stack them together in your right hand, and show them again. Turn your body a little to the left so everybody can see, and openly drop them into the right-hand pocket of your jacket—but really into the "ticket pocket" at the top of it.

Don't put your hand all the way into your pocket. Just spread the "ticket pocket" with the backs of your fingers, let the tags fall into it, and immediately remove your hand. This should be done with seeming carelessness, not as though you were being cautious about where they went.

Explain that your "sponsor" is the manufacturer of one of the four brands and that the survey is to test "whether silent commercials work," whether he will reach for one brand instead of the others "by some blind impulse." This is said to give a reason for having him choose blindly from your pocket instead of simply looking at them and choosing one.

Without deliberately showing that your right hand is empty, let it be seen that it is. Put it just far enough into the top of your right-hand pocket so your fingers cover the "ticket pocket." Hook your left thumb into the top of the whole pocket at the opposite side, the side toward the spectator, and spread the pocket wide.

Hold it open that way as you shake it, as though mixing the tags that rattle in the bottom of it, and say, "Just dip your hand into my pocket and take one of them. Mix them up. Don't take the first one you touch—unless you want to. But take just one—any one—and bring it out."

As soon as he takes one, remove both your hands from the pocket. Ask him to read aloud the name on the tag he has "chosen." Repeat it. Then say: "You have had a note in your pocket since we began this survey. Will you open it now, please, and read it to everyone?"

He reads your thanks for listening to the silent commercial and the prediction that he would choose "Toasties."

Telepathy for One

How it looks

You are alone with one of your friends, someplace where the person can sit at a table directly across from you, and you turn the conversation to psychic phenomena and telepathy.

"If you came up to me on the street and challenged me to read your mind, I know I couldn't do it," you say, "because you might be thinking any of hundreds of different things and I wouldn't know where to start. But if we both agreed in advance that you were to think of something specific—such as someone's name—Let's try it. Just for fun."

From your pocket, you take out a wallet, and sort through the cards in it until you find one with a blank side. "This will do," you say, pushing the card across to him, and giving him a pen or pencil if he hasn't one. "I'll turn my head and you just print someone's first name on the card. Print the first name of someone you're sure I don't know. Then turn the card so the writing is facedown and put it at the center of the table."

You turn your head or stand up and turn your back to him. When he says he has written the name and turned the card over, you sit facing him across the table again. "I'll cover it with this," you say, picking up the wallet and dropping it on top of the card. "I want you to imagine that there is a big red spot, right here." You point to the face of the wallet. "Fix your eyes on that to center your thoughts and then concentrate on the name."

Slowly you begin to "read" his thoughts. You get one letter of the name, then another, and finally reveal the entire name.

What you need

A large "secretary-type" wallet, about 4-1/2" by 8", with an inside pocket that will hold an assortment of cards

Half a dozen business cards (Preferably these should be of various kinds and sizes—some with one side blank, others penciled with notes—cards that normally might be carried in a wallet.)

Double-faced (sticky both sides) transparent tape

A pen or pencil

Sports jacket

The secret

The wallet has a small strip of double-faced tape stuck to one face of it. When you cover the person's card with the wallet and point to an imaginary red spot, the card sticks to the bottom of the wallet. You tilt the wallet up on edge as you explain how you want the person to center his thoughts on the "spot," and the card lifts with it so you can secretly read the name he has written on the card.

How you fix it

There is little to prepare. Start with the wallet on a table, turned like a book you were about to read, narrow ends top and bottom. Fasten a 1-1/2" strip of double-faced tape vertically to the outside center of that face of the wallet. Rub the ball of your thumb over the tape a few times to make it slightly less sticky. Then open the wallet and put the assorted cards inside it.

Put the wallet in the inside right-hand pocket of your jacket, so the taped side is toward your body, with the open edges of the wallet at the rear of the pocket. Have the pen or pencil clipped in that pocket.

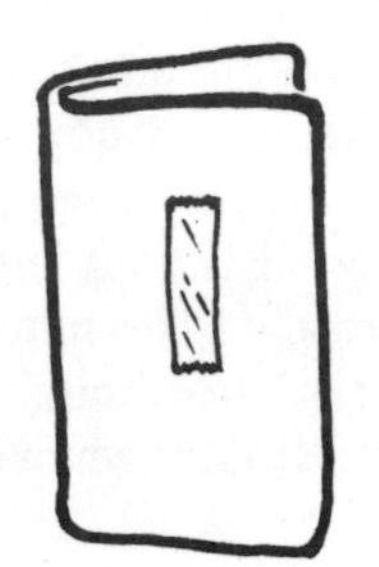

You attach a doublefaced tape to the back of the wallet.

What you do

With your friend seated directly across from you at a table, remove the wallet from your pocket with your left hand. Keep it upright, tape at the back. Transfer it to your right hand and put it on the table, with its taped side down so that its *long* edges are at the top and bottom. Open it, sort through the cards, select one with a blank side, close the wallet and leave it in that lengthwise position.

Slide the card, blank side up, across the table to him. Ask if he has a pen or pencil, and if he hasn't one give him yours. Turn your head or stand with your back to him and say, "Just print the name on the card. Print the first name of someone I don't know." You are telling him twice to "print" the name, to avoid handwriting that might be difficult to read quickly. "Then turn the card so the writing is facedown and put it at the center of the table."

When he has done that, sit facing him again and say, "I'll cover it with this." Pick up the wallet with your right hand at the long edge that is toward you and drop it on top of the card. As you do, glance to see that the tape will come in contact with the card. The wallet should lie horizontally, covering the card lengthwise.

When the wallet is tipped up on edge, the card sticks to the wallet.

"I want you to imagine that there is a big red spot right here," you say. Point to the center of the wallet and press down with the tip of your finger so that the card beneath it sticks to the tape. With your left hand, tilt the wallet up without lifting it off the table, and continue to tap the face of the wallet with your right finger, pointing to the imaginary "spot." Tell him, "Fix your eyes on that to center your thoughts and then concentrate on the name."

As you speak, secretly look at the card that is stuck to the back of the uptilted wallet and read the name he has printed. You should be able to gain the information at a glance, even if the printing appears upside down to you, which sometimes happens. The instant you know what the name is, drop the wallet flat again.

Pretend to get one or two of the letters and finally reveal the entire name. With your left hand, tilt up the wallet, and bring your right hand underneath to flick the card free of the tape with your fingers.

Lift the wallet away with your left hand, pick up the card with your right hand, and turn the card over. Read the name aloud as if to confirm that you "read his mind" correctly, and put the wallet away in your pocket as you hand him the card—to keep, if he wants it.

Toll the Hour

How it looks

You take a small envelope from your pocket and remove a card from it, on which there is a drawing of a numbered clock dial without hands. One of a group of spectators gathered around a table is asked to think of something that happened to him yesterday or that will happen tomorrow.

"It could be something trivial or something important," you say, giving him a pencil. "I want you to think of the hour of the happening—never mind the minutes—and draw in a hand to that hour on this clock. Just draw a straight line—an arrow—from the center of the dial to the hour."

While he is doing that, you turn your head so you can't see, and then ask him to place the drawing facedown on the table. Facing the group again, you slide the card flatly across the table and put it into the envelope, which you seal. Both sides of the envelope are shown so there will be no doubt that the clock dial is entirely covered from view.

"Your thought of that hour exists in two dimensions—in your mind and in the physical expression of it on the drawing sealed in this envelope," you say. "If I were to tear up the drawing, the thought would be physically destroyed." You tear the envelope and the drawing inside it into small pieces and discard them by dropping them into your pocket. "In a strictly physical sense, the hour is now lost. But, of course, the thought of that hour remains in your mind."

For a moment, you stand silent, and close your eyes. "In *my* mind," you say then, "I hear a clock tolling—chiming the hour." You slowly tap the end of the pencil on the table, sounding it one, two, three times. Opening your eyes, you tell the spectator, "The hour in your mind is three o'clock."

What you need

A 2-1/2" by 4-1/4" manila coin envelope with an end-opening flap (It should be of good quality paper, thick enough so it cannot be seen through.)
A blank card, cut slightly smaller than the envelope
Pencil, pen, and scissors
Sports jacket

The secret

Although the envelope is convincingly shown on both sides so it appears to have no openings, it does have a hole cut in the face of it. But the hole is so small that it is covered by the ball of your thumb. Through the hole you are able to see the center of the clock dial and enough of the "hand" that the spectator has drawn to tell the hour to which it points.

How you fix it

Start by drawing the clock dial with the pen. In the center of the card, make a circle about 2-1/4" in diameter. The size need not be exact, but the dial should be large enough so the numbers will be well spaced around it. Number it from one to twelve as a clock is numbered, with the numbers positioned carefully where they would be on the face of a clock.

At the center of the circle make a fairly large dot. Then enlarge the dot just a bit at the top, so the top of the dot points upward toward the twelve. This is done so that when the numbers are covered by the envelope you can tell from looking at the point of the dot whether the dial is upside down.

Card with a clock dial. The point at the top of the dot shows that the dial is right way up.

With the scissors, cut a small "window" in the face of the envelope so that the dot of the clock dial will be at the center of this opening when the card is in the envelope. Cut it only in the face of the envelope, not through the back. The "window" should be about 1/2" square so your thumb will cover it entirely. All you need to see is the inner end of the line the spectator will draw, starting at the dot, to tell which hour the "hand" points to.

To understand how it is handled, have the envelope containing the card lengthwise and facedown on a table, flap end of the

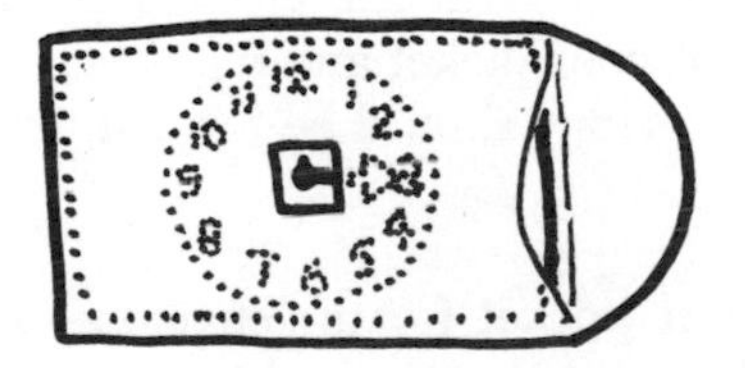

When the card is sealed inside, the window cut in the envelope reveals the hour.

envelope to the right. Pick it up by bringing the tips of your right-hand fingers against the back of the envelope and sliding the envelope toward you off the edge of the table, where you naturally grip it by bringing your thumb up underneath. As you take the envelope, your thumb comes up right over the hole. You can feel the opening to make sure it is well covered.

Now turn your hand over from left to right and show the face of the envelope. With the "window" hidden by your thumb, the face looks as unprepared as the back. After you have shown it, turn your hand from right to left and drop the envelope on the table, facedown as before.

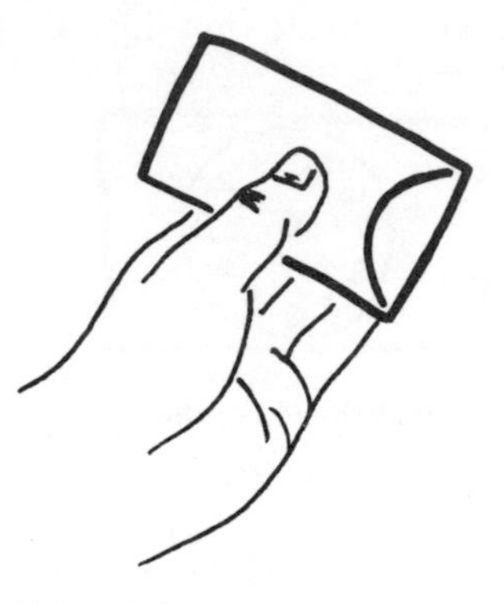

Your thumb covers the window hole.

Later, when you take it again to tear it, you pick it up almost the same way, but with your hand more to the right end of the envelope as you slide it back off the edge of the table and grip it from underneath with your thumb. That way your thumb does *not* cover the "window" and you can see the center of the clock dial through it as you hold up the envelope with its back toward the spectators.

Have the envelope, with the clock dial card inside, in the right-hand pocket of your jacket and the pencil with it. The "window" face of the envelope should be toward your body.

What you do

Reach into your pocket for the envelope. Feel for the "window," cover it with your thumb, and bring out the envelope. Casually show the face of it, turn it over, and drop it on the table with its back up.

Ask the spectator to think of something that happened or may happen to him, and to think of the hour of that happening. Keeping the envelope flat on the table, open the flap and draw out the card. Show the clock dial on it and slide the card over to him. Take the pencil from your pocket.

"In a moment, I'll ask you to draw in a hand to that hour on this clock—while I turn my head so that I can't see what hour you're thinking about." To demonstrate what you want him to do, you turn the pencil to its unpointed end so it won't make a mark and draw an imaginary straight line from the dot to one of the hours. "Just draw a straight line—an arrow—from the center of the dial to whatever hour you have in mind." You give him the pencil and turn your head away. "Have you done that?— Please turn the dial facedown on the table."

You face the group and slide the card over to the envelope. Open the flap and put the card in. Moisten the tip of your finger, wet the flap with it, and seal the envelope without lifting it from the table. Now pick up the envelope as previously explained, by sliding it toward you off the edge of the table so that as you take it your thumb comes up underneath and covers the "window" hole.

Feel to make sure it is well covered, and then turn the envelope to show the face of it. Don't say anything about it, but give everybody a good chance to see it. Hold it that way a moment and then turn your hand over and drop the envelope facedown on the table.

"Your thought of that hour now exists in two dimensions—in your mind and in the physical expression of it on the drawing sealed in this envelope." You point to the envelope and slide it back off the edge of the table so that your thumb coming up to take it from beneath does *not* cover the hole.

Lift the envelope that way, with its face toward you and its back to the spectators, and glance through the "window" to see in which direction the dot at the center of the dial is pointed. If it points up, the dial is positioned correctly. But if the dot points down, the twelve on the dial is at the bottom. In that case, turn your hand to bring the point of the dot to the top.

Look at the spectator and say, "If I were to tear up the drawing, the thought would be physically destroyed." With both hands, start to tear the envelope, and as you tear it look through the "window" to see where the clock "hand" is pointed. Imagine the clock dial and think around it—twelve, three, six, and so on—until you have mentally fixed the position of the pencil line at the right hour. Continue to tear the envelope to pieces, show the scraps in your hand, and drop them into your pocket.

"In a strictly physical sense, the hour is now lost," you say. "But, of course, the thought of that hour still remains in your mind."

Pick up the pencil the spectator has left on the table. Stand silent for a moment and close your eyes. Then say, "In *my* mind I hear a clock tolling—chiming the hour." Tap the pencil on the table to sound whatever the chosen hour is. Open your eyes, look at the spectator, and tell him the hour that is in his mind.

Symbolic Sight

How it looks

"The standard symbols for scientific testing of extrasensory perception are a circle, a cross, three wavy lines, a square, and a star," you say. "I have printed those symbols on these office file cards." You show each of the symbols and then hand all the cards to a spectator and turn your back.

"Mix them please," you tell him, "and when you're satisfied that they are thoroughly mixed, spread them all out facedown on the table so it will be impossible for me to see what is on them. Then just take any one—look at it and hold it with its face against your forehead while you think of that symbol."

You turn around and face him. After some effort, you announce which symbol he has in mind, and ask him to hold up the card and show it to everybody. Then you tell him, "Please put it back with the others and mix them on the table again. This time, while my back is turned, take three—any three you wish. Look at them, hold them against your chest, and then turn your own back to me."

When he says he has done that, you face the spectators while he stands with his back toward you. Again, you concentrate, and then say, "One of the symbols you have is the star [or whatever it may be]. Will you hold it up, please—and then the cross that you have—and the square."

For a final ESP experiment, while your back is turned again, you have him mix the symbols and spread them facedown on the table as before. You turn around, go to the table, take a red pen from your pocket, and draw a symbol on the back of each face-down card. Then you hold them up, one at a time, to show that your drawings match the hidden symbols on the faces of all five.

What you need

Five office index file cards, the standard kind with printed lines on one side and the opposite side blank (These come in various sizes. Small 3" by 5" cards, easy to carry in the pocket, may be used for close-up performances. For a larger group, 5" by 8" should be used, with bigger symbols drawn on them.)
A black marking pen and a red marking pen
A typewriter eraser
Sports jacket

The secret

This routine is strong, direct, and can be presented almost anywhere. Its secret depends on the use of the file cards. The fact that they are manufactured with lines printed on what will be used as the backs allows for marking them in a way that can be seen from a fair distance. The performer quickly knows, from the back of a card, what symbol is on the face of it.

How you fix it

First, for those unfamiliar with the standard ESP symbols, a coding system that is often used by mentalists should be learned. It is an easy one to remember. The circle is one continuous line, so it is thought of as 1; the cross or plus sign is made of two lines, so it is thought of as 2; the three wavy vertical lines are 3; the four-sided square is 4; the five-pointed star, 5. Memorize them in that order and always think of them that way: circle, cross, lines, square, star—1, 2, 3, 4, 5. Thus if you see a mark that indicates "1" it is the circle card, "3" is the wavy lines card, and so on.

The lined sides of index cards are manufactured with a *red* line at the top and *blue* lines spaced down the rest of the card. The

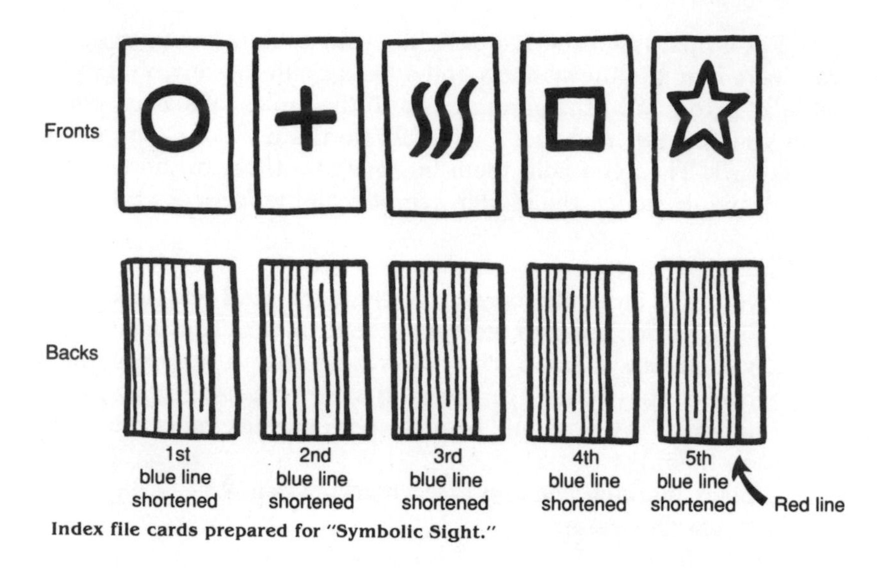

Index file cards prepared for "Symbolic Sight."

red line will be your key. No matter in what position a card is held or placed on the table, you will look first for the red line, then for the blue lines, to count them mentally from the red-line starting point.

Put one of the cards on a table with the *red* line at the top. Make sure the typewriter eraser is clean and erase a full inch from each end of the first *blue* line beneath the red one. Erase it thoroughly, so no trace of the printed line remains at the ends.

Turn the card over so the blank face is up and so the narrow edges of the card are now top and bottom. With the black marking pen, draw a circle as large as will fit on the card.

Put that card aside and take another. Erase an inch from both ends of the *second* blue line beneath the red one, then turn it over and draw a cross vertically on the face of that card. From the back of the third card erase the ends of the *third* blue line, and on the card's face draw three wavy vertical lines. Erase the ends of the *fourth* blue line from the fourth card and put a square on its face. Do the same with the *fifth* blue line on the fifth card, and draw a five-pointed star on its face.

Now try this: Turn all the cards facedown, spread them on the table and mix them around any which way, then look at the back of one of them. Count to yourself from the red line (no matter whether it is now at the left, right, top, or bottom) to the first blue line that has no ends. If it is the first line from the red one, the card has a circle on its face.

Try it from a distance. Prop up one of the cards against the back of a chair, as though someone might be holding the card, then stand several feet away. You still should be able to see the erased line clearly, so as to tell which one it is from the back.

The reason for erasing both ends of the blue lines is that one end may be partly covered by a spectator's fingers when he holds a card against his forehead, or ends may be overlapped when cards are spread on the table. Don't worry about the fact that the markings seem obvious to you once you know where to look for them. The spectator is kept busy doing things and looking at the faces of the cards. He won't be holding the cards long enough to compare the backs carefully, and even if he should notice that part of a line is missing it will appear to be an imperfection in the printing.

There is no setup for performing. Just have the stack of cards and a red marking pen in your pocket or on the table.

What you do

Explain about the standard ESP symbols and show each of the cards. Hand them all to the spectator, move away, and turn your back, and have him mix them and spread them facedown on the table "so it will be impossible to see what is on them." Ask him to take any one, look at it, and hold it with its face against his forehead while he thinks of that symbol.

Face him and look for the red line on the back of the card he is holding. Mentally count from that to the first blue line with missing ends. Announce what the symbol is, but don't make it seem too easy, and have him hold the card up to show it to everybody. Ask him to return that symbol to the table with the others and to mix and spread them around facedown again. Turn your back and invite him to take any three symbols he wishes, look at them, hold them against his chest. Then tell him, "Turn your own back to me."

Turn to face the audience while his back is to you. Pretend to be having trouble sensing his thoughts. Close your eyes and put the palm of your hand to your forehead a moment. Partly cover your eyes to prevent the audience from seeing the direction of your downward glance as you look down at the table. Look at the backs of the two cards that remain on the table. If you see from their backs that those are, for instance, cards 1 and 3, you know that the spectator is holding 2, 4, and 5—cross, square, and star. Call each of them and have him hold them up to show them.

Now turn your back once more while he spreads all five face-down cards on the table to mix them. Then go to the table, remove the pen from your pocket, and read the back of each of the cards in turn as you draw red designs on them. You have plenty of time to figure out each marking. Don't rush it. Hesitate as you start to make a design on one. Scratch it out and start over. Say: "I can't get them clearly—I'm afraid I missed on this one, but maybe I got a few."

Finally pick up one of them. Show the audience the face and then turn it to show your matching symbol on the back. Continue with the others. When you come to the last two, lift them together, one in each hand, with their faces toward you. Glance from one to the other to build suspense. Then quickly turn them both and hold them up high to show them.

Spy Hunt

How it looks

"Let's imagine we're all secret agents, international spies," you say to four spectators who have been asked to take part in an experiment with you. "We're all hunting for the secret plans that have been hidden among the papers in a hotel room."

You take a paper bag from your pocket, open it, and spill out on the table five small rolls of paper. "Five little strips of paper, all tightly rolled, each sealed with tape. Please look them over—but don't open any of them yet. You'll see that outwardly they appear identical. But one of these slips—only one—contains the secret plans."

Dropping them back into the bag, one at a time, you mix them thoroughly. "Imagine that the hotel room is dark. It would be too dangerous to turn on the lights. As spies, we are all after the same secret plans—the papers that are somewhere in that room. We all have an equal chance of getting our hands on them—unless one of us somehow might mentally influence the decisions of the others."

You ask each of the spectators in turn to dip his hand into the bag and take out one of the slips of paper. "Each of you has chosen one," you say, "and that leaves one for me." You take the last one that remains.

They all unroll their papers and hold them up for the audience to read what is written on them. Printed in big letters on one spectator's strip of paper are the words: LAUNDRY LIST. The others read: SUBWAY MAP, HOTEL BILL, SHOPPING LIST. You unroll yours and show it. On it are the words: SECRET PLANS.

What you need

Five strips of white paper, each about 15" long and 2-1/2" wide (You can cut the strips from a large sheet or from a blank roll of adding machine tape.)
A flat-bottomed brown paper bag, about 5" by 10"
Transparent tape
Broad-tipped black marking pen
Sports jacket

The secret

Although the paper strips are rolled and taped so they all look alike to spectators who casually examine them, the one marked SECRET PLANS is slightly torn, so you can tell it from the others at a glance. When you drop that one into the bag, you bend it in half, and later secretly draw it up beneath your fingers as you hold the bag at the top. It remains hidden under your fingers while each of the spectators takes one of the other slips from the bag, and at the end it becomes the only one left for you to take.

How you fix it

With the marking pen, in bold black letters as large as will fit on the paper, print the words SECRET PLANS on one of the strips. Roll it up tightly, end to end. Wind a piece of tape around the center to keep it rolled, leaving an end of the tape that you can bend down and stick together to form a little tab so it can be pulled loose quickly to open the roll.

Prepare the other strips the same way, printing on each in turn: LAUNDRY LIST, SUBWAY MAP, HOTEL BILL, SHOPPING LIST. Now take the SECRET PLANS roll, lift one overlapping end, and tear the paper slightly, right along the edge of the tape that binds it. A tiny tear is enough, just a fraction of an inch; it should look accidental, yet you will spot it instantly when that slip is mixed on the table with the others.

Drop all the slips into the bag, fold the bag, and have it in one of your pockets.

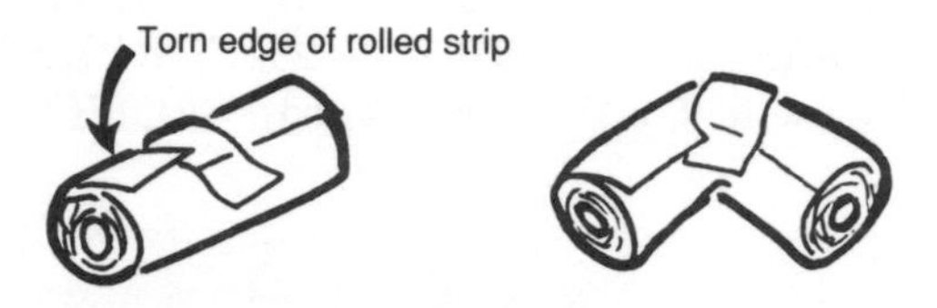

Bend roll of paper before dropping it into bag.

What you do

Invite four spectators to join you in a spy hunt for the secret plans and have two stand at each side of your table. Open the bag and spill the rolls of paper out on the table as you explain that each strip is sealed with tape and only one contains the plans.

Rest the bottom of the opened bag on the palm of your left hand. With your right hand, pick up the papers, one at a time, and put them into the bag. When you come to the torn one that you recognize as the SECRET PLANS slip, bend it between your thumb and fingers inside the bag as you drop it to the bottom with the others. Just quickly double it, squeezing hard, so the two ends touch, and immediately bring your hand out to pick up another slip from the table to drop into the bag.

When you have dropped them all in, shake the bag as you explain that you want to mix them thoroughly. Put your right hand into the bag again and mix them around in the bottom, feeling for the bent one. Draw that into your fingers, bring your hand up flatly against the inside of the bag, and take hold of the bag at the top with that hand. Your fingers remain inside at the top, your thumb outside at the back, and the slip stays hidden under your fingers, pressed against the inside of the bag at the top.

Holding it that way, shake the bag again, and ask one of the spectators to put his hand in and mix the slips around in the bot-

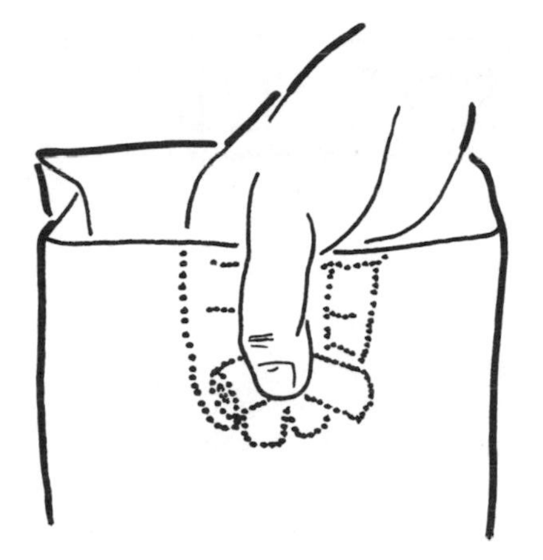

Your fingers hide the slip against the inside top of the bag.

tom. Have him take out any slip he wishes. When he has done that, ask each of the others to reach in and take a slip.

By the time you reach the fourth spectator, there will be only one slip still in the bottom of the bag instead of two, because of the one hidden under your fingers. But he is not aware of that, and to keep him from feeling around in the bag, you hurry him a bit. "Just dip your hand in, take one, and hold it high," you tell him.

As soon as he has a slip, move the bag away and let the hidden slip drop from under your fingers to the bottom of the bag as you shake the bag and put it on the table. "Each of you has chosen one," you say, "and that leaves one for me."

Let the audience see your hand is empty by making a casual gesture with it as you speak. Reach into the bag, straighten the slip between your thumb and fingers inside the bag, and take it out. Don't worry if it remains slightly bent. Just hold it up high and keep it in plain view.

Have each of the spectators unroll his slip. "Open it out between your hands and hold it up so everyone can read it," you say. "What's yours— Oh, I'm sorry— In the dark, you seem to have picked up the laundry list— And you, sir—have a subway map—but not the secret plans we were after. The next gentleman seems

to be on his way to do a little shopping—and you're stuck with the hotel bill. I *am* sorry about that."

Finally you unroll yours and hold it out between both hands to display the words: SECRET PLANS.

What's in the News?

How it looks

You pick up a newspaper and give each of three spectators one full, double-page sheet from it, keeping one yourself to demonstrate what you want done.

"Just tear a piece about this size from any part of any page," you explain, as you rip a piece from your paper. "Top, bottom, front, back—it doesn't matter what pieces we use. Then crumple the piece into a ball like this."

To demonstrate, you crumple yours into a ball and drop it into a glass, in which you collect the rest of the pieces. One of the spectators is invited to return to your table with you. You pour the balled-up pieces out of the glass, and he chooses one, which he opens and reads to himself while you stand away from him.

You then "read his mind" to reveal what the news story is about. He concentrates on the headline, and you tell him what it is. He is asked to think of the name of any person who happens to be mentioned in the news item, and you reveal that name. Finally he mentally spells out one of the words to himself, and you spell it aloud with him, letter by letter.

What you need

A newspaper, preferably tabloid size for easy handling
An "iced-tea" glass, about 6" high
A large pad and broad-tipped marking pen
A pencil

The secret

Although the presentation leads the audience to imagine that any part of the newspaper might have been chosen, you actually do the "choosing" yourself, and the spectator gets a news item you have read and made notes from in advance.

How you fix it

Start by looking through the paper you intend to use for a news item that meets these conditions: It should be at the top of the outside column of a right-hand page as you open the pages before you; the item should have a solid advertisement or picture on the back of it, not another news story or reading material; it should mention the names of only two or three people.

When you have found the news item you want, read it through a few times and remember as much about it as you can. At the top of the first sheet of the large pad, lightly pencil the headline, then list the personal names mentioned in the item, with a one-word reminder for each, to indicate who they are or what they do, and finally make a note of the very last word in the item.

Now remove the outside front double page of the paper and three more pages. Put the double sheet that contains your news story inside those, and then put the rest of the paper inside your page at the center. Refold the paper and have it on your table with the glass, the facedown pad, and the marking pen.

What you do

Show the newspaper and discard the front page as you explain: "We won't use the big headlines for this. Let's get down to the fine print." Peel off the next three double pages from the outside of the paper, one at a time, and give one to each spectator. Remove the fourth double page and put aside the rest of the paper.

As you demonstrate what you want the spectators to do, open out the double page you are holding. Unknown to the audience, the piece you want to save is at the top of the right-hand column. Just tear it out as you say, "Tear a piece about this size from any part of any page. Top, bottom, front, back—it doesn't matter what pieces we use."

Don't try to be precise or fussy about the tearing. Make it seem casual, as if you were ripping any piece from the paper. Hold the piece up for them to see its size and crumple it into a ball at least as big as a golf ball as you continue to show the spectators what to do.

While they are doing that, pick up the glass and drop your ball of paper into it. Then take the glass to the spectators and have all of them drop in their balled-up pieces. Because you put yours in first, it naturally remains at the bottom. The glass is too narrow and the paper balls too big to become mixed up, so there is no difficulty in remembering which it is.

Invite one of the spectators to return to your table with you. Tip the glass and spill the balls of paper out on the table, watching to see where yours falls.

Ask the spectator to pick up any two of them. If one of the two he picks up is yours, say, "All right. Now hand me one of those—either one you choose." But if neither of them that he first picks up is yours, say, "All right. We've eliminated two. Just throw those away. Now pick up the other two and hand me one of them—either one you choose."

Whichever way he starts, you have now brought him to the point either of handing you the piece you want or of keeping that and handing you the other one. If he hands you the one you want, you say, "Okay. We'll use this one then. You can throw the other one away." But if he gives you the other one, simply throw it away yourself and point to the one he still has in his hand as you say: "That's the one you've chosen to keep."

Tell him to unroll the ball of paper as you turn away from him. "Open it up and read either side to yourself," you say. "It doesn't matter which side you choose as long as there's a news item on it—a few paragraphs of information of some kind." Since there was only a picture or solid advertisement on the back of the chosen piece, he is forced to read the side you want him to read. "Is there enough of the story there so you can get an idea of what the news item is about?"

Close your eyes a moment and then, haltingly and in general terms, begin to reveal the subject of the news item aloud. Talk around it and gradually describe some of the details you remember. Pick up the pad and marking pen and say, "It may help if I try to jot down some of your thoughts as they come to me."

Hold the pad upright facing you and scribble a few words as you continue to talk about it. As you do, glance at your penciled notes at the top of the pad. Ask if the item includes a headline. Have him concentrate on it. Scribble again and then tell him what the headline is, not word for word, but the gist of what it says.

Ask him to glance through the item and to think of some person whose name may be mentioned in it. If there are three names, you now will have to fish a little to find out which one he is thinking about. From the notes on your pad, you know the three possible names, so you call out an initial or describe who a person is or what he does—keeping it vague until you know you have hit on the one he has in mind. Then quickly reveal the full name as you scribble it on the pad. While you are doing that, memorize the final note on your pad, the spelling of the last word in the news item.

"Now please look at the last sentence—the very last word," you say. "In your mind, spell that word slowly—to yourself."

Throw the pad facedown on the table. Face him directly and spell the word aloud as if you were receiving his thoughts one letter at a time. Repeat the whole word and ask: "Am I right? Was that the exact word you had in mind?"

Weather Forecast

How it looks

"One thing everybody tries to predict is the weather," you say, as you hold up a large card and read aloud the weather conditions printed on it in red: "Warmer, colder, cloudy, stormy, fair."

Turning to one of the spectators, you invite him to try to predict what tomorrow's weather will be. "Just make a guess. But don't tell us yet what it is," you say. "Look over this list of possibilities and decide in your own mind what kind of a day you think tomorrow will be. Let's see if I can pick up your mental forecast."

When he says he is thinking of one of the listed weather conditions, you turn the card so it faces you. "I'll make a little circle and put an X in it." Taking a black pen from your pocket, you mark the card without showing it to the audience. "All right. I've marked what I believe your forecast will be. You can tell us now. What's your guess—warmer, colder, cloudy, stormy, or fair?"

He calls out his mental choice—perhaps, "Stormy." You show

the audience the card. The word you have marked with an X is stormy.

"You were very positive about that," you say. "I got the thought clearly. If you're as good at predicting the weather as you are at projecting your thoughts, we'd better expect a stormy day tomorrow."

What you need

A 7" by 11" sheet of white posterboard
A red marking pen
A broad-tipped black marking pen that can be clipped into your breast pocket
A package of round white self-sticking removable labels 1" in diameter
Scissors
Sports jacket

The secret

You only pretend to mark the card. The circle and X mark are drawn ahead of time on one of the labels. This is hidden, in a way that will be explained, so that your thumb secretly rolls the label into place and sticks it on the card after the spectator has called out what he is thinking. The label makes it look as if you had marked the card itself, right opposite the word he had in mind.

How you fix it

The list of weather conditions should be printed with a wide margin at the left of the words. Start with the large card on a table, narrow ends top and bottom. With the red marking pen, print WARMER in letters about an inch high, beginning about two inches down from the top and the same distance in from the left. Print each of the other weather conditions directly below the previous one, with a good space between them. Turn the card with the printing side down and put it aside for a moment.

Take one of the self-sticking white labels and trim a tiny edge off the top and one side with the scissors. This is done to give the label a slightly irregular shape, such as you would make if you quickly drew a circle with a pen. With the *black* pen draw a circle on the label, all the way around just inside the edge. Then mark a large X in the center.

Stick the *left half* of the label firmly to the *back* of the large card about an inch down from the top left corner, but leave the right half of the label unstuck. Bend that free right edge leftward and crease it *slightly* at the center of the label, so the right edge remains unstuck and retains a curl. (If it does accidentally stick flat later you can easily peel it free with your thumbnail.)

Have the card faceup on the table and clip the black pen into the outside breast pocket of your jacket.

Attach label (with right side bent) to back of card.

What you do

Pick up the card and hold it at the sides between both hands to show the audience what is printed on it. Your left hand is at the *top* left side and the right hand at the *lower* right side, fingers of both hands at the front and thumbs at the back. The ball of your left thumb should be touching the label that is hidden on the back of the card.

Read aloud the list of printed weather conditions and invite one of the spectators to try to predict what tomorrow's weather will be. "Just make a guess. But don't tell us yet what it is," you say. "Look over the list and decide in your own mind. Let's see if I can pick up your mental forecast."

While you are talking, secretly press the ball of your left thumb against the free edge of the label so that the label sticks to your thumb. Roll your thumb to the left and the label will peel off the card and remain attached to your thumb. The patter allows time to do this slowly, and the slight movement of your thumb is concealed by the card and by your fingers at the front.

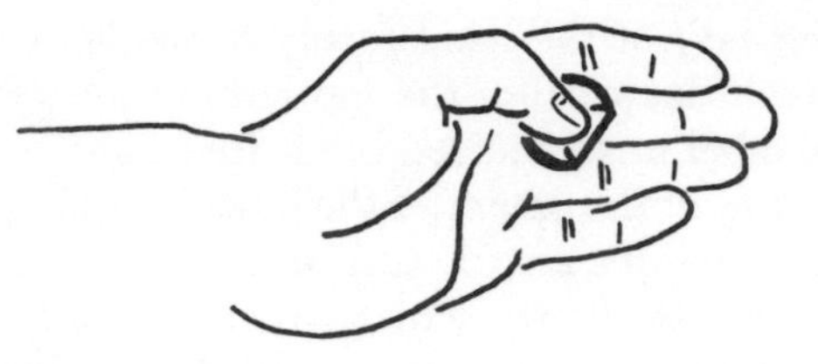

Your thumb lifts the label off the back.

When the spectator says he is thinking of one of the weather conditions, draw your left thumb, with the label stuck to it, in toward the palm of that hand. Keep the hand held up as it is. With your right hand turn the card around so it is facing you and grasp the top of the card again with the left hand. Hold the card up with that hand and drop your right hand to your side. This is the natural way you would turn the card around, and it should look like nothing more than that.

Keep the card facing you, held by your left hand. The fingers are at the front of it and the thumb behind, the label still stuck to your thumb. Bring your right hand over to your breast pocket and

Your thumb sticks the label to the front after the card is turned toward you.

remove the pen. Move the pen up and down the list behind the card as if debating which word to mark. Scratch your fingernail on the card as you pretend to make a circle and put an X in it, without actually marking the card. Put the pen away in your breast pocket again.

Now take the card with your right hand and drop your left hand to your side, keeping that thumb and the label attached to it hidden by your fingers. "All right. I've marked what I believe your forecast will be," you say to the spectator. "You can tell us now. What's your guess—warmer, colder, cloudy, stormy, or fair?"

When he calls out his mental choice, bring your left hand up to the side of the card again so that your thumb goes behind the card *directly opposite the word he has chosen* and your fingers are at the front. Hold the card, still facing you, between both hands. Secretly roll your thumb to the right, catching the edge of the label against the card. This will peel the label off your thumb and stick it to the card. Smooth the label with your thumb and press it firmly into place.

You can look down at the card as you do this, as if checking the prediction. Take your time and transfer the label properly. Finally turn the card around so the audience can see what appears to be the circle and X mark in front of the chosen word.

EIGHT

Card Magic

While magic hobbyists do all kinds of tricks, they do far more card tricks than any other kind. Half a dozen magic magazines and hundreds of books devote most of their space to card tricks.

Experts treat card trickery almost as a science. They discuss the most sophisticated principles in detail, debating the correct positioning of fingers or the proper holding of a pack, arguing the merits of new mathematical arrangements and psychological approaches. Serious hobbyists spend days perfecting moves that are designed mostly for showing to other hobbyists. At club meetings and conventions, card sessions go on day and night.

Others take the view that methods are really unimportant and that all that counts is the entertainment value. But whether they count themselves among the "finger flingers" or public performers, they all find fun in card magic.

During the centuries since card magic began, thousands of tricks have been invented. By conservative estimate at least fifty thousand variations of card tricks have been published in the last twenty-five years. Card magic is said to involve some two thousand basic principles and there are some individual tricks for which more than five hundred methods of performing have been devised.

But there are many people, including some magicians, who hate watching card tricks. Unless they are presented entertainingly, they can be a bore. The wrong place, the wrong time, or too much card magic will produce annoyance instead of pleasure. Long-winded tricksters that deal cards into endless heaps and piles or instruct watchers to remember several different cards at the same time will bore the audience as much as the fumbling trickster who does nothing more than dig out a chosen card that has been lost in the pack.

Yet even those who insist that they loathe card tricks usually will join in appreciation of one that gets right to the point. Like all good magic, a good card trick must have some element of surprise. Its presentation demands more than just, "Take a card and I'll find it." Almost anyone can learn to do that. Yet the simplest "take a card" trick can be really entertaining if it has novelty and an interesting plot.

Directions for card tricks always seem more complicated in print than when you actually try them. They usually make very little sense unless you follow them with cards in hand. All of them, even the simplest, require rehearsal—practicing what you are going to say as well as what you are going to do.

There is nothing more frustrating for the performer of card tricks than to come to the climax of one and then have the person who chose a card say he has forgotten what it was. To avoid that, whenever the plot of the trick allows, have the person show the chosen card to others around him, which will also keep him from playing a joke on you by saying at the end that the card wasn't his.

The Blind Man's Card Trick

How it looks

"Years ago there was a famous French magician who was completely blind," you say, as you show a pack of cards. "He couldn't see the cards at all, but he managed to do magic with them by means of touch alone."

You shake out a sheet of newspaper and hang its center fold over your arm, covering the pack of cards in your hand. "I'd like to give you my impression of one of the tricks he did—with my hands covered like this so there is no possible way that I can see the cards as I deal them."

You hand out the pack to be thoroughly shuffled, then take it back into your hands under the newspaper and deal the cards into four piles on the table. Putting aside the paper, you ask someone to turn over the top card of each pile. When he does, he discovers that all four top cards are kings!

"That could be just luck, to hit on all four kings in just one deal of a shuffled pack," you say. "But what about this?" Quickly you flip each of the four piles faceup. All four bottom cards are aces!

What you need

A pack of cards
A newspaper

The secret

The covering newspaper, instead of making the trick harder, lets you secretly hold a stack of cards while the pack is being shuffled.

How you fix it

Remove the pack from its case as you tell about the blind magician. Take the cards facedown in your left hand. With your right hand, shake open the newspaper, show it, and then bring the center fold over your left arm so that paper covers your hand and the cards.

What you do

Remove the pack from its case as you tell about the blind magician. Take the cards facedown in your left hand. With your right hand, shake open the newspaper, show it, and then bring the center fold over your left arm so that paper covers your hand and the cards.

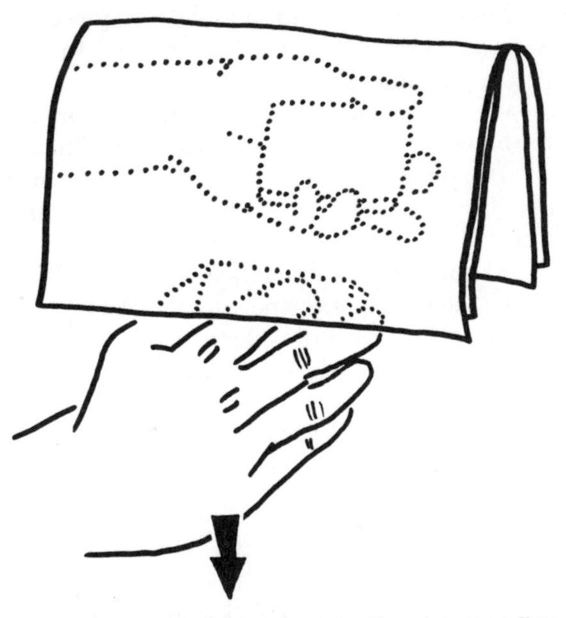

Your left hand keeps a bottom stack of cards under the newspaper. Your right hand brings out the pack to be shuffled.

Explain that with your hands covered there will be no way you can see the cards as you deal them, but say that first you want to have the pack thoroughly shuffled.

Reach under the paper with your right hand to bring out the pack and give it to someone. But as you take it, just leave a packet of cards from the bottom of the pack in your left hand. There is no need to count them; simply hold back a small batch that includes the stacked aces and kings. They remain hidden, of course, by the paper that hangs over your left hand.

When the pack has been well shuffled, take it with your right hand and put it back under the paper on top of the cards you have been secretly holding. With both hands under the paper, bring them above the table and start dealing out the cards. Deal four cards from the *bottom* of the pack facedown in a row from left to right across the table. Then continue dealing from the *top* of the pack, placing the cards down from left to right on the others until the entire pack has been dealt out into four piles. This leaves a king on top and an ace on the bottom of each of the four piles.

Put aside the newspaper and remind your audience that the cards were shuffled and that you couldn't see them. Ask someone to turn over the four top cards. Wait a moment for the first surprise to register—the four kings in a row. Then quickly flip over each of the four piles and show the four aces.

Comedy Card Force

How it looks

"Will you please choose a card?" you ask someone, as you take a pack from its case and spread the cards in your hands. "Any card at all."

Before he can reach for one, a two of clubs shoots out of the pack into the air and falls at his feet. "Oh, I'm sorry you dropped it," you say. "Please pick it up and show it to everybody—but don't let me see which card it is."

Everyone thinks it's a joke, because you obviously "forced" him to take the two of clubs that shot out of the pack at him. But you continue as if you had no knowledge of which card was "chosen." You ask him to keep it facedown so you can't see it, and to put it back on top of the pack.

"Just think of the card," you say. "I'm getting a mental impression of it. The picture is becoming clearer— The card is the king of hearts—am I right?" When he answers that you are wrong, you ask what card it was, and he says the two of clubs.

"Are you sure?" you ask. "I could have sworn it was the king of hearts." You turn the joke by holding up the top card to show that it *is* the king of hearts!

What you need

A pack of cards and their cardboard case
A rubber band
Double-faced (sticky both sides) transparent tape
Sports jacket

The secret

The two of clubs (or any card) is shot out by means of a rubber band around the lower half of the pack. When the card is put back on top, it sticks to the king of hearts, already on top with sticky tape on its back, so the two can be shown as one.

How you fix it

Turn the king of hearts facedown and fasten a small piece of double-faced tape to the center of its back. Put it and the two of clubs aside for a moment.

Prepare the pack by taking about half the cards and encircling them lengthwise with the rubber band. It should go around the entire packet, down the middle from end to end.

A rubber band around half of the pack.

Put the banded cards on a table and lift about half of them back toward yourself, as if you were opening a book endwise, stretching out the rubber band.

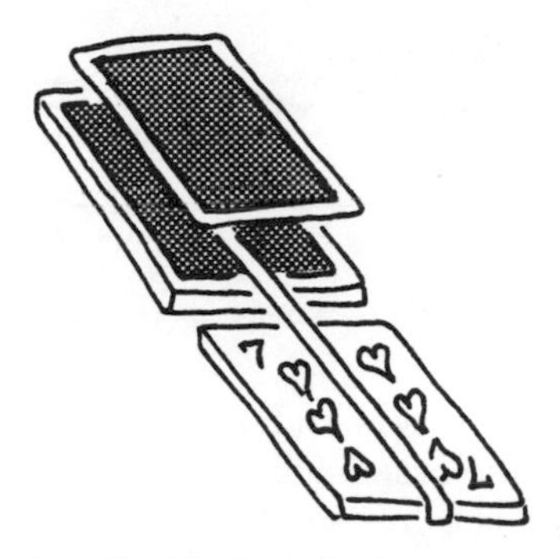

The banded half is opened out flat. The force card goes on top of the forward part.

Hold the two halves opened flat on the table, end to end, and place the two of clubs facedown on the forward half of the packet, on top of the band. Hold it there and close the top half of the packet upon it. (If you release the pressure, the band will shoot the two of clubs out from the rest.)

Set up the packet that way, with the two of clubs ready to shoot out. Hold it tightly and put the rest of the pack on top of the banded packet and the taped king of hearts facedown on top of the pack. Keeping the pressure, slide the entire pack facedown into the card case, with the "shooting" end toward the top end of the case. Close the flap and drop the pack into your left jacket pocket.

What you do

Take the cased cards from your pocket with your left hand. Press your left thumb tightly on the case. With your right hand, open the flap. Grip the end of the pack tightly between your right

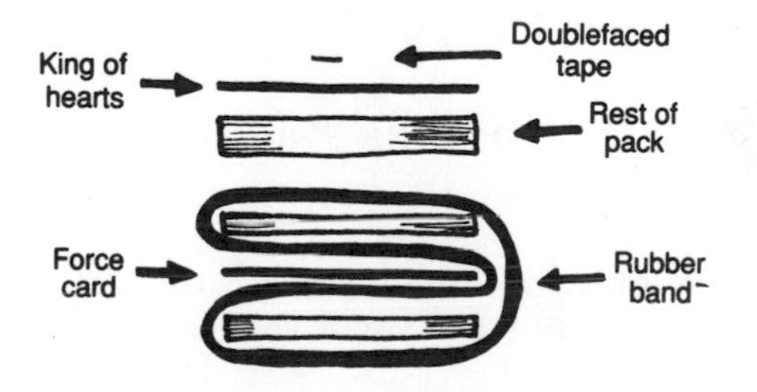

Side view: The rubber-banded half is on the bottom of the pack.

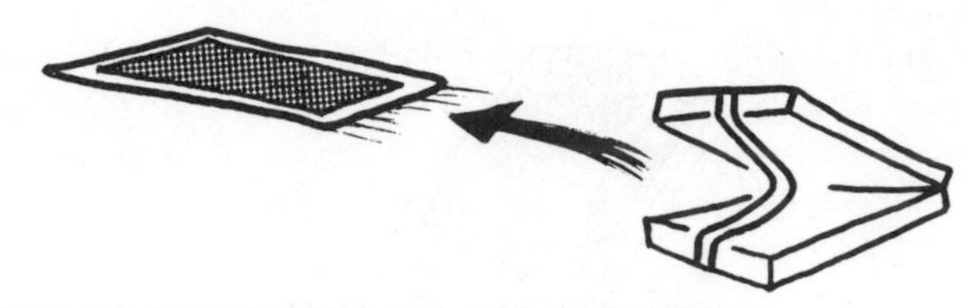

The rubber band shoots the force card out from the others.

thumb at the top and fingers underneath. Remove the pack, keeping it flat, and put the case back in your pocket.

Now take the pack in your left hand, maintaining the pressure. Spread out the top cards between your hands as you move toward some person and ask him to choose a card. While you are still a few feet away from him, release the pressure by simply loosening your grip on the pack. The two of clubs will fly out into the air and land on the floor. Square up the pack in your left hand.

Ask him to pick up the card and show it to everyone, but not to you. With mock seriousness, play along with the joke of not knowing which card it is. Tell him to keep it facedown so you can't possibly see it and to put it back on the pack. Hold out the squared up pack in your left hand so he can put the card on top of the taped king of hearts.

"Just think of the card," you say. Press down with your left thumb so the two top cards stick evenly together. "I'm getting a mental impression of it. The picture is becoming clearer— The card is the king of hearts—am I right?"

When he says you are wrong, ask what his card was. "Are you sure?" you ask. "I could have sworn it was the king of hearts." Thumb the stuck-together cards off the top as a single card. Show that it *is* the king of hearts. Toss it back on top of the pack, and put the pack away in your pocket.

Doubles Match

How it looks

"Instead of asking you to choose a card, this time I'll do the choosing," you say. "But first, will you please shuffle the pack? Shuffle them thoroughly."

You take back the pack after the person has shuffled. "Now I'll choose a couple of cards I like. It's all right if I look at them—I'm the magician." You look through the cards and remove two of them, placing them facedown on the table without showing them. "This one—and this one."

Holding out the pack, you ask the person to cut the cards by lifting about half of them off the top and putting them facedown on the table. You place the remaining half of the pack across his half. "I'll mark where you cut them. Remember, the cards were as you shuffled them. Now I'll show you the two that I chose."

You turn your cards faceup on the table. They may be, for example, the nine of clubs and the jack of hearts. "Let's see how you did." Turn over the top half of the pack and show that one of the cards he cut to was the nine of spades. "The card that matches mine—the other black nine."

Then turn over the top card of the bottom half of the pack, the other one he cut to. It is the jack of diamonds. "Again you matched me—the other red jack," you say. "I don't know how you did that, but it certainly is a strange coincidence."

What you need

A pack of cards

The secret

The two cards you choose match the cards on top and bottom of the shuffled pack and the cutting is done in a way that brings those original top and bottom cards to the center.

There is nothing to fix in advance.

What you do

Take back the shuffled pack and hold the cards facing you as you look through them. Secretly glance at the top and bottom cards. Remove the two *matching* cards of the same number and color, and put those facedown on the table without showing them. (If the top and bottom cards are the jack of clubs and three of hearts, for instance, you would remove the jack of spades and three of diamonds.)

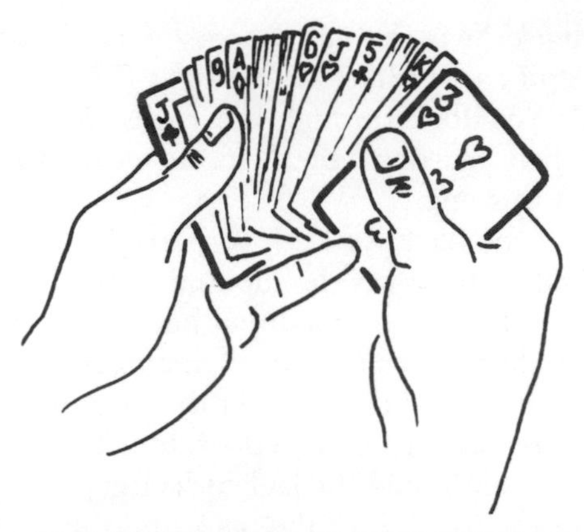

Look through the pack and remove the two that "match" the top and bottom cards.

Square up the cards and hold them facedown on your left palm. Ask the person to cut the pack by taking about half the cards and putting them facedown on the table. Immediately put your remaining half of the pack down *across* the top of his half, so the two halves lie crisscross on the table, and say, "I'll mark where you cut them. Remember, the cards were as you shuffled them."

That isn't *really* where he cut them, since all you have done is place the original bottom half of the pack across the original top half, bringing what were the original top and bottom cards of the pack together at the middle.

It is important at this point to distract the person's attention momentarily, so he won't realize the true position of the two halves of the pack. You do that by drawing his attention to the two cards you have chosen.

"Now I'll show you the two that I chose." Turn them faceup on the table, and say aloud which two cards they are. "Let's see how you did—"

On the table, place your cards crisscross on top of his.

Lift off what is now the top half of the crisscrossed pack and turn that half faceup on the table. Point to the face card and then to your matching card, whichever one it may be. "The card that matches mine—the other black jack."

Put that half of the pack aside, faceup on the table. Pick up the bottom half of the pack, point to the top card, turn it faceup, and show the second matching card. "Again you matched me—the other red three," you say. "I don't know how you did that, but it certainly is a strange coincidence."

Tell Me My Fortune

How it looks

"This is my fortune," you say, as you hold up a small glass with a bunch of pennies in the bottom. "A very small fortune in pennies." You rattle them around in the glass, put it aside on the table, and take out a pack of cards.

"Just for fun, I'd like you to tell me my fortune—with these cards," you say to someone. "Let's pretend you're a gypsy fortune teller."

You deal eight cards facedown in a row on the table and ask him to call out any number from one to eight. When he calls the number, you count to that card in the row and show it. "It happens to be a nine," you say. You turn over some of the other cards and show them. "You might have chosen this one, a three—or this one, a seven. But the card you chose is a nine."

Then you pick up the glass with the pennies, pour them into your hand, and drop them back into the glass one at a time as you count aloud. "One, two, three, four, five, six, seven, eight—exactly nine pennies. The same number as the card you chose. Thank you for telling my fortune."

What you need

A pack of cards
Nine pennies
A small glass that can be carried in your pocket, such as a "cheese glass" or a shot glass
A sports jacket and trousers with pockets

The secret

In this trick you ignore the suits, such as spades or diamonds, and use only the numbers on the cards. Eight cards are stacked in order on top of the pack at the start so that when you deal them out across the table every second card in the row is one of the nines. By counting from the left or right, according to the number the person calls, the "Chosen" card always is a nine.

How you fix it

Remove the four nines from the pack. Now take any other card from the pack and put it faceup on the table. Put one of the nines faceup on top of it, then any other card, then another nine, and so on, until you have a stack of eight cards: any card, nine, any card, nine, any card, nine, any card, nine.

Turn the whole stack facedown and put it on top of the pack. Slide the pack into its case to keep the cards in order and put them in one of your pockets. Have the small glass in another pocket and the nine pennies in your otherwise empty right-hand pants pocket.

What you do

Scoop the pennies from your pocket, making sure you get all nine. Take out the small glass and drop the batch of pennies into it. Hold up the glass, rattle the pennies, and say, "This is my fortune. A very small fortune in pennies." Rest the glass on the table, take out the cards, and ask someone to pretend he's a fortune teller.

You should be standing directly behind the table. Deal the eight prearranged cards facedown in a row from left to right, but *don't* count aloud as you deal. Put the rest of the pack aside, and say, "Will you please choose any number from one to eight? Just call out the number. Which one of these cards do you want?"

If he calls an even number (2, 4, 6, 8) start counting aloud along the row from your *left*, touching each card with the tip of your finger until you come to the number called. But if he calls an odd number (1, 3, 5, 7) start the count from your *right*. Either way, the card at the number called will be one of the four nines.

Pick it up, look at it, and hold it up to show it, as you say, "It happens to be a nine." Then pick up the cards at each side of that one to show that he might have "chosen" some totally different card, and say, "But the card that you chose was a nine." Quickly scoop up all the cards, drop them back on the pack, and put it away in your pocket.

Pick up the glass with your left hand and pour all the pennies into your cupped right hand. Hold that hand above the glass and slowly drop the pennies into it, one at a time, as you count them aloud. "Exactly nine pennies. The same number as the card that you chose," you say. "Thank you for telling my fortune."

Jumpers

How it looks

"I'm about to make an acrobat of your card," you say to someone who has freely chosen a card, looked at it, and returned it to the pack. "It will do a double somersault—flip itself over and land faceup in the facedown pack."

You snap your fingers and spread out the cards. There is a faceup card in the center, but *not* the chosen one. It is the joker.

"I should have known," you say. "That flipping joker is the biggest show-off in the whole house of cards." You turn the pack faceup and put back the faceup joker. "Let's try again. By the way, which card *did* you choose?"

He may answer that he chose the four of hearts. "Thanks for telling me," you say. "I never would have guessed." You command it to jump, and when you spread the cards facedown again, the four of hearts (or whatever card he chose) is faceup at the center. "Good. It finally got the word. As long as the magic is working, let's work it once more."

You turn the four of hearts facing the same way as the others and command it to flip. But when you spread the cards, the faceup *joker* has reappeared. "Oh, no," you say. "That flipping joker is back. That's enough. I'm going to put it away in my pocket where it can't cause any more trouble." You remove the joker and put it in your pocket. "Now jump, four of hearts—jump!"

Again you spread the cards, but the joker you just put away in your pocket is back in the pack and has reversed itself again. "If the joker can jump from my pocket to the pack," you say, "then the four of hearts should be able to flip itself from the pack into my pocket." Showing your hand empty, you reach into your pocket and take out the other person's chosen four of hearts. "And so it has. Now that's flipping good."

What you need

A pack of cards with both jokers (Most packs are made with duplicate jokers.)
Double-faced (sticky both sides) transparent tape
Sports jacket

The secret

One of the jokers and the chosen card become stuck together back-to-back, making an instant double-faced card that is joker on one side and the chosen card on the other side. When you put the joker away in your pocket the chosen card secretly goes with it, stuck to its back. It is the duplicate joker that is manipulated to appear reversed in the pack at the end. You are left with an ordinary pack; the taped joker is safely tucked away in your pocket.

How you fix it

Fasten a small piece of double-faced tape to the center of the back of one of the jokers. Put that taped joker *faceup* on the bottom of the *facedown* pack, and put the duplicate joker facedown on top of the pack. Slide the pack back into its cardboard case.

What you do

Remove the pack from the case, holding the cards flat so the faceup joker on the bottom will not be seen. Spread the cards between your hands to show they are all facedown, being careful not to expose the bottom card. Ask someone to choose any card, to look at and remember it, without letting you see it.

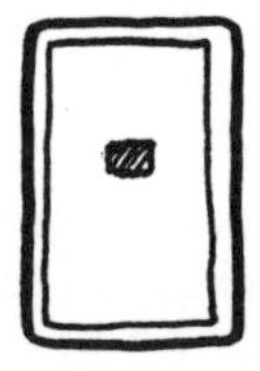

Double-faced tape on back of one joker.

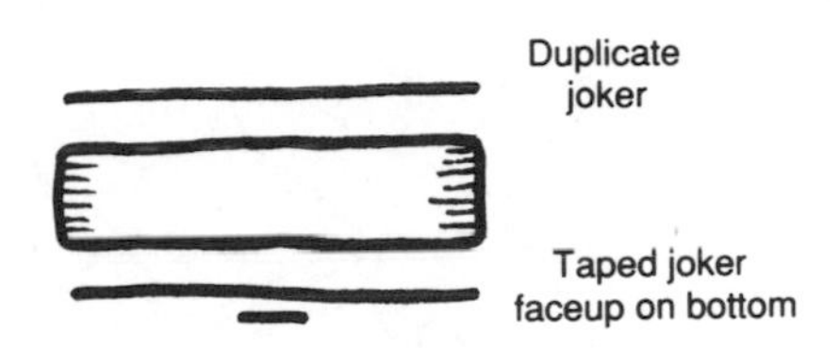

Preparation of the pack of cards for "Jumpers."

Square up the pack in your left hand. Draw about half the cards off the bottom, keeping those flat in your right hand, and hold out the cards remaining in your left hand so he can put his chosen card back on top of those. (This places his card directly above the facedown joker that was on top of the pack.)

Drop your right-hand cards on top of the left-hand cards to bury his chosen card in the pack. (This places the taped faceup joker on top of his card.) Square the cards so all edges are even and press down on the pack with your left thumb so the chosen card and faceup joker will stick together back-to-back in the center of the pack.

"I'm about to make an acrobat of your card," you say. "It will do a double somersault—flip itself over and land faceup in the facedown pack." You snap your right fingers over the pack and then spread the cards between your hands.

But you "discover" that the *joker* has turned faceup instead of his chosen card. "That isn't your card, is it?" you ask. "I didn't think so—I should have known. That flipping joker is the biggest show-off in the whole house of cards."

Separate the pack at the faceup joker, taking off all the cards above it and putting those on the bottom of the pack under the left-hand cards, which leaves the joker faceup on top. Square the pack and take the joker with your right hand, holding it flat. "I'll put it back faceup with the others." Turn the pack faceup in your left hand, spreading it slightly, and push the faceup joker into the center of the faceup pack. Square up the pack and turn it facedown.

"Let's try it again," you say. "By the way, which card *did* you choose?" He may answer that it was the four of hearts. (You really don't know what card he took until he tells you, but you jokingly imply that you knew all along.) "Thanks for telling me. I never would have guessed." Snap your fingers over the pack. "Jump, four of hearts—jump!"

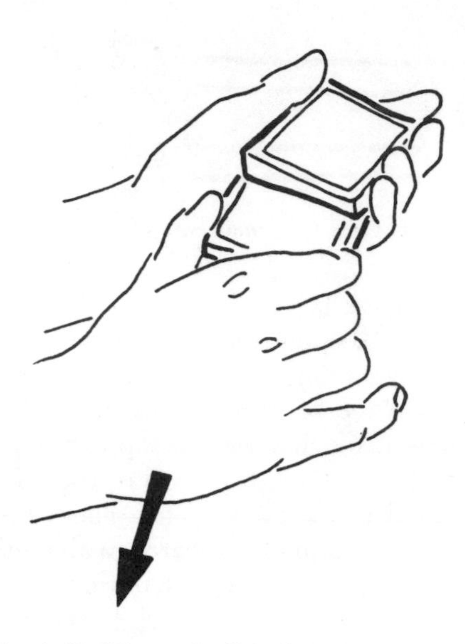

Your right hand takes half of the pack off the bottom.

Spread the facedown pack between your hands and show that the chosen card now is faceup at the center. "There it is! Good. It finally got the word. As long as the magic's working, let's work it once more."

Remove the chosen card with your right hand, keeping it flat so as not to reveal the joker stuck to its back. Turn the pack faceup in your left hand, spreading it slightly with your left thumb. Push the faceup chosen card into the faceup pack. Square the pack and turn it facedown. Snap your right fingers over it and command the chosen card, by name, to flip itself faceup again.

Spread the faceup pack between your hands and "discover" that the *joker*, instead of the chosen card, has reappeared faceup. "Oh, no," you say. "That flipping joker is back. That's enough. I'm going to put it away in my pocket where it can't cause any more trouble."

Remove the double card with your right hand. Hold it up close to you, keeping its joker face to the front. Turn your right side toward those watching so they can see what you do, and put it into

He puts his card on top of the duplicate joker. The taped joker goes on top of his card.

your right jacket pocket. Inside the pocket, separate the stuck-together joker and chosen card by thumbing them apart at the top edges and sliding a finger down between the cards. Show your hand empty as you take it out of your pocket.

At the same time, while your right side is turned toward the right and your left side is momentarily out of view, let your left hand drop to your left side with the pack.

With your left thumb, push the top card (duplicate joker) halfway down off the top of the pack, so the side edge of the card strikes against your leg. Move your hand down against your leg, the thumb still pressing on the back of the card; this maneuver will turn the card over. Square the cards with your fingers and then tip the entire pack faceup in your left hand. (This leaves the duplicate joker facedown on the bottom of the faceup pack.)

Bring the pack faceup in front of you, holding it flat, as you face front again. Spread the cards to show them all faceup, without revealing the bottom card. Square the pack, keep it faceup, and cut the pack by lifting half the cards off the top and putting those on the bottom. This secretly brings the reversed duplicate joker to the center.

The joker appears faceup in a facedown pack—the chosen card is stuck facedown to the back of the joker.

"Now jump, four of hearts—jump!" Snap your fingers. Spread the faceup pack between your hands and find the facedown card at the center. "There it is! Your four of—" Break off your words as you remove the facedown card. Turn it over, and "discover" that it is again the joker!

"Not that joker again. That's impossible—I just put it away in my pocket." Show the joker, toss it onto the table, and put down the pack. "Well, if the joker can jump from my pocket back into the pack, then your four of hearts should be able to flip itself from the pack into my pocket."

Snap your fingers over the pack. Show your hand empty, reach into your pocket, take the card nearest your body, and bring it out to show it is his chosen card. "And so it has. Now *that's* flipping good!"

(If you wish, you can have the person who chooses the card write his initials on the face of it at the start, so he can identify it at the end as the same card that jumps into your pocket.)

Envelope Card Rise

How it looks

This seemingly impromptu version of the classic trick of making cards rise one at a time from a pack requires no threads, attachments, or mechanical equipment. Any pack may be used, and the other props are simple and easily carried in the pockets for close-up performance.

Two cards are chosen and put back in the pack, which is then cut a few times so they apparently are well mixed among the others. The pack is placed in an envelope, the top is torn off, and two small holes are torn in opposite sides. A pencil is pushed through so that the envelope, with the pack in it, hangs suspended from the middle of the pencil.

As you hold the tip of the pencil, and transfer it from hand to hand to show both sides of the hanging envelope, the chosen cards rise up from the pack, one at a time.

What you need

A pack of cards
A personal-letter size envelope, about 3-3/4" by 6-1/2" (not the long ones used for business letters)
An ordinary full-length wooden pencil with sharpened point
A small rubber band
Sports jacket

The secret

The cards are pushed up from the back of the pack by secretly turning the pencil, which has a hidden rubber band around its center.

How you fix it

Twist the rubber band around the center of the pencil and put it point down, in the inside left pocket of your jacket. Have the cards and envelope in another pocket.

What you do

Spread the pack between your hands and have two cards freely chosen. Ask each person to look at his card, remember it, and show it to those around him without letting you see it. While the spectators are looking at their cards, square up the pack and hold it in your left hand. The facedown pack should be in dealing position, your thumb along the left edge and fingers up against the right edge.

With your right hand, pull the bottom half of the pack out from under, by gripping the rear end of that half between your right thumb at one side and first and second fingers at the other side. Draw the bottom half away and keep it in your right hand.

Hold your left hand out to the first spectator and ask him to put back his card. He puts it on top of the remaining cards in your left hand. Ask the second spectator to replace his card and extend your left hand to him so he can put his card back on top of the first one.

As soon as both cards have been replaced, bring your hands together to put the right-hand cards down on top of the left-hand cards. *But as you do that,* secretly bend the tip of your left little finger in so that the fingertip goes between the two halves of the pack.

This holds open a break of about a quarter of an inch right above the two chosen cards. This break, however, is not visible at the front and is concealed by your hands at the sides, so only you can see it at the rear.

Keep your hands together for a moment, pressing down slightly on the top of the pack with your right fingers to help conceal the break. The two chosen cards seem to have been buried in the pack and lost among the others.

Now you appear to cut the pack several times more, as if further mixing the cards, but you do it in a way that secretly leaves the two chosen cards on top. Simply lift off about half the cards above the little finger break and put them facedown on the table. Then lift off the rest of the cards above the break and put those on the first batch. Put the remainder of the pack on top of the others.

(This handling can be used in many other card tricks that require secretly bringing a chosen card to the top. It looks direct and convincing, and avoids suspiciously tricky moves.)

Show the envelope empty, put the pack into it, lick the flap, and seal it. Hold it up with its narrow ends top and bottom and tap it a few times on the table so the pack inside is squared up at the bottom.

Tear off the top end of the envelope, *just above the top of the pack,* tearing right across, and discard the torn-off piece. About an inch down from the torn top, tear out a small piece to make a hole at the right side. Directly opposite, at the left side, tear another small hole. They should be only big enough for the pencil to go through.

Hold up the envelope with your left hand, and with your right hand reach down inside your pocket and take the pencil at its center. Hold it between your first two fingers in front and thumb at the back to hide the rubber band and bring it out to show it. You can display it freely with the band concealed by your thumb and fingers, but do this casually. The pencil should seem incidental to the trick, nothing to focus attention upon.

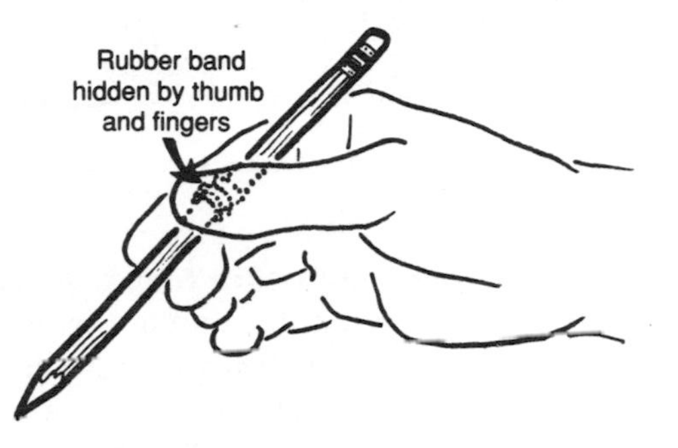

Pull out the pencil, holding it at the center.

With your left hand, turn the envelope so that what was the right side is facing you at the rear. Keeping your right hand at the center of the pencil, push the point in through the hole that is toward you. Glance down into the envelope and continue to push the pencil on across, *behind the pack of cards.* Push it on out through the opposite hole until the point extends far enough so the envelope is centered on the pencil.

Turn the face of the envelope to the front. Take the eraser end of the pencil between your right thumb on top and first two fingers underneath. Hold the pencil by that end and take away your left hand so the envelope hangs suspended from the center of the pencil. Ask the *second* spectator who chose a card to call out the name of it.

Very slowly, roll your right thumb back and down, rotating the pencil with a *slight* continuous movement between thumb and fingers. Rolling your thumb turns the rubber-banded pencil against the card at the back of the pack and gradually pushes it up until it rises from the envelope. *This should be done so the rolling of your thumb is not noticed.*

As you secretly rotate the pencil, slowly turn your right hand and arm out to the right until the back of the hanging envelope is

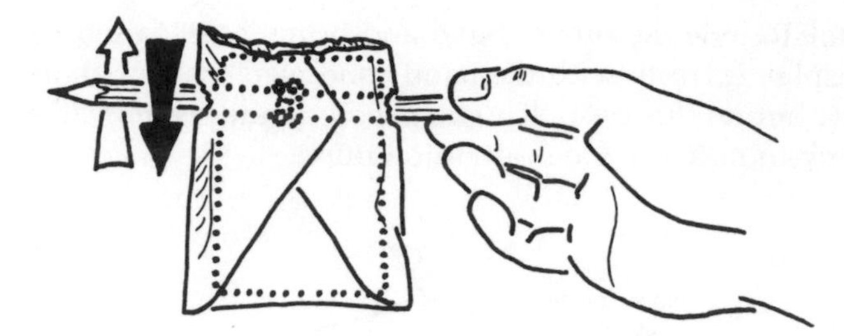

Your thumb secretly rotates the pencil. The rubber band rolls against the card.

toward those watching. Then slowly turn your arm back as it was, in front of you again. Grip the pointed end of the pencil between your left thumb and fingers and remove your right hand. Without a break, continue the rotation of the pencil with your left thumb and fingers as you turn your arm out to the left.

Transferring it from hand to hand allows you to get a fresh grip, because each thumb can give the pencil only about one full rotation. Moving the envelope back and forth helps hide the motion of the thumbs. Showing both sides of the envelope as the card continues to rise also adds to the mystery.

When the card has risen almost all the way, remove it from the envelope with whichever hand is free at the moment. Hold it up to show it and drop it on the table. Then ask the *first* person who chose a card to name his, and make that card rise from the envelope the same way.

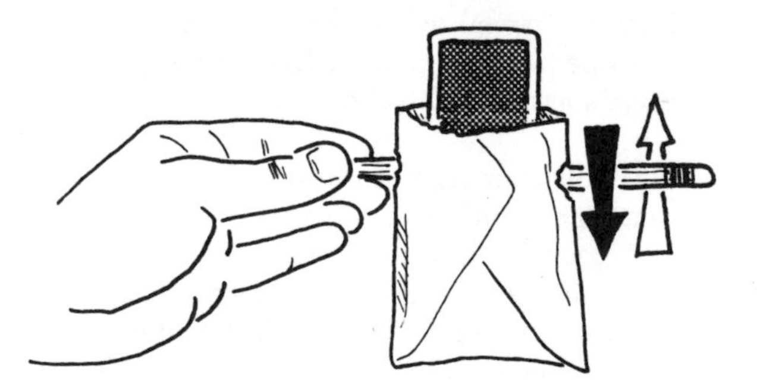

Your left hand takes the pencil and continues to rotate it.

Finally turn the side of the envelope toward you and withdraw the pencil, covering the banded center between your thumb and fingers as at the start. Show the pencil casually and tuck it away in your pocket. Take the pack from the envelope, spread the cards across the table, and toss the empty envelope on top of them.

NINE

Putting It All Together

It takes more than tricks, no matter how clever or mystifying they may be, to entertain people with magic. The secrets of the tricks a magician does are the least important part of a magic show. Tricks alone amount to no more than puzzling little toys.

What matters is not how a magician does his tricks, but how entertainingly he does them. His props serve somewhat the same purpose as the wooden dolls of the puppet stage, or the costumes and scenery of live theater; they are the means of creating illusion. People enjoy being fooled when the magician helps them pretend they are seeing something happen that they know can't really happen at all.

He must surprise them constantly, keep them always wondering what will happen next, and satisfy their desire to see things that seem to contradict the laws of nature, logic, and common reasoning. He may amuse them with the often ridiculous stories he tells, which nevertheless seem to come true through the fun of magic. He may joke about his "mystic" powers or even make fun of himself—or he may present his magic in a serious manner.

Each magician has to find for himself his own best style of presentation. He learns gradually, by giving shows, what will best please an audience. Some tricks that may be successful for others just won't suit him at all.

By trying them, he learns which to keep and improve upon and which to discard. He becomes a good magician by learning which tricks really entertain his audiences the most and then by working on those few until he makes each of them really his own.

That is why all tricks, including the very simplest, should be practiced and planned for their best effect. They should be put together in a planned routine that builds increasing interest. Even a seemingly impromptu show should be rehearsed carefully, so the magician always knows exactly what he is going to do next, exactly how he is going to do it, and exactly what he is going to say.

Doing magic can be the most fun when you don't have to worry over making a mistake or over the embarrassment of failure. Practice brings that ease of performance and peace of mind. It lets you forget yourself and concentrate on pleasing those who are watching you. They can't relax and enjoy themselves if you appear to be fumbling and nervous. If what you do is going to look magical, it must be done with seeming ease.

But practice and planning should be anything but a weary chore. There should be fun for you in trying the tricks on your own, in finding the satisfaction of doing a trick a little better each time you try, and in the enjoyment of seeing in your mirror what effects you are able to achieve.

How to Learn a New Trick

First read the full description of the trick all the way through, and think of it in terms of the surprise or amusement it will have for the audience. Then read it through a second time and pay particular attention to how it is done. Make sure you understand what is done and why.

But don't try to memorize any of the moves in detail until after you have made up all the necessary props. Learn the moves by reading the instructions with the needed props at hand. Go through each move. Then try to do it without looking at the book.

Think the trick over and experiment a little. See if you can find an easier or a better way of doing it, a method that may suit you better and still produce a strong effect.

When you have learned the working, then plan the presentation. Don't copy it exactly from the book or parrot the words that are suggested for patter. Try to bring something of yourself to each trick, so that it expresses your own personality.

But finally decide on one planned way of doing it and then practice that until you have it down so well you don't have to think about what you are doing. Try it in front of an audience and then work on it again to make it stronger, smoother, more entertaining.

Don't attempt to learn too many tricks at once. Try them out, just for fun, if you wish. But settle on a few and build those into a planned routine. Some of the world's greatest magicians have achieved fame with just a few tricks they could do really well.

A full-length mirror will help you during early practice sessions, but when you reach the point of dress rehearsal, it probably is better to rehearse without one. Instead, imagine an audience, and put on your show exactly as you would if the audience were there. Pretend you are inviting members of the audience to assist you. Talk to them, do everything the way you would in a real show, down to the handling of the very smallest prop you will use.

Planning Your Shows

Whether you intend to entertain a fairly large audience or just a few friends who ask you to show them a trick or two, your performance should be planned. Perhaps the best way is to work up two or three acts to suit various occasions.

One act might include the kind of small magic you can carry in your pockets to show almost anywhere, on the spur of the moment. A second act might be made up of larger tricks, but only the kind you can take out of a suitcase or do without any advance setting up. Your third act could be designed for shows where you will have a chance to set up your props behind a curtain or screen.

You will find that when you put five or six tricks together as an act you probably will have to make changes in the working or arrangement of some of them. One of your pockets may become too crowded, for instance, with things to be concealed in it, or you may find that the props for one trick are in the way of the apparatus for another.

These are things that have to be worked out as you build each act, which is why the act should be rehearsed as a whole after the individual tricks are learned. Another reason is that the tricks must be blended together in some logical order, so that the best spot for each one is chosen in relation to the others.

Your acts should have variety, both in the kinds of tricks they include and the props that are used. For example, you probably wouldn't want to do two production tricks or two vanishing tricks one right after the other. You wouldn't want to use two tricks that work by the same method any more than you would want to show the same trick twice to the same audience. Remember, in planning your acts, to think always in terms of what will be the most surprising or unexpected.

Once you have made up your acts, don't be tempted to add anything you haven't planned and rehearsed in advance. Naturally you'll want to try new tricks from time to time. But build the new ones into the framework of the act. Gradually drop out one or two weaker tricks and replace them with others.

Have all the things you need for each act ready in one bag or box. Then make up an index, using an office file card or notebook page for each trick. Write the name of it, the brief effect, any special performing conditions, such as whether you can do it when the audience is on all sides of you, and a complete list of all the props needed and where they are to be placed. On the back of the card or page, write a brief outline of the moves and patter.

Routining Your Act

Most magicians agree that your opening trick should be short, quick, and right to the point. Something magical should happen fast. An audience will judge you by the first impression you make. But above all, an opening trick should be one you are completely sure of doing well, something you can do every time without any chance of failure.

It need not be deeply mysterious or puzzling, as long as it creates fun and some kind of surprise. Certainly it shouldn't be your best trick, because then you won't be able to top it with what comes afterward. It is far better to open with a small trick you do perfectly than with an elaborate one that may go wrong.

Your second trick should be one that lets your audience become better acquainted with you. It may be the kind in which you invite the assistance of some member of the audience, or one involving a humorous story that gets across your personality. At this point, your aim is to get the audience thinking, "He's a nice fellow and pretty clever, too. This is going to be fun."

For your third trick, you might choose a longer one, the kind that has some real mystery, one of the features of your act. Then vary the following ones, to produce different kinds of surprises and build toward the climax.

Your show should end with your best trick, whatever it is.

Many acts finish with an elaborate and colorful production, but this should depend entirely on your own style of presentation. Do what you know goes over better than anything else that you do, and end your act right there. Don't drag out the ending.

There is an old show business saying: "Always leave them wanting more." It applies to magic as well as to other types of acts. Don't go on doing trick after trick. Bring your act to a climax and a definite conclusion, even if you are performing a routine of pocket tricks for just a few friends. Accept the applause you have won and "quit while you're ahead."

Performing Conditions

Some tricks cannot be shown when there are people behind you or at the sides. Others require you to start with things concealed in your hands. These problems should be thought out ahead of time. Consider the place where you will give the act and plan your routine accordingly.

But don't fuss and worry over some little thing that may go wrong. Very often, your audience won't notice it at all. If they do, they may think it was planned that way. The magician always has an advantage in that an audience never knows what he intends to do until he does it.

Have fun with your magic. If people see that you enjoy doing it, they're more likely to enjoy watching you. And that's the best reward magic has to give—the ability to create pleasure for others as well as for yourself.

Other Magic Books by Bill Severn

Magic Wherever You Are
Magic and Magicians
Shadow Magic
Magic in Your Pockets
Magic with Paper
Magic Shows You Can Give
Packs of Fun
Magic Comedy
Magic Across the Table
Bill Severn's Big Book of Magic
Bill Severn's Magic Trunk
Magic in Mind
Bill Severn's Magic Workshop
Magic with Coins and Bills
Bill Severn's Big Book of Close-up Magic
Bill Severn's Guide to Magic as a Hobby
More Magic in Your Pockets
Magic with Rope, Ribbon and String
Bill Severn's Impromptu Magic
Magic Fun for Everyone